D0983884

Envoys Extraordinary

WOMEN OF THE CANADIAN FOREIGN SERVICE

Margaret K. Weiers

DUNDURN PRESS
Toronto • Oxford

Edited by Michael Power
Printed and bound in Canada by Webcom

The publisher wishes to acknowledge the generous assistance and ongoing support of the **Canada Council**, the **Book Publishing Industry Development Program** of the **Department of Canadian Heritage**, the **Ontario Arts Council**, the **Ontario Publishing Centre** of the **Ministry of Citizenship, Culture and Recreation,** and the **Ontario Heritage Foundation**.

Care has been taken to trace the ownership of copyright material used in the text (including the illustrations). The author and publisher welcome any information enabling them to rectify any reference or credit in subsequent editions.

J. Kirk Howard, Publisher

Canadian Cataloguing in Publication Data

Weiers, Margaret K., 1928–
    Envoys extraordinary : women of the Canadian foreign service

Includes bibliographical references.
ISBN 1-55002-241-5

1. Women diplomats – Canada – Interviews. 2. Diplomatic and consular service, Canadian. I. Title.

JX1730.Z7W45 1995   327.71'0092'2   C95-931835-6

Dundurn Press Limited	Dundurn Distribution	Dundurn Press Limited
2181 Queen Street East	73 Lime Walk	1823 Maryland Avenue
Suite 301	Headington, Oxford	P.O. Box 1000
Toronto, Canada	England	Niagara Falls, N.Y.
M4E 1E5	0X3 7AD	U.S.A. 14302-1000

Contents

To the men in my life — R.J.W., Bob, and Max

ACKNOWLEDGMENTS

To write is to be in self-imposed solitary confinement. It matters not whether the writer is in a crowded newsroom full of clattering machines and chattering people or in a secluded study with a "do not disturb" sign on the doorknob. When the blank sheet of paper goes into the typewriter or, more likely today, the empty screen comes up on the computer, the world disappears and the writer is alone to put thoughts into words.

Before that definitive moment, however, many people cross the writer's path to help assemble material, provoke thought, stimulate ideas, and provide moral and even financial support. So it has been for me; now is the time and this is the place to say "Thank you."

I am very grateful to the Canadian Research Institute for the Advancement of Women in Ottawa for giving me one of its 1992 research grants. The money helped defray expenses for travel to Ottawa, New York, and Halifax; the recognition buttressed my belief that this was a book worth writing.

Librarians are a writer's best friends and I have many to thank. Jane Barrett and her associates at the library of the Canadian Institute of International Affairs were helpful and encouraging. Gayle Fraser, the institute's curator of the John Holmes papers, gave me access to them. Carol Lindsay, chief librarian at the *Toronto Star*, was never too busy to answer a question. Ruth M. Thompson, former director of library services at the Department of External Affairs, made many useful suggestions.

My thanks, too, to those cheerful and helpful men and women whose names I do not know, librarians at the Robarts Library at the University of Toronto, the Metropolitan Toronto Reference Library, the External Affairs Library in Ottawa as well as the entire staff of Richview, my neighbourhood branch of the Etobicoke Public Libraries.

Two individuals in Ottawa were unstinting in sharing their time and expertise. Paulette Dozois, archivist in the historical resources branch, government archives division of the National Archives of Canada in Ottawa, helped in two ways. She steered me through that venerable institution's filing system so that I could find documents on my own. She also found documents for me. John Hilliker, head of the historical section, corporate communications division, External Affairs and International Trade Canada, and author of the official history of the department, was a fountain of information and gave me permission to quote from his book. I am profoundly grateful to both of them.

Other individuals at External whose help I appreciate are Paul Frazer, now minister-counsellor at the Canadian embassy in Washington; E.R. (Ted) Johnston, former coordinator of access to information and privacy, whose letter of introduction opened the door to many interviews; Marlene Picard, head of the department's employment equity program; and Carol N. Markham and Debra Hulley of *bout de papier,* the quarterly journal published in Ottawa by the Professional Association of Foreign Service Officers.

Many thanks also to my friends: Lorna Marsden for the concept of the book; Linda Silver Dranoff for lawyerly tips; Ann Jamieson for hospitality in Halifax. And to my family: Bob, my husband, for soothing my anxiety attacks, keeping watch on expenditures, and taming a temperamental printer; and Bob, our son, for his vote of confidence.

My deepest gratitude goes to all the women who agreed to be interviewed for this book; without their candour and co-operation, the entire enterprise would have been impossible.

I also acknowledge with thanks the following permissions to quote:

From *Storm Signals* by Charles Ritchie. © 1983. Reprinted by permission of Macmillan Canada.

From *Mike, the Memoirs of the Right Honourable Lester B. Pearson, Volume I, 1897-1948* by Lester B Pearson. © 1972. Reprinted by permission of University of Toronto Press.

From *The Canadian Diplomat, An Essay in Definition* by Marcel Cadieux. © 1963. Reprinted by permission of University of Toronto Press.

From *Undiplomatic Notes, Tales from the Canadian Foreign Service* by Sidney A. Freifeld. © 1990. Reprinted by permission of Hounslow Press.

In November 1993, the Department of External Affairs was renamed the Department of Foreign Affairs by Prime Minister Jean Chrétien's government. For the sake of historical continuity, I have used the original name throughout this book. Unless otherwise indicated, all quotations in this book are from interviews conducted by me.

Margaret K. Weiers
Etobicoke, Ontario, 1995

INTRODUCTION

A DISTINGUISHED MINORITY

Jules Léger's remark was puzzling, possibly paternalistic, and ultimately prophetic.

It was early in September 1955. I was a new foreign service officer who was being posted to New York. Until my assignment, I never had a passport of any kind, let alone a red diplomatic one. I was expected to do double duty in what, to a neophyte from the prairies, was the most exciting city on the continent, if not in the world. As a vice-consul at the Canadian Consulate General, I was to help my colleagues in the information section tell the folks of New York, New Jersey, Pennsylvania, and Connecticut everything they ever wanted to know about Canada. Later in the month, when the annual session of the United Nations General Assembly opened, I was accredited as an adviser to the Canadian delegation with the specific duty of assistant press officer. My background as a journalist qualified me for the assignments. Since I had joined the External Affairs department a mere six weeks earlier, there had been no time to take the customary training program. Indeed, such an early posting was almost unprecedented and caused some envy among my fellow probationers who had to endure at least two years of Ottawa bureaucracy before spreading their wings in foreign skies.

Jules Léger was then External's deputy minister – the precise title is Undersecretary of State for External Affairs, shortened in conversation and documents to USSEA – and it was his custom to have a brief chat with officers going on postings. In his office in the East Block on Parliament Hill, I answered his gentle questions about my university years in Saskatoon and my work as a newspaper reporter in Regina. At the end of our short meeting, he said to me as I was leaving, "I have just one piece of advice for you: stay a journalist."

The remark had the effect of a cold shower. Here I was, excited at the prospect of starting a new career in what I imagined to be the glamorous world of international diplomacy, and one of its foremost Canadian practitioners was telling me to go back to my former occupation.

As it turned out, that is exactly what I did. After two fascinating years in New York – the press office at the Canadian delegation to the U.N. was a hectic place as Lester B. Pearson stickhandled his way through the 1956 Suez crisis to score the unexpected goal of a Nobel Peace Prize – I left External because that is what women officers had to do when they married. Much later, after achieving some success as a reporter and writer of features and editorials for the *Toronto Star*, I reflected on what Léger had said more than thirty years earlier. Was he such a good judge of character that in a few short minutes he knew me better than I knew myself and concluded that I was not cut out to be a bureaucrat? Or was he making a subconscious judgment of me as a woman, reflecting the conventional wisdom of the day that, with rare exceptions, women were not suitable to be diplomats?

In May 1989, at lunch in a Toronto restaurant, I told this anecdote about Léger and my brief diplomatic career to Lorna Marsden, then a Senator and a professor at the University of Toronto. She is now president of Wilfrid Laurier University. Her instant reaction was that I should write a book about my experiences. I demurred. Unlike many journalists, I had no grand ambition to write a book. My career in the foreign service was far too short and much too undistinguished to provide enough material even for a newspaper column. A book was out of the question.

Marsden's remark, and a note which she wrote me a week after our luncheon, got me thinking that other women's careers in the Canadian foreign service *did* merit recording. Her note said, "I am quite serious in saying I hope you write a book about your years in the foreign service or other people's years in the foreign service. It may seem to be a difficult thing to do but it is an extremely valuable record for women now and in the future. I am always so grateful to those who write about women who have lived in recent years rather than in the distant past."

Because I was then writing editorials on international affairs, I knew a number of officials at External well enough to ask them what they thought of a book about female diplomats. No one dismissed it as a flight of fancy; many, indeed, thought such a book long overdue; some began to suggest names of persons to be included. I was encouraged to give the project serious thought.

I had read books on Canada's international relations and the memoirs and biographies of Canadian diplomats, and it often struck me that women – unless they were mothers, wives, daughters, secretaries, or hostesses – were rarely mentioned. I knew from my own experience in External and in journalism that there had been some remarkable women in Canada's diplomatic service; unlike the men, they had not written their memoirs, nor had anyone written their biographies. I soon discovered, as I began more intensive research, that there was very little material of any kind about women in the foreign service or about international diplomacy as a career for women.

Léger's remark about remaining a journalist came back to haunt me, as evidence mounted that diplomacy was a man's world to which women came late, on tiptoe, and in single file. In Canada, the doors to a diplomatic career – like those in many other professions and occupations – were opened to women only during the Second World War when the men, who otherwise would have been preferred, joined the Armed Forces. Even then, the doors were merely ajar; the women who started with External in the war years did not have the rank or the pay of officers, though they did officers' work and did it with imagination and dispatch. Not until 1947 were women permitted to write the foreign service examinations and become diplomats on an equal basis with men.

The ban on married women foreign service officers persisted in External until 1971, sixteen years after the government removed restrictions on married women in all other departments of the federal public service. It was the double standard in all its glory: married male diplomats could and did take their spouses and children to any corner of the world where Canada had a mission, but married female diplomats, even when their spouses were willing, could not do the same. Supervisors often offered lame excuses, as Lois and Stuart Beattie discovered. Both of them were foreign service officers. They married after joining the department, but Lois had to resign when Stuart was posted to Bonn. A dual posting was out of the question. "What would we do about the allowances?" she was asked. (The obvious solution – pay allowances for entertainment on an individual basis and pro-rate the housing allowance since they were sharing accommodation – apparently didn't occur to anyone in authority.) So Lois went to Bonn as Stuart's spouse and was promptly offered a job in the Canadian embassy as a locally engaged employee. She turned it down, not wanting to work as a press aide if she could not continue as a diplomat.

Officially sanctioned discrimination has been excised from the External Affairs department but discriminatory attitudes linger. A woman who completed a questionnaire for the government's 1988 task force on barriers to women in the public service observed, "In an interview with External Affairs, I was told, 'You would make a better wife of an ambassador than an ambassador.'" Another woman told the task force about encountering cultural barriers at External and explained, "It is not that they are awful people, but that they see women differently and do not provide adequate opportunities for women's advancement."

Condescension to women is not confined to External. In 1969, Margaret Meagher was sent as ambassador to Stockholm on the most important assignment of her diplomatic career. She headed the Canadian team negotiating with representatives of the People's Republic of China the terms on which the two countries would resume diplomatic relations that had broken off in 1951, in the aftermath of the Communist revolution and the outbreak of the Korean War. The *Toronto Star* published a story on Meagher's assignment with the headline, "Our girl in Stockholm presents her credentials," and it printed a photograph that showed her, all long and shapely legs, getting out of the official car.

Margaret Ford, a former foreign service officer who had postings to Dar-es-Salaam and to Canada's U.N. mission in New York, before she left External for an executive position with the National Transportation Agency, took a critical look at the career complaints of women in the foreign service and concluded that they were legitimate. In the Fall 1990 edition of *bout de papier*, published by the Professional Association of Foreign Service Officers in Ottawa, Ford wrote:

> Virtually all women would testify that paternalistic and even chauvinistic attitudes still exist in the department to some degree. A good number of male officers still seem to have difficulty, at least to some extent, in accepting women as peers or superiors and in relying on them in the same way as their male colleagues. Women have found most male supervisors to be less comfortable with women and, consequently, less at ease as their supervisors, often treating them somewhat differently from their male colleagues. For instance, I know of at least two cases where the particular head of post took each of his male officers with him on official tours, but never the women FS at the post. In my own experience at headquarters, none of my supervisors ever had lunch with me on a one-to-one basis, although we often lunched in somewhat larger groups. In other cases, I and

other women have rarely been asked to accompany our supervisors to appointments with senior-level officials. Many useful learning experiences were thus missed ...

The system tends in particular to be conservative and risk-adverse in staffing women, because they have generally less access to the "old boys' network" and are consequently less well-known and have less credibility in comparison with their male peers. The end result is that women often do not get the same type of challenging assignments as many of their male colleagues. It is frankly easier to assign a woman to a job for which she is overqualified than to persuade a supervisor to accept her in an assignment where she has the qualifications but is unknown or untested. By contrast, a good number of my male colleagues have been given active boosts to their careers by being staffed by Personnel into high profile jobs, often as stretch assignments for high profile supervisors. Not surprisingly, they have done considerably better in terms of appraisals and promotions, not just because they are able officers, but because they acquired the on-the-job experience needed to make them even more effective. (pp. 21-22)

John W. Holmes had a distinguished career in External from 1943 to 1960, before becoming a professor at the University of Toronto and counsellor to the Canadian Institute of International Affairs. He dodged the issue of discrimination against women in a paper, "The Canadian foreign Service at Middle Age," which he delivered at a colloquium at Leeds University in November 1982.

There are other problems of discrimination in a country like Canada. Women were the chief victims. They were not allowed at all in the service before the last war. Since then they have had equal entry, but the numbers have been small. There have been and are women ambassadors and high commissioners. Whether the dominance of males in the higher ranks is attributable to lack of available females or ingrained prejudice is a question the author has not the courage to answer. The Canadian situation, however, is not unique in the world.

Flora MacDonald, Canada's first female foreign minister, found that even her exalted position did not provide immunity from thoughtless slights that unwittingly reflected a particular mindset.

> People out in the field, in the various posts, didn't quite grasp that their minister was a woman. I remember going to a conference, to the Commonwealth heads of government meeting in Lusaka, with Mr. [Prime Minister Joe] Clark and we stopped in the Cameroon on the way to Lusaka and we were met at the airport in Douala by a group of officials. This was the first time a Canadian prime minister had ever made an official visit to any African country, and Cameroon being bilingual, and the kind of rapport or close connections it has with Canada, there was a very good turnout at the airport.
>
> When we went in to the air terminal, the prime minister and Maureen McTeer were leading, with the protocol officers who'd come out to the plane to greet them, and I followed. We were taken into the building and there was a room for a large group of people, and a smaller room where the prime minister and the foreign minister of the Cameroon were waiting to greet us and talk to us. Mr. Clark was shown into that room and the others went in to the larger room. And as I came along, my ambassador said to me, "Would you mind waiting in the other room with the women?" It was the kind of thing that just absolutely rocked you to the soles of your feet.
>
> I was very angry and I was prepared to turn around and get back on the plane and go right back to Canada but I remember muttering to someone, "Next posting for him is Patagonia."

MacDonald held other portfolios besides External and found in them a much more open attitude towards women.

> I think there is a kind of traditional elitism built into External that is perhaps only now being broken, a kind of borrowing from the British scene as to what the foreign office was really all about. It had the cream of the crop, the people who were hand-picked, the feeling that

we're just a little bit better than anyone else and the "we" were always male. I think that attitude permeated the department for a long while and to some extent still exists.

The male elite to whom MacDonald referred may have been reluctant to regard women as equals, but they relied heavily on them in non-diplomatic roles. Charles Ritchie, in the conclusion to volume four of his celebrated diaries, *Storm Signals: More Undiplomatic Diaries, 1962-1971*, noted the duality.

> Women diplomats in the higher ranks are still something of a rarity in all Foreign Services. In our own Foreign Service we have had a handful of distinguished women diplomats – too few and far between. The unsung heroines of the Foreign Service are the women in its administrative and secretarial ranks, without whom the whole operation would speedily collapse. (p. 139)

Rare they may have been, but it was not hard to find women who had beaten the odds and carved niches for themselves in the Canadian foreign service. Everyone I met during my own short stint in External spoke highly of Elizabeth MacCallum and Margaret Meagher. They were seen as role models by every new female foreign service officer of the 1950s. Agnes McCloskey's name was familiar from books; her reign of terror as the department's first accountant got under men's skin and earned her a mention in the memoirs and the histories. Marjorie McKenzie had had the temerity to write the foreign service examinations seventeen years before women were officially permitted to write them. Although she tied for first place, she had to be content with a secretary's title until 1947. MacCallum, chargé d'affaires in Lebanon in 1954, was the first Canadian woman to go abroad carrying the credentials of a head of post. Meagher, who went to Israel as ambassador in 1958, was Canada's first female ambassador. The British, on the other hand, did not have a female ambassador until 1976, when Dame Anne Warburton was posted to Denmark, although they had planned to send Dame Barbara Salt to Israel in 1962. Illness prevented her taking up the post. The U.S., meanwhile, was ahead of both Canada and Britain. Frances Elizabeth Willis, the first American female career officer to become an ambassador, went to Switzerland in 1953.

The six Canadians in the first part of the book, whom I call the trail-blazers, all began their foreign service careers as clerks or secretaries and rose through the ranks to become officers. Four of them joined the department before women officers were recruited. The other two – Pamela McDougall and Janice Sutton – simply found it expedient to start at the bottom. Their ability, intelligence, and performance made promotion to officer status right and inevitable. Indeed, it would have been a shocking waste of resources to have left McDougall and Sutton languishing in clerical and secretarial roles. As a deputy minister told the task force on barriers to women in the public service, "Brains are passed out randomly, and 50 per cent of them land up in women's heads. Why would you limit yourself to half the supply, and take the bottom half to fill your positions when you could have the top of the other half?"

For the second part of the book, I sought the achievers – women who were or had been heads of post or had otherwise made their mark – who could be interviewed in either Ottawa, Halifax, or New York. A very representative group of women was available and agreed to participate. Included were Canada's first female ambassador to the United Nations in New York, the first woman to enter External as an officer after 1947, married women with children, and women with experience in trade, immigration, and development as well as in the conventional political work of a Canadian diplomat.

In the third part of this book, younger women – the contenders – talked to me about their experiences and aspirations as they climb the diplomatic ladder. At the time of our interviews in mid-1992, only one had reached the head-of-post level. Lucie Edwards was appointed high commissioner to Nairobi, following in Margaret Meagher's footsteps. As bright, capable, and well-educated as their predecessors, these young women are ready to take in stride the changes wrought to conventional diplomacy by modern technology. The computer modem and facsimile machine have replaced the diplomatic courier, and international travel is so easy that heads of government can be their own envoys at summit meetings. This has the potential to make traditional diplomatic exchanges irrelevant if not superfluous.

Whether achiever, contender, or trail-blazer, a female diplomat is still in a minority, subject to a type of constant critical scrutiny not visited upon her male colleagues. Dorothy Armstrong, after twenty-two years in the service, found that she always had to prove herself. "I think it will be this way in our lifetime," she said. "I have hopes for the next generation, however." Janice Sutton simply became discouraged. "When I looked at my career, six postings and all those divisions I had worked in, every time it was a whole new ballgame, a whole new set of responsibilities, a whole new set of colleagues, a whole new hierarchy, I had to prove myself all over again. And I got tired of that."

All the women in this book are career foreign service officers. I deliberately excluded women who have been political appointees to high diplomatic posts, including the only woman who has ever been high commissioner in London. Jean Wadds, a former Conservative MP, was sent to London when Joe Clark was prime minister, and, by all accounts, she served both him and his Liberal successor, Pierre Trudeau, with diligence and distinction. I excluded the political appointees not because they were not capable or deserving; as a deputy minister once said, "You can break a glass ceiling more easily from above than from below." I excluded them because it is the career foreign service officer who is in it for the long haul; it is the career officer who provides continuity in foreign policy and who represents Canada abroad as governments change and partisan political fortunes wax and wane.

As Charles Ritchie observed, officers are not the only women in the foreign service. Clerks and secretaries – generally called the "support staff" – the majority of whom are women, make an important contribution; at posts abroad, they are often more visible to the local population and so more identifiably Canadian than the ambassador. But to include them in this book would have made an unwieldy tome; as women, they were always accepted in support roles and did not begin their careers at such a disadvantage as the female officers.

This is not a book about foreign policy. It is a book about women who stayed the course and are still on it, influencing, developing, shaping, and implementing Canadian foreign policy at home and abroad. It is a story, often told in their own words, of twenty-two remarkable women. With charm, grace, dignity, and intelligence, these women survived that most quintessential of Canadian establishments, the Department of External Affairs.

PART ONE

The Trail Blazers

Marjorie McKenzie

CHAPTER ONE

A WOMAN AHEAD OF HER TIME
MARJORIE McKENZIE

In January 1950, Marjorie McKenzie sent a wry note to Marcel Cadieux in the personnel division of the Department of External Affairs. The note was attached to the department's weekly bulletin on Ireland, which reported, among other events, the appointment of Josephine McNeill as Ireland's minister to The Hague, making her second-in-command to the Irish ambassador in the Dutch capital. McKenzie's note read: "Women's rights and Ireland forever! Please file this where it will do the most good. Personally, however, I shall insist on an ambassadorship."

McKenzie never achieved her goal and never lived to see another of her sex reach that pinnacle. McKenzie died in November 1957, and Margaret Meagher's appointment to Israel as Canada's first female ambassador did not occur until 1958. It was not lack of qualifications, ability, or experience that prevented McKenzie from becoming an ambassador. She was just a woman ahead of her time.

Born in North Bay, Ontario, in 1895, Marjorie McKenzie followed the pattern of many women of that era who did not get married immediately after high school. She went to Normal School, and in 1915 she began teaching in a succession of Northern Ontario schools. At the same time, she studied for a bachelor's degree, taking extramural courses from Queen's University. She gave up her teaching post in 1919 to attend Queen's full-time, and she received her BA the following year.

Apparently, McKenzie had not found teaching all that fulfilling. Corolyn Cox, in a *Saturday Night* article published in 1945, wrote that McKenzie considered herself a flop as a teacher and reckoned that she had done her students a favour by leaving the classroom. Cox did relate one pedagogical success: to augment her sparse income while studying at Queen's, McKenzie tutored H.D.G. Crerar in German and did it well enough to enable him to pass an Imperial Staff College examination and go on to command the First Canadian Army during its 1944-45 campaign in Northwest Europe.

Meanwhile, McKenzie pursued her extramural studies toward an MA in French and German while working as a clerk, typist, and proofreader at Jackson Press in Kingston and writing occasionally for the *Whig* newspaper.

The event that propelled McKenzie into the diplomatic career that was to occupy her for the rest of her life began innocuously enough. In 1923, the dean of arts at Queen's, Dr. O.D. Skelton, was looking for a secretary. One of McKenzie's professors, the head of the German department, John Macgillivray, suggested that she apply.

The man who was soon to become the legendary undersecretary of Canada's External Affairs department was so impressed by McKenzie that he hired her at the end of their first interview. When Skelton left Queen's to go to Ottawa in 1924, he took McKenzie with him and she joined the department as a temporary senior clerk-stenographer at an annual salary of $1,320. It was decent pay for the time; the starting salary for junior-level officers in External three years later was $2,520 a year. McKenzie stayed with Skelton until his death in 1941 and worked for his successors until 1946, rising to the post of head clerk at $3,000 a year. On 1 October 1947, she was promoted from head clerk to foreign service officer grade two (FSO2) and received a $660 increase to her annual salary.

That date – 1947 – marked a watershed in the history of External Affairs. The government finally lifted the ban on women officers that had existed since External's first undersecretary, Sir Joseph Pope, set the rules for recruitment when the department was established in 1909. Several other women who had been doing yeoman service in External Affairs during the war years also became foreign service officers at this time.

An unsigned memorandum from the undersecretary's office was put in McKenzie's personnel file in September 1947. It contains this assessment:

> Miss McKenzie performs duties comparable with those
> of senior members of the diplomatic staff and should, if
> it were possible to appoint women as members of the
> diplomatic staff, be rated as one of the senior members.
>   Miss McKenzie has custody, in co-operation with
> other members of the department, of certain documents

of particular secrecy and which cannot, for security reasons, be filed with regular departmental records.

It is considered that Miss McKenzie, who successfully qualified in the Third Secretary examinations many years ago and who performs duties equivalent to those of a senior diplomatic officer, would have been recommended long ago for appointment in the diplomatic ranks were it not for the fact that the department has not yet taken steps to recommend the inclusion of women in such service.

McKenzie was one of a hardy band of pioneers, which included Elizabeth MacCallum, Agnes Ireland, Margaret Meagher, Hilda Reid, Dorothy Burwash, and Mary Dench. By 1946, they had begun to prick the collective conscience of the department. Referring to McKenzie, MacCallum, and Burwash, in a pre-1947 memorandum, Norman Robertson wrote: "It is certain that, were these three employees men, we would have taken steps to regularize their positions in much higher grades of foreign service officer. Most of their work could in fact be considered that normally undertaken by a First Secretary."

The women had been doing officers' work ever since they joined the department as clerks in the mid-1940s. It was the time of the manpower shortage of the Second World War. They met all but one of the requirements set out by the Civil Service Commission in advertisements announcing the first competitive foreign service examinations in 1927. Candidates were expected to be university graduates or have equivalent experience, to be trained in political economy, political science, or international law, to know a foreign language, and to be well-spoken. The only problem was that officers had to be men. External was still following the guidelines proposed by Pope to a royal commission in 1907: "I recommend that a small staff of young men, well educated and carefully selected, be attached to the department ... and that they be specially trained in the knowledge and treatment of these subjects. In this way we shall acquire an organized method of dealing with international questions which at present we wholly lack."

In those early days, if women wanted careers in the foreign service, they had to settle for jobs as clerks and secretaries. Even then, their presence was only grudgingly accepted. When a 1907 royal commission on the civil service asked Pope about the employment of women, he replied, "Speaking generally, I do not think it desirable, though I know of several exceptions. But I am speaking of the general principle, because I find that as a rule women clerks claim the rights of men and the privileges of their own sex as well."

In the intervening years, attitudes had changed sufficiently that in 1946 a high-ranking departmental official, Escott Reid, made a bold suggestion. Following the 1947 foreign service examinations – the first ones which women were allowed to write – Reid urged the department to adopt a policy that "a certain number of vacancies *must* be filled by women." (Emphasis his.) In the conclusion to his memorandum, Reid referred specifically to the women who had been doing officers' work for clerks' pay during the war years:

> I feel very strongly that since these women have been in the service for some considerable time and have done excellent work, it is not fair to ask them to continue any longer with the classification of clerks, and with indefinite promises that their position will eventually be regularized.

Despite Reid's urging and his support for affirmative action, long before that phrase was coined, External hardly welcomed women officers with open arms. T.W.L. MacDermot advised caution in a 1947 memorandum to Lester B. Pearson, then the department's deputy minister. While allowing that women ought to be permitted to write the examinations, MacDermot also warned that a large number of female applicants should be discouraged. Practically all of them, he argued, would find themselves unsuccessful "in view of (a) the overseas preference and (b) the difficulty of absorbing any large number of women officers in the department." The memorandum did not elaborate on the precise nature of those difficulties. It is possible to conclude, however, that they had little to do with women's capabilities and much to do with the traditional view that diplomacy was men's work.

The reluctant MacDermot went on to say, "the only women we are likely to wish to appoint after this examination are a few already in the department who could probably be approved by virtue of their highly specialized knowledge and experience ..."

For Marjorie McKenzie, writing the 1947 examination was little more than a formality. After all, she written it once already, in 1930, when she knew full well that she could not be an officer. She did it to establish standing for a promotion within the non-officer ranks.

There is a revealing memorandum on the results of that 1930 examination, in a file at the National Archives of Canada. On a list ranking "the more promising candidates" according to the test results, there is this intriguing paragraph: "1. Miss Marjorie McKenzie, Ottawa, secretary to the USSEA (Under-Secretary of State for External Affairs); graduate of Queen's university, and specially equipped in French, German and Spanish; appointments were stated to be open to men only, but Miss McKenzie wrote to establish standing; she was tied for first place in the written examination."

McKenzie got her promotion – to principal clerk – in 1936. But as John Hilliker observed in his book, *Canada's Department of External Affairs, Volume I, The Early Years, 1909-1946*, her talents were such that she exerted much more influence on the department than was apparent from her rank and title. Hilliker wrote:

> McKenzie's interest was not in the administrative process but in the substance of foreign policy and the quality of written expression. Responsible for overseeing the paper flow through the under-secretary's office, she was well placed to comment on ideas coming forward from the department. Enjoying Skelton's trust, which made her the keeper of his confidential records and the author of some correspondence for his signature, she could expect to receive an attentive hearing for her opinions. (pp. 103-104)

Marjorie McKenzie did not become an ambassador, and she was never posted abroad, even after becoming an officer. Her entire foreign service career, which lasted until her death on 21 November 1957, was spent at External's headquarters in Ottawa. But she was far from confined to the undersecretary's cramped and cluttered outer office that for so many years was her little corner in Parliament Hill's East Block. When Prime Minister W.L. Mackenzie King attended the Imperial Conference in London in 1926, McKenzie accompanied the Canadian delegation as their stenographer. Two years later, at the 1928 Imperial Conference, McKenzie became the delegation secretary. She and Agnes McCloskey were two important women members of the Canadian delegation to the Imperial Conference that followed the coronation of King George VI in London in 1937. In the department's official history, Hilliker described her role:

> McKenzie provided liaison with the conference secretari-
> at, circulated schedules and reminders to delegates about

> meetings, organized and supervised stenographic work, ensured that documents for Canadian use were on hand regularly and in sufficient quantity, and otherwise ensured effective Canadian participation. She kept a complete set of all records, which she organized for future reference on her return to Ottawa. (p. 201)

Organizing documents and making note of their significance were nothing new for McKenzie. When the Conservative government of R.B. Bennett took office, on 7 August 1930, Bennett followed the example of his Liberal predecessor, Mackenzie King, and kept the External Affairs portfolio for himself. But Bennett, who became prime minister at the beginning of Canada's Great Depression, was preoccupied with economic matters and had little time to devote to international affairs. To keep him *au courant* with world news, Skelton sent him a weekly five to twelve page summary of events. The summary was prepared by Marjorie McKenzie. She perused material from the British Foreign Office and the Dominion Office in London, correspondence and reports from Canadian posts abroad, and articles from foreign newspapers. She then judged what was significant and put it together in readable form.

By the time Norman Robertson became undersecretary, following Skelton's death, McKenzie's duties as a secretary had disappeared, and she had become what the headline on Corolyn Cox's magazine article called her, "Safekeeper of the Secrets and Conscience of External Affairs." John Hilliker described her work:

> Marjorie McKenzie had long since given up secretarial duties in order to concentrate on other tasks: keeping up a set of working files, preparing correspondence, writing periodic resumes of current events, summarizing British documents, and copying King's marginal notes onto the departmental copies of papers before the originals were returned to Laurier House. She also continued in her role as commentator, via marginalia of her own, on drafts coming up from the department for the undersecretary. (p. 243)

That McKenzie also jealously guarded her turf as the custodian of secret documents is evident from her marginal notes on a 1942 document. Elizabeth MacCallum had just joined the department and had been assigned to work with McKenzie in the undersecretary's office. Saul

Rae, a newly recruited young officer who was Robertson's special assistant, wrote Robertson a long memorandum containing detailed suggestions for a complete overhaul of the filing system in the deputy's office. McKenzie did not take kindly to Rae's proposals.

He recommended that close relations be established with the department's file room, giving it information "as to the nature and presence of secret material," and added that "A notation should be placed in the general files indicating, if necessary, that these are incomplete and that further material may be seen on application to the custodian of the secret material." McKenzie's sharp rejoinder was "Definitely not, in some cases."

Rae's observation that "The filing of secret material should not be done on a purely personal basis, but should be based on some system which can be transmitted to and understood by others" drew this comment from McKenzie:

> I am well aware of this, and the filing system in the deputy's room is at least as systematic and comprehensible as that in the department. There has, however, never been any one available who was willing to learn it, consequently it's in a mess which will take a considerable time to put in order. This process will not be helped by talking it over with a lot of people who aren't familiar with the material. I know what I want to do and I want to be let alone to do it.

Rae ended his memo with the suggestion that Elizabeth MacCallum (whose name is misspelled as "Macallum") "be asked to compile the raw material of the Departmental Bulletin, under my guidance ... since I am not able to give the time to it which it now deserves."

To that suggestion and the entire document, McKenzie's response was blunt:

> Miss MacCallum has enough on her hands at present. If Mr. Rae can't carry on the Bulletin, perhaps one of the other 3d. secs. [third secretaries] could.
>
> It's nice of Mr. Rae to give so much thought to arranging my future for me. I think, however, things will go more smoothly if he will continue to look after his own business and leave me to look after mine. I didn't get Miss MacCallum brought in here and hand over the

more interesting half of my work to her just in order to load myself up with a lot of new work which doesn't interest me in the least, and which I'm much too lazy to tackle.

Shortly afterwards, McKenzie softened her language if not her position. She wrote a memo to Hume Wrong, then head of the Commonwealth and European division:

> You may have noted my immediate reactions to Mr. Rae's memorandum on organisation of material filed in and around the Deputy's room. This is an attempt to follow up with a more considered statement in diplomatic language. While it is really a matter for Mr. Robertson, you may wish to look through it in connection with the memorandum by Mr. Rae now in your possession. I should like it brought to Mr. Robertson's attention, as I am anxious to ensure that no decisions vitally affecting my own work are taken behind my back or without a clear understanding of my views on the subject.

McKenzie was on Robertson's staff and closely followed the proceedings at the first of two wartime Quebec conferences in 1943 and 1944 between U.S. President Franklin Delano Roosevelt and British Prime Minister Winston Churchill at which Mackenzie King acted as host.

Corolyn Cox described McKenzie as an apparently shy, private person, rather frail-looking, and untidy. In a Karsh portrait, she appears determined and angular, with a clear outward gaze.

Charlotte Whitton, in a radio broadcast on station CFRA in Ottawa, three days after McKenzie's death, paid her this tribute:

> Her entire life was one of challenge, a steadfast will of strong purpose against a frail body, frequently racked with pain, and rarely free from nagging ill-health, but all cheerily borne with a delightfully dry wit which would break through her grave reserve and almost submerging shyness. Informed, competent, discerning in her judgment of public affairs, she revealed a rare sensitivity in her few but delicately framed poems, published in a small chapbook for personal friends.

But what distinguished Marjorie McKenzie was her life of integrity of mind and spirit – this was utter and complete and nothing spurious could long survive in her cool, just and quite unconscious appraisal. She herself was so simply sincere that the meretricious and insincere shrivelled in her presence. Her life and service in the young Department of External Affairs in a country itself young in international relations is not likely ever to be recognized to the fullness of its worth.

That McKenzie never became an ambassador was only partly due to the tenor of her times. Her failing health and her responsibility to care for an elderly relative prevented her from being sent abroad even in a junior capacity after she became an officer. In a posting information sheet, dated 28 May 1957, she explained her reluctance to leave Ottawa:

I have bronchiectasis and chronic sinusitis which make me abnormally susceptible to influenza and pneumonia and subject to occasional bleeding from the lungs, usually very slight but requiring care while it lasts. My ability to continue working seems to depend on ready access to a well-stocked drugstore, a competent doctor, and sometimes to a good hospital. I have a dependent aunt living with me, 92 years old, somewhat crippled, and with an apparently arrested breast cancer which needs careful observation.

And on a characteristically self-deprecating note, she added, "I do not think I would be much use at any post abroad, owing to anti-social tendencies, a cloistered life, and a natural aversion to work."

Her colleagues certainly did not detect any aversion to work. Chester Ronning, who rated her performance when McKenzie was a desk officer in the department's Commonwealth division in 1953, said, "Miss McKenzie's knowledge, especially of our Commonwealth relations, is more profound than that of any other officer of the department, without a doubt." Indeed, Ronning thought so highly of her ability and her work that he supported her desire to remain in the Commonwealth division and urged the department to give her time off – a few months to a year – to write a book on Canada's relations with Commonwealth countries.

Ronning was not the only senior officer to praise McKenzie's work in the Commonwealth division. One of her tasks was to prepare briefing papers for members of the Canadian delegations attending meetings of Commonwealth ministers. In December 1949, she wrote a lengthy paper analysing discussions that had taken place during a meeting of Commonwealth prime ministers in October 1948. Her supervisor, H.F. Feaver, called the paper "comprehensive." The undersecretary, Escott Reid, who commended it as "a first-rate job which will prove extremely useful," had it circulated to the delegates who were to represent Canada at the Commonwealth conference in Colombo in January 1950. Although the memo is now more than forty years old, it was impossible to secure its release through Access to Information. Except for a few fragments and some introductory headings, the five-page document – still stamped secret – is covered in the heavy black blobs of the censor's felt pen. The official explanation for continued confidentiality is that the document contains critical assessments of the leaders of foreign countries.

Despite McKenzie's praiseworthy performance and sterling record, Ronning's recommendation to keep her in the Commonwealth division or give her leave to write a book went unheeded. Instead, in 1954, she became the first woman in External to assume the responsibility of a division head when she was appointed acting head of the Historical Research and Reports division. In a 1955 rating report, assistant undersecretary John W. Holmes credited McKenzie with good judgment and reliability. He said that she had "one of the best prose styles in the department. Her verbal style is terse but by no means ineffective." That was high praise indeed from a man who was himself a trend-setter among the department's prose stylists and a thorn in the side of those who did not meet his exacting standards.

Two months after McKenzie's death, an anonymous colleague summed up her work and influence, in the January 1958 edition of the department's monthly bulletin, *External Affairs:*

> Her essential characteristic was courage; courage both physical and intellectual. For years she fought against such ill-health as would have defeated – or at best soured – most of us. Yet, up to a few days of her death in hospital, she called for work to do and wrote with the same vigour and effect as she had in comparative health. Against the twin dangers that beset the civil servant – compromise with standards of accuracy and of style – she conducted what was perhaps an unconscious, but certainly an effective, one-woman campaign. She was a relentless pursuer of the truth, whether it was a date or an interpretation. Nothing stopped her, once started:

neither the clock nor elusive evidence. Because of the same intellectual honesty (combined with a wry humour), her style of writing was the constant enemy of "officialese" and "gobbledygook." This was in part because she sought to clarify rather than to confuse, and in part because her writing was an intriguing blend of precise phrases, abrupt condemnations, and down-to-earth remarks.

The size of the department multiplied many times during her period in it, and a decreasing proportion of its workers were conscious of this small and unostentatious person. Those who did know her capacities thought little of her rank or particular position, but rather of her judgment and her ability to find and to analyse the material needed for subjects covering a wide field. She "ventilated" subjects in a more accurate sense than the usual one, for she let fresh air into everything she touched.

Miss McKenzie had intellectually few illusions, and the illusions she had came from her generous heart. She would appear to be gruff and critical, but her warm smile would break through and melt any such impression. She had no automatic respect for authority, but was ready to give help to all those who sought it; and ready co-operation to those whose abilities she admired.

Wherever Marcel Cadieux first filed McKenzie's January 1950 note about the Irish minister, Josephine McNeill, it ended up in a National Archives file labelled *Recruitment of Women as FSOs in External Affairs.* How much good it did before it arrived there is not known; it is entirely possible, though, that McKenzie sent it to Cadieux because she wanted to make a point with him more than with anyone else who might read it. Cadieux, who later became undersecretary, was far from being a staunch advocate of the employment of women officers in External.

In 1948, as head of the department's personnel division, Cadieux wrote a memorandum on the selection of foreign service officers that said:

Women are eligible for appointment but a very small number should be admitted for the following reasons:

(a) They are very likely to marry and thus create early vacancies and therefore additional problems from the point of view of recruitment.

(b) They cannot be sent to all posts as easily as men and their usefulness abroad is not comparable in all missions to that of men, other things being equal. The admission of women in the Foreign Service should therefore be limited to exceptional cases when there are definite employment possibilities at headquarters or in the few large missions abroad where the work can be done indifferently by male or female officers.

In another memorandum later that year on the same subject, Cadieux referred to setting a policy on "the recruiting of girls as foreign service officers." Even in those unenlightened days, adult women aspiring to be diplomats must have flinched at being called "girls."

Cadieux's attitude towards female foreign service officers changed little over the years, despite McKenzie's subtle efforts. In his 1963 book, *The Canadian Diplomat*, Cadieux described the typical diplomat in terms at once picturesque and one-dimensionally masculine:

Everyone is familiar with the classic portrait of a diplomat: meticulously dressed, restrained in speech, punctilious in social relationships, at ease in any company, a man of the world, resourceful, even somewhat crafty, often cynical or at least mildly sceptical, little given to enthusiasm – in brief, remote, refined, but, taken all together, oddly ripe for caricature, not a lovable person. (pp. 19-20)

In time, the male mandarins of External would discover what Marjorie McKenzie's 1950 memo to Cadieux implied – that there were women who fitted the mould of the classic diplomat just as well as men did, and, in the course of their work, there were women who were perfectly capable of breaking a few moulds too.

CHAPTER TWO

EYE ON THE BOTTOM LINE
AGNES MCCLOSKEY

Many books have been written by and about the men who have had distinguished careers in Canada's diplomatic service. Unfortunately, women are barely mentioned in those books, unless they were wives, secretaries, socialites or celebrities. The men's female colleagues rated little more than a sentence or two or were relegated to an entry in the book's index.

The one notable exception to this generalization is Kathryn Agnes McCloskey. Her name appears not only in books about the early history of External Affairs, but also in the diaries of the men who led the department during its golden age, and in a vast clutter of departmental memoranda still on file in dusty boxes at the National Archives of Canada. So large did McCloskey loom in the consciousness of External's male mandarins that Sidney A. Freifeld devoted an entire chapter to her in his 1990 memoir, *Undiplomatic Notes: Tales from the Canadian Foreign Service*.

McCloskey arrived in the fledgling department on 27 December 1909. It was not long before her first name disappeared into a deliberately ambiguous signature – K.A. McCloskey – which she adopted so that correspondents would not ignore her because she was a woman. As she told Madge Macbeth of *Mayfair* magazine in a 1943 interview, she could not write stern letters to hard-nosed businessmen "using a meek sign-off like Agnes." Nor did she bother to set the record straight with correspondents who addressed her as "Dear Sir."

McCloskey remained in External – making waves and rousing resentment – for nearly forty years, retiring reluctantly at the end of May 1949.

Agnes McCloskey

She was not the first woman in the department. Grace Rankins had been there for three months when McCloskey was hired to replace another woman, Nellie Grey, who apparently lasted only four months as a temporary employee. (In those days, most women in the federal public service were hired as temporary employees; in 1921 the restriction on their tenure was codified by requiring women to resign when they married.)

But McCloskey was the first woman to get a diplomatic posting abroad. When Canada opened its consulate-general in New York, in 1943, McCloskey was appointed a consul representing External. Hugh D. Scully, the first consul-general, and two trade commissioners completed the staff.

It was the culmination of a career that began very modestly. Sir Joseph Pope, External's first undersecretary, had asked the Civil Service Commission for "a lady typewriter" and the commission sent him Agnes McCloskey, who had written the civil service examinations earlier in 1909. She was not much interested in a teaching career, even though she had earned a teacher's certificate at Ottawa Normal School.

Born in Chesterville, Ontario, in 1883, McCloskey had a conventional but sound education for a woman of her day. After elementary school in her home town, she spent three years at Gloucester Street Convent in Ottawa and took supplementary classes in physics and chemistry at St. Patrick's College. She never did learn to type; she bluffed her way into the typist's job at External by admitting archly to a civil service examiner that she did not know "everything" about typewriters. She managed to pass a simple typing test using the hunt-and-peck system; her lack of any more efficiency at the typewriter certainly did not hinder her career. Indeed, that and a complete ignorance of shorthand may have enhanced her prospects because nobody then or later could consign her to the typing pool or label her a stenographer. McCloskey was a bright, independent, and determined young woman who started out as a grade one clerk at a salary of $500 a year.

External was a minuscule department in 1909. McCloskey and Rankins, six men, and the undersecretary were its total staff. There were no posts abroad. Prime Minister Wilfrid Laurier managed foreign policy out of his office. In the resulting atmosphere of family informality, people tended to do whatever needed to be done without benefit of flow charts or job descriptions. McCloskey drafted letters for Pope's signature and began doing the department's accounts because, as she told a newspaper reporter, "I had a flair for mathematics and somebody was needed for the job."

In 1919, McCloskey, seeking reclassification and a pay increase, described her duties in a three-page, double-spaced, legal size memorandum to Pope. She said that she had worked on practically every post in the office and had been doing the work of an accountant for several years. With three, sometimes four, clerks to help her, she was drawing up the pay list for eighty permanent and temporary employees in Ottawa, keeping attendance records, arranging clerical appointments, buying supplies and equipment, arranging newspaper subscriptions and telephone and telegraph services, ordering printing and stationery, and guarding the petty cash for the department's Ottawa headquarters. She was the clerk in charge of supplies for External proper, for the Passport Office and the Prime Minister's Office.

Extending her reach beyond Ottawa, McCloskey supervised the expenditure of a $250,000 budget that was apportioned to meet administrative costs of posts in Paris, London and Washington, various consulates, several boards and commissions, as well as pay for entertaining official visitors to Ottawa.

There was a positive though not immediate response to McCloskey's long memorandum. It was not until 1 April 1921 that she was appointed departmental accountant grade one and her salary rose from $1,200 a year to $1,500. The salary range for senior clerks at the time was $1,320 to $1,600 annually.

McCloskey became External's chief accountant in 1931. She is warmly described in an article by Corolyn Cox in *Saturday Night* of 8 May 1943:

> As accountant of the department she arranged the financial matters covering each newly opened office, from the purchase of buildings to setting up of staff, furnishing of offices and residences, regulation of expense accounts. Still everybody remained "family," and Agnes, guardian angel for them all, sent cheques to children left in Canadian schools by parents on foreign service, rented suddenly abandoned apartments anywhere from Russia to New Zealand, always had an amazing assortment of house keys, private letters, powers of attorney, and other personal oddments stowed away in the drawers of her desk, finding time to execute bits of family business for our representatives in far away places. She was, in a word, an *institution* in the East Block. She is also what you call "a chip off the old block." There is a right and a wrong way of doing things, and Agnes believes in things being done right. Many a youngster, newly expanding his wings in Canada's foreign service, has had them summarily clipped by the lady who both sat on the Personnel Board that selected him for the department and decided where he should go, and then handled his expense account.

McCloskey's close scrutiny of expense accounts was a major reason why so many officers – all men – resented her and her influence in the under-secretary's office. The chapter about McCloskey in Freifeld's memoirs is called "The Penny Pincher of External"; Charles Ritchie called her "our female Talleyrand"; and J.L. Granatstein, in *The Ottawa Men, The Civil Service Mandarins, 1935-1957*, described her as an "unpopular and tyrannical accountant who had arrogated to herself total control of the department's administration." (p. 4)

Freifeld chronicles some of the ways in which McCloskey clipped the wings of young diplomats whose names would later become household words in Canada's foreign service. She docked Jules Léger a day's pay because he arrived late on his first day in the department. She refused to pay a living allowance to George Ignatieff in London until the high commissioner himself, Vincent Massey, intervened. She balked at paying the full cost of moving D'Arcy McGreer's five stepchildren to Tokyo.

The most glaring example of McCloskey's parsimony is recorded in an oft-quoted letter from L.B. Pearson at Canada House in London to Norman Robertson in the department in Ottawa. According to a 1940 file, while Hitler's bombers were raining their nightly devastation on London, Agnes McCloskey in Ottawa was filling pages of her ledgers with hand-written calculations on how much officers' allowances could be cut during wartime. After all, the usual rounds of official entertaining could not be conducted when bombs were falling, could they? McCloskey recommended, and the department concurred, that allowances be cut by 10 percent in all countries except those requiring U.S. dollars, where the cuts would be 5 percent. Pearson's reaction is quoted in full in the first volume of his memoirs:

> Dear Norman,
> Just a few words on last week's sequence of exciting events.
>
> *Monday, August 12th*
> British official figures show cost of living up 33%.
>
> *Tuesday – breakfast*
> No eggs (3/ -dozen)
>
> *Tuesday, 11 a.m.*
> Notice from landlord that rent is due (no reduction).
>
> *Tuesday – lunch*
> Three Canadian soldiers to lunch (no reduction).

Wednesday
Letter from my wife to effect that it is expensive to maintain household in Canada (including keeping 3 children not our own).

Thursday
Air raid shelter for 1 1/2 hours during day.

Friday
Suburban station next to mine hit by bomb in evening – streets nearby machine-gunned.

Saturday
Cable from External: 'Your allowances are cut by 10%.'

Sunday
Cable from External (after a heavy night bombing): 'You are all much in our minds.'

PS Please get us out of your minds at once. We don't want another cut. (pp. 183-84)

Officers may have been the most articulate complainers, but they were not the only targets of McCloskey's tightfisted ways. She kept tabs on the number of pencils used by stenographers and rubber finger guards used by file clerks and called to account anyone she deemed was using too many.

McCloskey had fans as well as critics in official Ottawa. Before the Conservative administration of R.B. Bennett changed the government's accounting systems in 1932, Agnes McCloskey gave External a record for efficiency that caused the auditor general to acknowledge that External was "one of the most air-tight and satisfactory systems in the government departments."

As John Hilliker recorded in the official history of External's early years, McCloskey ran a one-woman show before the Consolidated Revenue and Audit Act came into effect. She did not welcome the changes. "Agnes McCloskey was determined to remain the focal point of the department's financial operations," Hilliker observed. "Thus she wanted to deal herself with the auditor general, who performed the post-audit of departmental accounts and reported to Parliament on the government's financial management." (p. 147) Calling McCloskey's accounting system one of "personal control," Hilliker said that it was "designed to discourage curiosity on the part of the supervising agencies while maintaining her own and the department's reputation for probity and efficiency. Her effort seems to have been successful, for the auditor general found little in the department's financial operations to complain about, apart from the practice of charging against public funds some of the costs of travel to Canada by wives of 'certain' heads of post." (pp. 147-48)

Hilliker recounted in some detail how McCloskey's accounting methods drew the auditor general's approbation:

> To meet the department's financial needs, Agnes McCloskey devised a simple system, but one effective for operations on a modest scale. She herself prepared the annual estimates of the cost of headquarters operations and also of the revenues earned by the department, mostly through the sale of passports. Each post was required to anticipate its own yearly financial requirements (not including salaries and allowances of Canadian-based staff, which were paid from Ottawa). These figures then became the basis for the money voted by Parliament to support the department's operations.
>
> Once the money was voted, McCloskey was strict in allocating it according to the budgets already prepared. Although the vote included provision for unforeseen contingencies, she was reluctant to draw upon this, and she also seems to have disliked requesting supplementary estimates. Posts therefore were expected to stay strictly within their budgets and, if they went over the limit on one type of expenditure, to find a counter-balancing saving elsewhere. (p. 147)

Conscientious as Agnes McCloskey undoubtedly was – one news report said that she was accustomed to working twelve hour days, seven days a week – she did not spend all her time poring over ledgers, revising budgets, and blue-pencilling expense accounts. She also travelled, usually at her own expense, when she found her workload threatening a nervous breakdown.

While she made many visits to England and Europe, one of her most memorable trips started in Japan. She had been invited to visit the Canadian Legation in Tokyo by the minister in charge, Sir Herbert Marler. Sir Herbert and Lady Marler were McCloskey's friends. Aboard ship en route to Japan, McCloskey met the King of Siam and found common interests among fellow-travellers who were members of the Conference on Pacific Relations. Having sailed across the Pacific, she did not let the outbreak of the Sino-Japanese war prevent her from going on to China. She merely bypassed Manchoukuo, where the war raged, and went straight to Beijing.

She also made official trips. In 1937, she was a member of the Canadian delegation to the Imperial Conference in London that followed the coronation of King George VI. As the delegation's administrative officer, McCloskey sometimes must have felt that she had never left Ottawa. These were her duties, according to Hilliker: "It was her task to keep track of the expenses of the members of the party, their transportation arrangements, the hospitality they offered, and their lodging requirements. She also had to arrange for office equipment, suitable space for briefings and meetings, telephone, cable and mailing facilities, newspaper distribution and so on." (pp. 200-201)

Although McCloskey gave public credit for her success to the training and inspiration provided by two of her superiors in the department, Sir Joseph Pope and Dr. O.D. Skelton, she possessed no false modesty. In 1922, McCloskey wanted a promotion, and Pope supported her submission to the Civil Service Commission in a memorandum that said, "an injustice has been done to a very hardworking and worthy official who, by the highly efficient performance of her duties, renders me great and lasting service."

Dr. W.J. Roche, chairman of the Civil Service Commission, sent a terse reply to Pope, on 27 June 1922:

> I have no doubt that, as you say, Miss McCloskey is a most efficient employee, but pardon me if I also say that she is a most persistent one, and has undoubtedly used the influence which she claims to possess by bringing all the pressure possible to bear on the Commission to attain her ends.

Efficient as she was in building her fiefdom and maintaining her power, Agnes McCloskey could not sustain them as the Second World War catapulted Canada into assuming greater and more widespread international responsibilities and External expanded to meet them. Firmly entrenched in the department, McCloskey was a roadblock to improved administration in a growing department because, wrote Hilliker, "The practices she had devised, which had worked well so long as the department's operations were simple, were inadequate to the volume and complexity of work arising from the war. Her unmodified practices became, in the view of senior officers, an obstacle to departmental efficiency, the more so because she insisted on consulting the undersecretary frequently on minor matters." (p. 267) Indeed, the frustrations McCloskey inflicted were so great that Norman Robertson actually drafted a letter proposing to resign as undersecretary. He wrote, "I have come to the conclusion that the job is not one which I am cut out to do satisfactorily. It is in large and growing measure, an administrative post, requiring qualities of temperament which I, unfortunately, lack ... I believe I can be a more useful member of the public service in an advisory than in an executive capacity."

In the end, Robertson did not have to send his letter; his tenure as undersecretary was preserved by one of his senior officers, Hugh Keenleyside, who had the bright idea of posting McCloskey to the new consulate-general in New York. In Washington, Pearson greeted the news by writing in his diary, "For anyone who has had to pry expense accounts out of her, the significance of this move will be obvious. In the legation, it overshadowed all the war news; even the advance of the 8th Army had to take second place."

Newspaper and magazine articles at the time heralded McCloskey's posting as a history-making first for women. However, historians have been more sceptical. Louise Reynolds, in a study for Hilliker's book, reviewed the circumstances of McCloskey's posting and concluded, "All of this adds up to the fact that Agnes's posting to New York, while an honour to her, was brought about as much by the necessity to move her out of the East Block as by anything else. She might even be said to be a victim, the first notable one, of lack of adequate managerial direction in the department."

McCloskey spent nearly five years in New York, apparently enjoying the perquisites of her office but chafing at the loss of her independence. Reynolds and Freifeld observed that her relations with Hugh Scully were not easy. A memorandum about McCloskey from T.W.L. MacDermot to Pearson, dated 29 January 1948, said, "It is clear that her feeling against the Consul General is so strong that she will now disregard the consequences of satisfying her resentment as far as possible."

Offered early retirement in 1947 – her years of service by then entitled her to a full pension – McCloskey characteristically declined. External responded by sending her on an inspection tour of Canada's posts in Latin America in 1948. She sailed from New York, through the Panama Canal to Lima and Santiago, then went overland to Buenos Aires, and by ship again to Rio de Janeiro and Havana. Reynolds described the result:

Agnes's report, when compiled, dealt with office administration, personnel requirements and personal problems
of staff. It is a sensible, a sensitive report, yet one that
she would not have cared to share in implementing herself before having had the experience of a posting. Her
time in New York had, undoubtedly, changed her viewpoint and she was even known to complain about her
own allowances.

If External's management had had the wit and imagination to send
McCloskey on an inspection tour years earlier, her sensitivity and common sense might have prompted her to ease up on what seemed to management harsh and unreasonable scrutiny of their budgets and expense
accounts. Freifeld's assessment is indicative: "'Public Service' to the core,
mindful of the need for efficiency in government, overzealous and sometimes misguided in applying regulations, Agnes McCloskey was nevertheless a loyal and dedicated person, kindly of heart and privately helpful to
colleagues in difficulties or wounded by her austerities." (p. 71)

Had there been an Agnes McCloskey in External Affairs in the early
1990s, officials might have been spared the embarrassment of critical
news stories about extravagant travel expenses, costly club memberships,
and high living at posts abroad. She died in 1975, two years after
External left the East Block for the new Lester B. Pearson building.
Unfortunately, her ghost does not haunt the tightly guarded fortress on
Sussex Drive.

CHAPTER THREE

MADAME LE CHARGÉ
ELIZABETH MACCALLUM

The name of Elizabeth Pauline MacCallum deserves to be as well-known and well-remembered as those of Norman Robertson, Lester Pearson, George Ignatieff, Escott Reid, Hume Wrong, Arnold Heeney, John Holmes, and all the others inscribed in the pantheon of Canada's golden age of diplomacy. But MacCallum's name is not there. Even though she possessed impressive intellectual, scholarly, and professional credentials that were equal to those of many of her male colleagues, she had to enter the department of External Affairs by the back door, as a principal clerk in 1942. And even though it was wartime and the government could not recruit enough men for an expanding department, it was unthinkable to hire women as officers in the foreign service. Instead, bright, capable, and well-educated women were taken on as clerks and secretaries and given officers' work. They proceeded to do it brilliantly enough that External's old boys' network finally had no choice but to admit them to the diplomatic ranks.

Elizabeth MacCallum was an outstanding member of that group of extraordinary women who joined External during the Second World War. Born in 1895 in Marash, Turkey, where her Canadian parents were Presbyterian missionaries, MacCallum learned Turkish and Arabic and acquired an abiding love and understanding of the Middle East and its people which she ultimately transformed into her life's work.

The road from a tiny Turkish village to the East Block of Ottawa's Parliament buildings was long, had many turns, and not a few detours.

Elizabeth was a teenager when her parents came back to Canada. She attended high school in Kingston, Ontario, and then obtained a first-

National Film Board of Canada/National Archives of Canada/PA193221

Elizabeth MacCallum

class teacher's certificate at Normal School in Calgary, Alberta. From 1915 to 1917, she taught in prairie schools and helped with local farm work during the manpower shortage of the First World War. She then returned to Kingston, enrolled at Queen's University, and earned a master's degree in English and history in 1919.

A long detour took MacCallum to Dawson City, Yukon, where she taught for two years. Next it was post-graduate study in history and political science. MacCallum went to Columbia University in New York and found, to her immense satisfaction, a stimulating intellectual atmosphere where female political science students were not regarded as peculiar aberrations who had to be tolerated when they could not be ignored. They were accepted as equals.

She attended Columbia in two spurts, 1921-1922 and 1924-1925. In the intervening years, she worked as assistant secretary of the Social Service Council of Canada and assistant editor of the journal, *Social Welfare*, to finance her continuing studies. While at Columbia, she augmented her income by doing private tutoring. Later, when applying for work with the Canadian public service, MacCallum described one such undertaking in words that revealed her compassion, her skill as a teacher, and her unwillingness to suffer fools. She wrote that she had been "preparing a backward child to enter Lincoln School, Teacher's College. The girl had been given up as a hopeless moron by a leading New York psychiatrist, but was able after this year of private tuition to enter Grade 8 at Lincoln School and did successful work later at Radcliffe College." Given a glowing recommendation from her professors at Columbia, MacCallum joined the research staff of New York's Foreign Policy Association in 1925. She took part in the organization's study of diplomatic affairs and weekly debates among policy-makers, cementing her reputation as an expert on the Middle East.

Anne Trowell Hillmen, in an obituary tribute to MacCallum in the summer 1985 edition of *bout de papier*, described those New York years:

> It was heady stuff; the electric atmosphere of the exchanges; the possibility, ever present, of violence; the excitement of rubbing elbows with the best minds of the era; the thought that, maybe, just maybe, some good could be done in an already very dangerous world ...
>
> From 1925 to 1931, MacCallum worked in the Foreign Policy Association's Research Department. In this work, too, she was a pioneer; the department was then getting under way. She was one of six writer-researchers; they were given scope and intellectual freedom but expected to hold to the highest standards of objectivity and productivity. The more than twenty "monographs" she produced in these six years, mostly on Middle East affairs but ranging all the way to Australian politics, are masterpieces of thorough research, rigorous fair-mindedness, and clear, crisp writing. On Palestine, for example, she understood the complexity and divi-

sions that centuries of history had wrought. The claims
of the Jews were honourable and understandable. But
weren't the claims of the Arabs just as honourable and
understandable? (pp. 14-15)

More than six decades later, students of Middle Eastern affairs can
still find nuggets of knowledge, insight, and understanding in
MacCallum's articles. One on the Palestine conflict, published in *Foreign
Policy Reports* in October 1929, mentions the rioting, looting, and blood-
shed that occurred the previous month when bands of Muslim
Palestinians attacked Jewish groups and British administrative buildings.
MacCallum examined the sources of the conflict between Arabs and Jews
from a strong historical perspective going back to Kings Saul and David.
She observed, "Prior to the British occupation, Jews and Arabs in
Palestine lived together in tranquillity."

Another article, in August 1930, was a comprehensive review of the
various agreements that led to Iraq's drive for independence from British
rule. The truth of MacCallum's comment – "The Kurds of the north
were not anxious to be included in an Arab state" – was confirmed in the
images of Kurdish refugees fleeing Saddam Hussein's Iraq in 1991.
MacCallum found that when the British in 1919 started asking the
inhabitants of Iraq what kind of self-government they wanted, resentment against British occupation was so strong and excitement was at such
a high pitch in the Shi'ite holy cities that inquiries in the region had to be
discontinued. And both the Kurds and the Shi'ites opposed a proposal for
conscription in 1927 because they did not want the Sunni Muslim
minority in power in Baghdad to have a powerful army at its disposal.
When MacCallum wrote that the Kurds of the north "were not certain
that the Arab majority would always permit them to enjoy an undisputed
autonomy," she was describing a situation in 1927. More than sixty years
later, as the Kurdish people flee oppression, MacCallum's words sound
prophetic.

Looking at the Middle East in 1928, MacCallum found Turkey pre-
eminent and independent; Persia adapting to western ways and consider-
ing social reform; Egypt still occupied by British troops and its parliament suspended; Iraq seeking membership in the League of Nations;
Palestine without even a legislature; Syria evolving a constitution;
Lebanon with two years' experience of a constitution; Transjordan yet to
try representative government; and Arabia independent but "primitive in
its social organization." She also saw the beginning of the long-running
Arab-Israeli conflict. "Arabs in Iraq," she wrote, "whether nationalist or

not, were watching the establishment of a Jewish National Home in Palestine with an unfriendly eye ..."

Anyone seeking a deeper understanding of the roots of latter-day Arab nationalism could do worse than look up a thirty-five page supplement to *Foreign Policy Reports* of March 1926, entitled "The Near East, A Survey of Political Trends in 1925." It was written by MacCallum and the Foreign Policy Association's research staff. The supplement covers political and economic developments in Egypt, Arabia, Iraq, Syria, Transjordan, Palestine, Turkey, Armenia, and Persia. It even contains an historical tidbit for feminist readers. There was a woman in the Armenian cabinet in 1925. She is identified only as Mme. Vardanian, and her responsibility, not surprisingly, was the welfare of women and children.

MacCallum was often impatient with the U.S. press, taking it to task for ignoring the affairs of Arab nations unless there was violence. One can only imagine what she would think of today's thirty second television "bites" that not only report the violence but also seem to glorify it.

To sum up, MacCallum's monographs for the Foreign Policy Association make it clear that she had a deep, thorough knowledge of the Middle East and a sensitive, objective understanding of the nationalisms struggling to surface against British – and French – colonialism. It was a knowledge and understanding that would serve both her and Canada well in her future as a diplomat.

There was to be yet another detour on the road to that future. By 1931, MacCallum was ready for a change of pace and an opportunity to recharge her batteries. She was convinced that intellectual activity should be balanced with physical endeavours; so she retreated to a two-acre market garden in Uxbridge, Ontario, where she remained until her money ran out in 1935.

That year Italy was threatening to invade Ethiopia. Against that backdrop, the World Peace Foundation of New York asked MacCallum to make a study of Ethiopia's relations with Britain, France, and Italy. The results were published in a book, *Rivalries in Ethiopia*. She then gave a series of radio talks and lectures based on her Ethiopian research which earned her a fee of $50 for a single night. Many years later, MacCallum told a Queen's University oral history interviewer that the money from one lecture was more than the income generated by her market garden in its best year. (She spent her farming profits on a barrel-sprayer for apples.)

MacCallum returned to Ottawa in 1936, where two more curves awaited her on the road to External. She worked for the League of Nations Society for four years and then for the Canadian Legion's Education Service for two. In 1942, at the age of forty-seven, she reached her East Block destination and her diplomatic destiny. In applying to External, MacCallum had named as a reference the former director of the research department of the Foreign Policy Association, Raymond Leslie Buell. By June 1942, Buell was an executive in the editorial offices of *Fortune* magazine. His letter on the magazine's letterhead is in MacCallum's personnel file in the National Archives of Canada:

> I have the highest regard for her meticulous scholarship as well as her ability to write clearly and persuasively – a combination which is very difficult to find. She was regarded as one of the leading specialists on Near Eastern Affairs in the United States, but is at home in almost any field of international relations and politics. She is a person of charm and culture, having a fine co-operative spirit ...

MacCallum's first tasks at External sounded mundane for one of her intellect and ability: marking and clipping newspapers, doing research and some anonymous writing. Of the latter, she said in retrospect, "It gives you very much greater freedom to do good work if you're anonymous."

However, it was not long before her knowledge and experience of Middle Eastern affairs made her External's expert on the region, and she began briefing colleagues and preparing policy papers. Occasionally, her authorship of a paper did become known. One on Palestine was sent to Prime Minister Mackenzie King in May 1944 by Hume Wrong, then an assistant under-secretary. Wrong's covering note says, "Miss MacCallum has made a detailed study of the arguments advanced by the Canadian Palestine Committee, in the course of which she has explained the Arab point of view."

As the Second World War continued and knowledge of Nazi Germany's annihilation of the Jews became widespread, there were increased demands on the British government to transform Palestine into a Jewish national state where Jews alone would have responsibility for immigration and development. MacCallum reviewed the history of those demands and the British response to them, analysed representations made to the Canadian government by the Zionist Organization of Canada and the Canadian Palestine Committee, and made many incisive, thoughtful observations. These observations were very useful to the King government as it formulated Canadian policy on what would become the state of Israel.

Palestine was a British mandate. In 1939, the British government issued a White Paper designed to ease Arab-Jewish conflict at a time when there was increasing pressure for the establishment of a Jewish national home. The White Paper proposed self-governing institutions that would lead to an independent Palestinian state in which Jews and Arabs would share authority. One of the paper's most controversial proposals was to set a quota on immigration. For five years, the number of Jewish immigrants to Palestine could not exceed 75,000 a year. After 31 March 1944, the Arabs were to be given a veto on Jewish immigration. Winston Churchill, then an opposition MP, argued that neither Arabs nor Jews should be given responsibility for determining the rates of immigration. In his view, authority over immigration should remain with Britain. He argued further that Britain's main obligation in Palestine was to facilitate the establishment of a Jewish National Home.

The White Paper was implemented in February 1939, but there was no change in immigration. As MacCallum wrote, "Because of the difficulty refugees have experienced in escaping from Nazi dominated territory, only 60 percent of the full quota of 75,000 legal immigrants had been admitted to Palestine by December 1943. It was accordingly announced that until the full total had arrived the principle of Arab consent would not be invoked."

Jewish groups in Canada and Britain mounted protests. The president of the Zionist Organization of Canada, in a presentation to the Canadian government in May 1939, objected to a policy limiting Jews forever to one-third of the population of Palestine, closing parts of the country to Jewish settlement altogether and giving the territory independence, which he saw as meaning the establishment of an Arab government.

In her analysis and response to an oral brief, which the Canadian Palestine Committee had presented to King, MacCallum made a number of comments that illustrated her ability to draw conclusions about current events based on a thorough knowledge of history and politics:

> Any interest Canada may have in the White Paper derives, therefore, from its membership in the United Nations and the responsibility it will share for establishing a just and durable peace ...
>
> The designation of minority status as a "wrong" suffered by the Jewish people seems to be based on the popular illusion that the Jewish dispersion was forced. On the contrary it was voluntary. Only a fraction of the

Jews remained in Palestine at the time of the Roman conquest in Titus' reign. Attracted to Alexandria and other parts of the Mediterranean world more prosperous than their own, they had already established themselves in many other regions, from which they later spread out through Europe. The real wrong they had to endure was not minority status but the restrictions and persecution imposed on them in the Middle Ages, continuing in modified form in later times and culminating in the unparalleled atrocities of our own day ...

For the Mandatory Power there is apparently no escape from the charge of "appeasement," which will be heard no matter what it may do. To satisfy any Arab demand whatsoever will be to "yield to a truculent people who have resorted to arms." To grant any Zionist request, on the contrary, will be "to appease a worldwide clamour, insistently brought to the attention of every western nation by its Jewish citizens." ... It is important, however, to distinguish clearly between "appeasement" of an expansionist power like Germany and any measures which may be taken to give Arabs the right to govern themselves in their own homeland or to allow political Zionists a chance to experiment with an independent Jewish state as an aid to solving the Jewish problem ...

It is most unfortunate that a case as urgent and just as that of the political Zionists should be made to depend so frequently on assertions no reputable historian would regard as adequate. It is true that there is little knowledge on this continent of what has actually happened in the Near and Middle East in the past 50 years, and that it is consequently easy to manipulate the record so as to encourage the view that Arab claims in the present controversy may be dismissed as all but irrelevant. It is obvious, however, to any who have followed developments attentively that a just decision would have been much easier to arrive at today had the literature of the controversy been less imaginative.

With scarcely two years' experience in External and not yet an officer, MacCallum did not make specific policy recommendations in her memorandum. Instead, she remarked that Canada might be expected to help both Arabs and Jews achieve nationhood and political independence. Nearly fifty years later, MacCallum's views remain relevant to Canada's present-day relationships with Israel and its Arab neighbours.

Noting a conflict of interest not just between Zionist Jews and Arabs but also between Zionist and non-Zionist Jews, MacCallum said that it affected not only the well-being of the three groups "but also the stability of postwar arrangements as a whole." Expanding on the theme, she wrote:

> If political Zionists should be denied the right to estab-
> lish an independent Jewish state, their chief aim would
> be frustrated ... only an independent Jewish state can be
> counted on in future to offer a free haven of refuge in
> cases where international pressure may prove insufficient
> to put a stop to persecution. Nothing short of such a
> haven will give Jews the protection history has shown
> they need from the barbarity of European governments
> ...
>
> Non-Zionists also are bitter over the proposal to
> regulate Jewish immigration into Palestine in accordance
> with Arab wishes at a time like the present, when it is
> possible at any moment that there may develop a most
> urgent demand for accommodation of refugees from
> Europe. They are also opposed, however, to the demand
> for transforming Palestine into an independent Jewish
> state. The eagerness with which Poles, Rumanians and
> Bulgarians are inclined to support this demand and – on
> a different level – the interest shown in it by Canadians
> who consciously or unconsciously discriminate against
> Jews socially, professionally or economically, gives sub-
> stance to the fear that anti-Semitism is preparing to
> clothe itself in the respectable garb of a philanthropic
> policy, that in western democracies there will result the
> discrimination against which Jews have had to fight so
> long and hard a battle ...
>
> Non-Zionists maintain that no matter how clear a
> distinction is drawn legally between Palestinian citizen-
> ship and the allegiance Jews outside Palestine owe to the
> governments under whose jurisdiction they live, in prac-
> tice there would develop an irredentist frame of mind as
> the result of the establishment of an independent Jewish

state ... In all countries a new barrier would be raised between Jewish minorities and their fellow-citizens, setting them apart – in the western hemisphere particularly – from all other minorities ...

If now the United Nations decide to establish an independent Jewish state, into which millions of refugees may pour from Europe, the Arabs believe a wedge will be driven between the component parts of the state or federation they themselves are trying to establish ... the Arabs fear that Jewish domination may not stop short at the boundaries of any state which may be carved out in response to Jewish demands ...

Arabs regard it as a matter of essential justice that Europe itself should make reparation to the Jews for the sufferings it has inflicted on them. If the establishment of an independent Jewish state is regarded as the best permanent solution of the Jewish problem, the logical thing to do, they hold, is to force Germany to alienate territory for the purpose. If the United Nations hesitate to do this on the ground that it would cause resentment and lead to future wars, precisely the same objection stands in the way of forcing the Arabs to alienate part of their patrimony – and in the latter case resentment would be increased by the knowledge that it was not the Arabs who had been responsible for the existence of a Jewish problem in Europe. If, on the contrary, Germany were merely asked to place a large fund at the disposal of the Jews, much of it to be used for the expansion of the Jewish National Home in Palestine, this again would mean that Arabs were being required to help pay for crimes they had not committed.

MacCallum concluded her memorandum with some observations about an alternative to Britain's White Paper. This was a proposal to divide Palestine into two states, one Jewish, one Arab.

The partition proposal ... will not satisfy many groups in the Zionist movement which are already mobilizing against it on the ground that the territory offered is utterly inadequate for the purpose it must fulfil. Neither will the proposal be acceptable to the Arabs, since it will serve to drive the Jewish wedge more firmly than ever into a strategically important part of the Arab heritage. Similarly, it will not remove the dangers threatening non-Zionist Jews. If the partition proposal is adopted, however, there is a possibility that in conjunction with a more liberal immigration policy in Canada and the United States, the opening up of opportunities for Jews in the Soviet Union, and the provision of special facilities for the rehabilitation of Jews in Europe, the compromise may prove successful.

At the United Nations in 1947, the General Assembly adopted the partition solution by a vote of thirty-three in favour, thirteen opposed, ten abstentions. Canada voted in favour of it, Britain abstained and the Arab and Muslim states were opposed. Six months later, the state of Israel came into existence. What influence Elizabeth MacCallum's thoughtful memorandum had on Canada's ultimate decision to support partition is not known; what is known is that Hume Wrong, for one, urged caution. When he sent MacCallum's analysis to the prime minister's office, Wrong observed:

I would myself be loath to see any strong advocacy by the Canadian government of a particular solution of the Palestine problem. No matter what may be done about the White Paper, Palestine will remain, for a long time, a troubled area in a region of the world in which it is most unlikely that Canada will have any very direct interest.

Twelve short years later, Canadian soldiers were on their way to the Sinai as United Nations' peacekeepers, demonstrating that Wrong was right about the region being troubled but wrong about Canada's interest.

Elizabeth MacCallum, meanwhile, had gone to the San Francisco Conference in 1945 as a member of the Canadian delegation and took part in negotiating peace settlements between Libya and Ethiopia. It did not seem to bother her that she was a clerk doing an officer's work. As Hillmen wrote:

External Affairs seemed to Elizabeth the ideal job. She had bright, energetic colleagues, most with the same university background. There she could also specialize in the life and politics in the Middle East. Her work was both intellectual and all-absorbing, perfect counterpoise to her contemplative existence in Uxbridge. (pp. 14-15)

When the ban against female officers was lifted in 1947, MacCallum became an officer and the department's one-person, unofficial Middle East division. In Ottawa, she exerted great influence in forming and shaping Canada's Middle East policy. At the United Nations in New York, she gave wise and invaluable advice to the Canadian delegation. Hillmen described MacCallum's role:

All material with even a remote bearing on Middle Eastern questions passed through her hands. Whether in New York ... or in Ottawa, she was respected for her expertise and for her strong-minded determination to ensure a balanced and humane approach to the problems of the region. She was directly involved in the negotiations surrounding the partition of Palestine, the internationalization of Jerusalem, the setting up of Canada's first mission in Beirut, and the Suez crisis. (pp. 14-15)

Except for five months' temporary duty in Athens, in 1951, MacCallum's career kept her based in Ottawa until 1954. She then became the first Canadian woman to go abroad as a head of post, opening the new Canadian Legation in Beirut, Lebanon. The post was not an embassy; so MacCallum was not an ambassador but chargé d'affaires ad interim. Thereby hangs a tale.

When the Lebanese foreign ministry learned that a woman was to head Canada's new legation, the chief of protocol wanted her title listed in the feminine form, Madame la Chargée d'Affaires. External initially agreed. But the Papal Nuncio and the British ambassador in Beirut both argued that the title "chargé" described a function, not a person, and should not be altered to the feminine when the person carrying out the function was female. MacCallum herself preferred the masculine form because she found that her fellow diplomats – all male – were treating her as a lady instead of a colleague.

In Ottawa, Yvon Beaulne of External's protocol division held out for the feminine form while Jules Léger, the undersecretary, pointed out that the question was one of diplomatic usage, not grammar, and suggested consulting Paris. Upon learning that when Clare Booth Luce was appointed U.S. ambassador to Italy the Italians used the masculine form of the title, reserving *ambasciatrice* for its customary designation of an ambassador's wife, and that several other countries alternated between attaché, attachée, chargé and chargée, E. D'Arcy McGreer of the protocol division recommended to Léger that MacCallum be called "Madame le Chargé."

Léger informed her of the decision in December 1954. He said that External would pay the cost of having new cards and invitations printed with the masculine form of the title. The undersecretary went on to advise her to pay calls on other mission heads in the absence of their wives, and to attend official functions herself. There was to be no misunderstanding about the identity of the Canadian representative.

MacCallum had her cards and invitations reprinted and sent External the bill. But her greatest satisfaction had come earlier when she presented her credentials to the Lebanese foreign minister, Alfred Naccache, on 19 October 1954, and told him, "It was a source of great happiness to me when the Secretary of State for External Affairs invited me to undertake this mission to a country whose history and development have been a subject of interest to me for many years." In his reply, Naccache noted that MacCallum was the first woman to head a diplomatic mission in Lebanon.

Although she carried out her diplomatic and consular duties with characteristic wisdom and dedication, MacCallum's deafness proved a much greater problem in Beirut, with all the social responsibilities devolving on a head of post, than it had in Ottawa.

She had never tried to hide her hearing problem. In the application form which she completed before she became an officer in 1947, she described the state of her health: "Hard of hearing, but able to take part in conversation and conferences on almost equal footing with persons of normal hearing, with the help of a hearing aid." Indeed, part of the reason for the Uxbridge farm years was to give her relief from the constant strain her deafness caused her in New York. She found country people to be much more considerate than her urban associates. She once described conversation as nervous torture, with her body "like a wired grand piano pulled to the utmost ... each sound like a hammer hitting ... everywhere."

After two years in Beirut, MacCallum returned to Ottawa. External wanted her to head the new, now official, Middle East division. She was not well enough to accept and in 1957 took a leave of absence, effectively retiring for health reasons in July 1958. But she was sorely missed in External, and when her health recovered later that same year, the department asked the Civil Service Commission to reinstate her with the rank of foreign service officer 5. Supporting the request, D.L. McGivern of External's personnel division wrote, "Miss MacCallum is a specialist on Middle Eastern matters and her services are especially required at this time because of the present political situation in the Middle East which it is expected will be a continuing one for some time." Léger backed McGivern's assessment: "In fact, she has special qualifications which are not otherwise available to this department."

MacCallum returned to External until her 65th birthday on 20 June 1960 when she retired formally. Even then, she did not entirely cut her ties with the department; until 1977 she worked occasionally on contract for the historical division while also pursuing other activities.

Immediately on her retirement, she returned to her beloved Turkey where she studied Turkish literature and worked on village development. At age 82, she became a community volunteer at Ottawa Civic hospital, working with the elderly, especially hearing-impaired patients. She taught herself sign language; she played the piano in concerts for patients; she gardened, took up jogging, and maintained a lively interest in people and world events until her death on 12 June 1985, a week before her 90th birthday.

MacCallum never married. Her deafness was one reason. As she told the Queen's university oral history interviewer, the strain of conversation imposed by marriage would have been intolerable for her. Marriage also might have cost her her life's work because in her day women officers who married had to resign from External.

Over the years, honours came to MacCallum. In 1952 her alma mater, Queen's, gave her an honorary doctorate of laws. In Centennial year, 1967, she was among the first to receive the Medal of Service of the newly established Order of Canada; she later became an officer of the order. But unlike the male mandarins who were her colleagues during Canadian diplomacy's halcyon years, Elizabeth Pauline MacCallum never wrote her memoirs. It is an omission that deprived Canada and Canadians – in particular Canadian women – of an important chapter in their history.

CHAPTER FOUR

AMBASSADOR EXTRAORDINARY
MARGARET MEAGHER

On the 400-mile highway from Nairobi to Kampala, an official car pulls up to the side of the road about ten miles outside the Ugandan capital. A slender woman in her mid-fifties steps out from behind the wheel, and a tall, burly African clambers from the rear passenger seat. The woman seats herself decorously in the back as the African buttons his shirt collar, dons a tie and a chauffeur's cap, raises the Maple Leaf flag on the car's front fender, climbs behind the wheel, and drives the Canadian High Commissioner to Uganda into the city in proper form.

Passersby might have seen this tableau several times in the years between 1967 and 1969 when Margaret Meagher was Canada's high commissioner in Kenya and Uganda and travelled regularly from her residence in Nairobi to Kampala. Usually, she made the trip by air: "Nairobi was a centre for air traffic in all directions and we could easily go to Entebbe," Meagher said in an interview. But because she loved to drive and always had her own car, she sometimes drove, taking her chauffeur in the official car because it was an official trip. "And he was perfectly happy, more than happy, to sit in the back seat while I drove," Meagher said. The roadside switch outside the capital illustrates how this distinguished Canadian diplomat was able to combine a sense of dignity with informality while never losing her human warmth amid the protocol demanded by her official position.

Meagher had many official positions during her thirty-two-year career in the Department of External Affairs and almost everywhere she went she broke new ground. She was the first female Canadian diplomat

Courtesy of Margaret Meagher

Ambassador Margaret Meagher with Israeli Prime Minister David Ben Gurion in 1960.

to become an ambassador – to Israel in 1958. In Tel Aviv and on postings to Vienna, Kenya and Uganda, and Cyprus, Meagher was the first woman head of mission. In Vienna she became the first woman to chair the board of governors of the International Atomic Energy Agency. In Kenya, besides being the first female high commissioner, she was also the first one from Canada to live in Nairobi. And from 1973 to 1974, Meagher capped her trail-blazing career by becoming External's first female foreign service visitor at Dalhousie University in Halifax.

With that appointment, she came full circle to Halifax where it all began. Margaret Meagher was born in the Nova Scotia capital in 1911. A student of French, German, and political science at Dalhousie, she nurtured her abiding interest in international affairs by joining the campus League of Nations Society. After graduation in 1932, she organized and became the first president of the Halifax youth unit of the League of Nations Society. She also became a teacher and taught in Halifax public schools for ten years. In the meantime, she earned an MA in French and German and took graduate studies in political science. "Had the foreign service been open to women at that time, it would have been my first choice and I would have applied. But since I couldn't do that – it was out of the question – I didn't give serious thought to it. Why should I? I knew it was impossible. So I taught school and I enjoyed it in a way but I would certainly have chosen External had I had the opportunity."

That opportunity came during the Second World War. Dr. Robert A. MacKay, who had been her political science professor at Dalhousie and who later became a diplomat himself, telephoned Meagher one day to say that External was holding a special examination for female university graduates. The department wanted to hire women as temporary clerks for the wartime emergency. They would do the work of junior foreign service officers. Meagher wrote the examination, did well, and started in 1942 as a grade 4 clerk at a salary of $1,620 a year. That was 60 percent of what probationary third secretaries earned. But it was the officers' work that mattered. "That was the carrot," she said. "I wouldn't for a moment have been attracted to go to Ottawa to do a clerical job in any department, even External. But the idea that, never mind the rank, I could be doing diplomatic work appealed to me enormously. The first day I was in External I came back to my lodging and I thought, eureka, this is where I belong."

Meagher was assigned to a special section (later a division) created to deal with issues arising from the internment of civilians and prisoners of war in Canada as well as the internment of Canadians in Germany, Japan, and Italy. While the defence department was responsible for administering prisoner-of-war camps in Canada, it fell to External to communicate with the International Red Cross and the protecting powers representing enemy governments about the welfare of military prisoners and civilians interned in Canada, and to monitor the treatment and condition of Canadians held in Germany and other enemy and enemy-occupied countries. Because Japan had not signed the Geneva Convention that set the rules for prisoners of war and interned civilians, the Allied countries had great difficulty trying to help their nationals who were imprisoned by the Japanese.

The section was so swamped that everyone worked overtime; for a fledgling diplomat, it was excellent on-the-job training. "I could not have had a better introduction to the workings of External Affairs," Meagher remembered. "Mr. Rive [Alfred Rive, the division head] gave me all sorts of opportunities to spread my wings, as he did with all his staff. It was a very busy time, the pressures were enormous and it was only by pushing all of us – including himself – to our limits could he ensure that his division kept up with the load. This was good for all of us and we all co-operated to the full."

One particular assignment led to Meagher's first posting abroad. In 1944, the governments of Canada and the other Commonwealth countries negotiated with the German government an exchange of sick and wounded prisoners of war. Meagher had to organize the practical details of the exchange. The International Red Cross had chartered a Swedish ship, the *Gripsholm*, to transport the prisoners, and it was agreed that a Canadian civilian, George Magann, a senior officer at the Canadian embassy in Washington, would be on board. Meagher replaced Magann for the three months he was absent from Washington. In the summer of 1945, as the war in the Pacific drew to an end, she did another three-month stint in Washington, working with the Americans on the repatriation of Canadian prisoners of war from Japanese camps.

Years later, when External was compiling a reference book on the war to serve as a guide for future emergencies, Meagher was asked to write a history of the special division. A draft of her account, now unclassified and stored in the National Archives of Canada, describes the bureaucratic nightmare of diplomatic decision-making when twelve government departments and five non-governmental agencies have to be consulted to implement an international agreement. Meagher wrote:

> I recall one particular example in connection with negotiations for an exchange of civilians with Germany. Joint approaches were to be made by the British Commonwealth and U.S. governments to the German government proposing an exchange of British and U.S. civilians held in German custody against an equal number of German civilians in British and U.S. territories. Before committing the Canadian government to this scheme an interdepartmental committee was called which was attended by representatives of all the departments concerned ...
>
> The entire committee, including the service representatives ... were very much in favour of the exchange which would result in the repatriation of Canadian civilians from enemy territory. No objection was raised at the committee and it was unanimously decided to recommend that Canada should go along with the U.K., the rest of the Commonwealth and the U.S.A.
>
> After obtaining the necessary approval, the Commonwealth and U.S. governments were informed of our decision and in due course the proposal, specifi-

cally including Canada, was delivered to the German government. This proposal was accepted in principle by the German government and there remained only the details to be negotiated.

At this point the Special Division received a letter ... in which we were told that the Intelligence Committee [made up of representatives from the armed forces and the RCMP and responsible for gathering information about subversive activities] had considered this proposed exchange at their latest meeting and that, for security reasons, they could not agree to the repatriation from Canada of uninterned German civilians. There was no doubt in our minds that the withdrawal of Canadian participation in the exchange, or the attempt to alter the proposal by adding a limiting clause in regard to Canada, would not only have prevented the return of Canadian citizens from Germany but might well have wrecked the entire scheme and probably jeopardized all future repatriation movements.

The project was saved when the Intelligence Committee retreated in the face of a sharp letter from Hume Wrong, acting undersecretary in External, warning of the consequences and pointing out that the prospective German repatriates would be subject to a thorough security screening before being allowed to leave.

Meagher wrote her account of the work of the special division from the Canadian embassy in Mexico, where she had been posted as third secretary in 1945. Although she was still a clerk, she was the first woman to be sent abroad with diplomatic rank, in a move more pragmatic than policy-making.

Hugh Keenleyside, the Canadian ambassador in Mexico City, had asked External for an additional staff member, and Wrong, the acting undersecretary, asked Meagher to go to Mexico City as a vice-consul. Meagher readily agreed but Keenleyside demurred. He told Wrong that he wanted someone to do more than consular work and that the Mexicans would not take Meagher seriously unless she was on the diplomatic list. (As a vice-consul, she would not have been on the list.) A typical Canadian compromise ensued: Meagher went to Mexico City as an accredited diplomat – third secretary – while Ottawa maintained her status and pay as a clerk.

"There was no question of changing the salary, that really wouldn't have been legal," Meagher recalled. "There were no women foreign service officers and it required a change in government policy to do that so my pay was going to be my grade 4 clerk's pay. The only question that arose was, what are we going to do about the allowances? It didn't seem to occur to them, or I guess to me either, that it should just be the same as the third secretary [male] would get."

In the end, somebody chose an arbitrary figure – now forgotten but less than the men were getting – and asked Meagher to try it. After three months, she realized that the amount was insufficient, wrote Wrong to say so, and promptly got an increase that permitted her to maintain a standard of living suitable to a foreign diplomat in Mexico City.

Meagher found her three and a half years in Mexico to be valuable training. She tried her hand at nearly all the activities usually performed by a foreign service officer abroad. She did consular work and reported to Ottawa on political and economic conditions, labour relations, defence, and other matters as they related to Mexico. On two occasions – for the only time in her diplomatic career – she played the role of naval attaché as she made the intricate arrangements for official visits of Canadian naval vessels to Acapulco.

Meagher was in Mexico in 1947 when the government decided to allow women to compete for positions as foreign service officers. She wrote the examination at the embassy and then went to Ottawa on leave, staying with the Keenleysides who had returned earlier. The results came quickly. The Civil Service Commission informed Meagher that she had passed the written examination and invited her to appear before the Oral Board the next day. The interview was gruelling, an ordeal which every prospective foreign service officer anticipated with dread.

Meagher was more than equal to the challenge. She was as successful in the oral examination as she had been in the written one, and with so much experience already under her belt, she became an officer with the rank of second secretary. She was so highly regarded by her male supervisors that subsequent promotions came regularly. (Then, and for many years into the future, all department and division heads as well as heads of mission abroad were men.)

Norman Robertson, who was Canada's high commissioner in London when Meagher was a counsellor at Canada House, foresaw the day when she would be a head of mission and praised her judgment and her ability to work with people and to earn their affection.

Other colleagues were similarly approving, though one was rather graceless in expressing himself. David Willcock, in a feature in *WEEK-*

END Magazine 25 October 1958, quoted a senior External official as saying, "Margaret thinks like a man. And she brings to her job all the intuition and understanding of a woman as well." Charles Ritchie, in one of his famous published diaries, was less patronizing. "Margaret Meagher is staying with us," he noted in December, 1969, when he was high commissioner in London, "She is very good value, down-to-earth in a Nova Scotian way." Praise indeed from a fellow Nova Scotian.

Returning from Mexico in 1949, Margaret Meagher spent four years in Ottawa and undertook a variety of assignments in External's American, United Nations and economic divisions. She represented External on an interdepartmental committee overseeing Canadian participation in the Colombo Plan. The plan had been established by Commonwealth countries to provide economic and technical assistance to their members in South and Southeast Asia. It was an experience that served her well when she had to keep an eye on Canadian aid projects in Kenya and Uganda eighteen years later.

Posted to Canada House in London in 1953, Meagher sharpened her skills at diplomatic reporting and solidified her admiration of Norman Robertson. "He was one of my heroes in the department," Meagher said.

> He was undersecretary when I joined and undersecretary for a long time; he was my high commissioner in London; and I just felt it was an enormous privilege to work closely with Norman Robertson which I didn't do in the department because he was up there in the rarefied atmosphere. But in Canada House I did. He always took anything I had to say, any reports, very seriously, we had long talks about things, and I was personally very fond of him. I think he was one of our really big brains, a really profound intelligence, very modest, not one for pushing himself and his views but highly regarded by the U.K. Foreign Office and anybody else that he worked with. We all had tremendous respect for Norman, but affection too.

It was not long before Robertson's vision of Meagher as a head of mission became reality. In April 1957, she was sent to Israel as chargé d'affaires at the Canadian embassy in Tel Aviv (the ambassador, with dual accreditation to Greece and Israel, lived in Athens). She expected to stay two years. The two years stretched almost to five, her longest stay in any of her posts, because during her tenure as chargé the government decided to appoint a resident ambassador to Israel. How Margaret Meagher became Canada's first ambassador to Israel, and the first Canadian woman to hold ambassadorial rank, provides an amusing example of what can occur when the niceties of diplomatic protocol are observed.

Meagher had been performing well as chargé and had a good relationship with Foreign Minister Golda Meir and other Israeli officials as well as with her Canadian colleagues and the diplomatic corps in Tel Aviv. Yet she was still surprised at the offer of an ambassadorship. The idea had never crossed her mind.

But Meagher could not just switch hats and change her calling card to read "ambassador" instead of "chargé d'affaires." First, she made an official call on the foreign ministry to ask for the Israeli government's formal acceptance of her as Canada's ambassador. This is called an *agrément*. The director-general of the ministry, Walter Eytan, found the request amusing, but he assured her that it would be granted. "I think it was something quite unusual to go and ask for *agrément* for yourself," Meagher said.

It was a perfectly choreographed diplomatic dance. Canada's chargé d'affaires to Israel was called home, ostensibly for consultations, and the Canadian ambassador was sent to Tel Aviv once the formal agreement arrived. "I was a new person, a different person, as it were," Meagher said. "While I was still in Canada and after the announcement was made, I got so many telegrams and letters from people in Israel, it was very heartwarming." One she particularly cherished came from the chargé at the U.S. embassy. Recalling the 1949 appointment of Perle Mesta as U.S. envoy to Luxembourg and her instruction to call her madam, the American chargé telegraphed Margaret Meagher: "Delighted to call you madam." And when the world's only female foreign minister, Israel's Golda Meir, visited Ottawa in October 1958, she spoke warmly of Canada's first female ambassador: "I cannot tell you how happy we are to welcome Miss Meagher as our ambassador, not because she is a woman but because in her own right she has been so highly respected and really loved. We are really delighted she is coming back. We couldn't have wished for anybody better."

Meagher remained in Israel until 1961. She was challenged by the diplomatic work in a never-dull political hot spot; she was intrigued by the Israeli sociological experiment of bringing Jews home from everywhere in the world; and she was enchanted by the opportunity to visit ancient cities and travel throughout the Middle East where western religion, civilization, and culture have their roots.

During her last year in Tel Aviv, shortly after Cyprus became independent and the newest member of the Commonwealth, Meagher was also accredited there as Canada's high commissioner. She presented her credentials in the spring of 1961 and travelled around the island, noting its scenic beauty, its monasteries, and its ties to Greek mythology and the history of the Crusades.

In 1962, Meagher went to Austria as Canada's ambassador, very conscious again that she was the first and only woman ambassador in Vienna, often called the cradle of diplomacy. She appears in a photograph taken at a New Year's reception given by the Austrian president for the diplomatic corps. It shows every head of mission with three or four staff members; Meagher is the only woman in the entire group.

George Hardy, a former diplomat now retired in Victoria, was second secretary at the Canadian embassy during Meagher's tenure and found her "extremely capable and very pleasant." He continued:

> The office ran like clockwork, my reports were read, discussed and signed without difficulty. Cocktail parties and formal dinners went smoothly, although I don't recall how the male-female seating arrangements were resolved at the latter functions. Indeed, this seemed to be the only "problem" of concern to the Austrians (protocol, you know!). We, of course, were well aware of this but Margaret never mentioned it to me. Indeed, I don't recall ever having had a better ambassador.

Meagher took a diplomat's social obligations in stride as easily as she took the professional duties. Nor was she hindered by being single. "I sometimes wonder," she said, "if it wouldn't be more difficult for a single man to be head of post. I mean, being a woman, you have a natural interest in the running of the house, in menus, in that kind of thing. It's terribly important to have good domestic staff and getting them is, to some extent, a matter of luck. Once you get them it's not luck any more, it's the way you treat them and handle the situation." (Meagher treated her domestic staff so well that her chief steward in Nairobi asked to be her butler in Stockholm. She agreed and paid his air fare when he returned home for occasional visits to his family.)

Much as she enjoyed living in Vienna, with its rich musical and cultural life and its opportunities for travel – often by car – to nearby European cities and the surrounding countryside, Meagher said that she would have been seriously under-employed had she been only the ambassador. Luckily, she was also a governor on the board of the International Atomic Energy Agency whose headquarters are in Vienna. As a country with expertise in nuclear power generation and other peaceful uses of atomic energy, Canada is a permanent member of the agency's board, along with Britain, France, the former Soviet Union, and the United States. During her time in Vienna, Meagher occupied Canada's seat on the twenty-five-country board, and in 1964 the members elected her its first female chairman. In addition, she headed the Canadian delegations to the annual conferences of the agency's full membership.

Service on the atomic energy agency was by no means Meagher's only experience with multinational organizations and conferences. Between 1948 and 1967, she was a member of Canadian delegations to sessions of the United Nations Educational Scientific and Cultural Organization, the International Telecommunications Union, the U.N. Economic and Social Council, the disarmament subcommittee of the U.N. Disarmament Commission, and the United Nations General Assembly. In 1964, she headed the Canadian delegation to the Trade and Development Board of the United Nations Conference on Trade and Development. Those assignments took her at various times to New York, Mexico City, Santiago, Tokyo, London, and Geneva.

In 1967, Margaret Meagher went to Kenya. Because she was the first Canadian high commissioner to reside in Nairobi, it was up to her to find an official residence and to arrange for it to be furnished and decorated. The office had been set up by an administrative team from Ottawa, but Meagher lived in a hotel until the house was ready.

Jomo Kenyatta was president of Kenya when Meagher was there, and she learned from Kenyan friends that he cited her position as high commissioner as an example to Kenyan women of what they could accomplish. "There were some very well-educated, very intelligent women and he wanted to see them start things going," Meagher observed.

She found diplomatic life in Kenya and Uganda very different from that in Vienna and later Stockholm.

> The most important and most frequent contact we had with Kenyan officials had to do with Canadian develop-ment projects and programs and this gave me a very practical reason for talking to people, for consulting with them, for going to look around the country to see what was happening. And I found this attracted me particular-ly because several times in my earlier career I had had to do with the theories of economic development and even

projects and plans from the Canadian end, such as the
Colombo Plan. Now I was seeing it at the receiving end.

Meagher was especially enthusiastic about two specific aid projects in
Kenya. In one, retired Canadian air force officers were training Kenyans
to become air traffic controllers. The other was more far-reaching. It
involved Canadians from McGill University helping to set up a medical
school at the University of Kenya. Professors from McGill went to
Nairobi to teach pediatrics; Kenyan graduate students went to McGill for
post-graduate work in their specialty and returned to their country to
practise and teach.

Her assignment to Sweden, in 1969, was the high point in
Meagher's diplomatic career. She was given the task of directing the
Canadian team in negotiations with the People's Republic of China. The
major issues were mutual recognition and the establishment of diplomatic relations.

Meagher was still in Nairobi when the stage was set for the talks.
Acting on instructions from Ottawa, Arthur Andrew, Canadian ambassador in Stockholm, initiated contact with Beijing. Andrew asked the
Chinese chargé in Sweden if his government were interested in establishing relations with Canada and, if so, in what capital where both countries
were represented would it prefer to conduct the negotiations? The
Chinese replied that they were interested, suggested Stockholm as the
site, and presently sent Wang Dong as their ambassador.

However, Arthur Andrew was coming to the end of his tour of duty
in Stockholm; so External turned to Margaret Meagher. "They asked me
if I would be willing to consider going to Stockholm as ambassador and
said that, if so, they would like me to be there at a certain time and
would I give up any idea of coming home on leave because these negotiations with the Chinese had just started and Ottawa did not want an
interruption."

At preliminary meetings, Andrew and Wang had set the ground rules
and procedures for the negotiations, agreeing that they would be conducted in strict confidentiality and that the negotiators would have nothing to do with the media. Meagher, meanwhile, was still in Nairobi. She
thought that "This will be a very interesting and different kind of thing. I
negotiated in the U.N. context but never this way, on a one-on-one basis.
I hope it's not all over before I get there."

She recalled how the talks went after her arrival in Stockholm in
September 1969.

You don't get many occasions to do that sort of thing and while, of course, I followed very strictly my instructions from Ottawa as the Chinese ambassador did his from Peking, just the same I think the role of negotiator is important in the give-and-take, in the establishment of confidence with your opposite number. And the Chinese ambassador and I got along very well.

There were times when I was rather discouraged. I wasn't sure we were ever going to get a successful conclusion to it. But the personal relations between the ambassador and myself were excellent and the negotiations were carried on – we each had a team with us – always in a very civil manner. There were no raised voices, no pounding tables, nothing like that. And I appreciated that and was terribly interested in the negotiating process.

In October 1970, thirteen months after Meagher arrived in Stockholm, the negotiations ended successfully without fanfare. "The agreement took the form of a mutually agreed text of a press release which the Chinese ambassador and I both signed," Meagher said. "So that, I think, was an accomplishment and I don't take credit for the substance of the negotiation but I take some credit for carrying it out. And I think it was important, not only to achieve the resolution of the problem but also to start out our new relationship on the basis of some confidence and the only two people who were talking to each other at that stage were the Chinese ambassador and I in Stockholm."

When Wang Dong, her opposite number in the Stockholm negotiations, was sent to Ottawa as China's ambassador, Margaret Meagher had been retired from the foreign service and was living in her native Halifax. On a visit to Ottawa, she dined with the Wangs at their residence. When they subsequently made an official visit to Halifax, Meagher was invited to a gala dinner, and the Wangs, bearing gifts, called on her at home.

Meagher's retirement in 1974 simply meant focusing her energy and talent in other directions. In the first year, she was a member of the Canadian delegation to the United Nations World Food Congress in Rome. At various times, she represented the Atlantic provinces on the board of trustees of the National Museums of Canada, and she was a member of the board of governors of the Atlantic School of Theology and the Nova Scotia College of Art and Design.

Her alma mater, Dalhousie, bestowed upon her an honorary Doctor of Civil Law degree in 1970; two other Nova Scotia universities, St. Francis Xavier in Antigonish and St. Mary's in Halifax, gave her honorary doctorates in 1974 and 1975. And the country which she had served so long, so faithfully, and so well officially recognized her achievements when she was made an officer of the Order of Canada in 1974. Margaret Meagher, so often the first woman among her peers in the diplomatic corps, was truly a pioneer. She reflected on this during an interview in the dining room of her comfortable Halifax home.

> Not only was I the only woman head of mission everywhere I went – in both Israel and Austria, however, one other female colleague was accredited toward the end of my assignment – but there were very few women members of any rank in the diplomatic corps. One had to be conscious of this – it was rather noticeable! I was never self-conscious or worried about it but it was, I suspect, one more reason why I was determined to do a good job. I was, after all, blazing a trail and whether I performed well or fell flat on my face might have had some influence, at least for a time, on the appointment of other women. In retrospect, I like to think that my record made some small contribution to the cause of equal opportunities for women in the Canadian foreign service. My strongest motivation, however, derived from my very deep loyalty to Canada and to External and I would never, consciously, have let down either of them.

CHAPTER FIVE

FROM CLERK TO ROYAL COMMISSIONER
PAMELA McDOUGALL

Most of the women who began their diplomatic careers as clerks did so because government policy until 1947 barred women from joining External as officers. But Pamela McDougall, the second Canadian woman to become an ambassador, rose through the ranks because, as she said in an interview, "It had never occurred to me that I might be a foreign service officer."

She could have had a career as a research scientist. Born in Ottawa in 1925, McDougall attended Glebe Collegiate before studying chemistry at Mount Allison University in New Brunswick. She had summer jobs at the National Research Council in Ottawa, and, after completing graduate studies at the University of Toronto in 1946, she worked at the council for a year as a researcher in organic chemistry. However, following a year's study at the Sorbonne on a French government bursary, McDougall abandoned science. "I really didn't want to continue in a laboratory," she recalls, "and when I came back from France I just simply went out and looked for a job."

Having relatives in the civil service and being an Ottawa resident, she naturally took her search to the federal government. Because she spoke French and had travelled, somebody suggested External Affairs and somebody else told her to learn stenography.

Fortunately for the future diplomat, she then met a wise woman in External's personnel division who said, "Learn stenography? You'd be crazy. We'll see if we can get you appointed as a clerk and then you can go on from there, you can write exams."

Ambassador Pamela McDougall, in September 1971, at the entrance to the newly completed Canadian embassy in Warsaw, with one of the Polish architects who helped design the building.

Starting as a grade 3 clerk, McDougall was assigned to the consular division. She said, "I was handling correspondence, I was doing jobs a lot of junior foreign service officers were required to do – they hated them probably – I found it quite interesting so the time wasn't wasted." Indeed, as a clerk she was offered her first posting abroad, to a new consulate the department was opening in Germany. Again, she was advised, "No, don't do that, don't disappear into the boondocks while you're still thinking about trying to qualify as a foreign service officer."

She stayed in Ottawa and wrote examinations, becoming first a junior administrative assistant and finally, in 1952, a foreign service officer grade one. She spent about eighteen months in the department's United Nations division before her first diplomatic posting abroad.

Getting that assignment gave McDougall an insight into how External officials sometimes treated women. The department initially wanted to send her to Berne. Then it occurred to someone in personnel that the man being considered as the new head of post in Switzerland was not likely to accept a female officer on his staff. His attitude reminded McDougall of an earlier incident of discrimination against women by Canadian diplomats. McDougall was studying at the Sorbonne when the Canadian embassy gave a reception to honor Canadian novelist Gabrielle Roy, who had come to Paris to accept the Prix Femina for *The Tin Flute*. Of the Canadian students living at the Cité Universitaire, McDougall recalled, "All the men got invited to the reception for Gabrielle Roy and none of the women, which I thought was just horrendous." McDougall wasted no time letting her friends at the embassy know what she thought of such a slight to the female students.

Instead of Berne, McDougall went to Bonn as third secretary. In her own view, she came out the winner because she found Bonn "a far more interesting and more important posting than Berne." She had her reasons for feeling this way.

From 1953 to 1957, Germany was an exciting place to live and work. The German people, having recovered from the post-war occupation, were full of energy and had embarked on what was to become an economic miracle. They were rebuilding their war-torn cities and eagerly implementing a new, democratic constitution. Germany was taking steps toward a rapprochement with the rest of Europe that would ultimately lead to European Union. The country joined the North Atlantic Treaty Organization in 1955. Subsequently, a NATO contingent of Canadian troops was stationed on German soil. It was also a time of heavy German immigration to Canada. All these events engaged McDougall's interest and intellect during her four years in Bonn. By comparison, Berne looked like a dull political backwater, notwithstanding the proximity of the Alpine ski slopes.

Posted back to Ottawa, McDougall dealt with human rights in the U.N. division, worked on the French desk in the European division, and then spent a year as the senior political advisor to the Canadian delegation on the International Supervisory Commission for Vietnam.

An international conference in Geneva in 1954 had produced accords to end hostilities between France and the Vietminh in Indochina. It established a commission composed of representatives from Canada, India, and Poland, to supervise the ceasefire zone on the 17th parallel between North and South Vietnam; to ensure the free movement of people; to facilitate the release of prisoners; and to stop any illegal movement of troops and arms. Every young, single foreign service officer in External in the mid-1950s could expect a tour of duty in Indochina; men were the first to go, but women eventually had to take their turn.

McDougall remembers the assignment as both horrible and fascinating. There were many small irritants such as the Army officer in charge of the commission who barely tolerated the diplomats from External, and the administrator who appropriated McDougall's staff car and took over the cockroach-ridden but spacious and attractive room in the Continental hotel in Saigon that she had left for her successor, Vivienne Allen. Regular trips to Hanoi were a nightmare; on one of them McDougall contracted amoebic dysentery. A bout of hepatitis confined her to her hotel room for six long, wretched weeks.

"But it was a fascinating experience. I travelled in Vietnam, travelled in North Vietnam to some extent, went to Cambodia and was able to see Angkor Wat, met some interesting people, worked with some very worthwhile people, enjoyed the Indians," McDougall recalled. "I think I'm probably one of the few Canadian foreign service officers that wasn't entirely put off the Indians during their time in Indochina."

There was considerable tension among the Indians, Poles, and Canadians on the commission. Some of it arose when the Indians chaired commission meetings and field trips; they sought unanimous agreement on every issue. The Poles, meanwhile, insisted on reporting what they saw as violations of the Geneva agreements by the anti-communist parties but ignored breaches by the communists. The Indians usually backed the Poles. Canadians, more critical of the communists, also disagreed with the Indians about the fate of South Vietnamese anti-communists should the communist north win free elections in a unified Vietnam.

In 1958-1959, when McDougall was in Indochina, the commission was in a holding pattern, little was being accomplished, and the Indian representatives wanted to do nothing that would upset India's friendly relationship with the Soviet Union, one of the countries to which the commission reported.

Most Canadians were frustrated by the lack of progress and by the Indians' attitude, but McDougall, perhaps because of her innate warmth and empathy, adopted a philosophical and detached viewpoint as she observed the games that were being played. She later remarked, "I found my Indian colleagues interesting and comparatively easy to get along with and I didn't get too worked up about their machinations, which were probably no worse or more surprising than those of all the other players in this tedious interval between two wars."

It was the first time that McDougall had worked in such an international setting, participating in multilateral discussions and negotiations. She called it "an excellent experience ... well worthwhile." She did not know it then, but the assignment in Indochina, working with Indians and Poles, was also good preparation for future postings to New Delhi and Warsaw.

Based in Ottawa for almost two years after returning from Saigon, McDougall spent some time in the Far Eastern division and then was sent on an inspection tour of Canadian posts abroad. "I think in 14 months," she said, "I was out of the country something like four months just travelling from one post to another. I was in South America, in the Caribbean, I was in Europe, Eastern Europe. It was a great opportunity to see what made a post tick and what bothered people."

On that 1960-1961 inspection tour, McDougall discovered a camaraderie among the personnel that was founded on a feeling of confidence about Canada's role in international affairs. People complained about salaries, allowances, medical care, housing, and the difficulties of educating children, but no one questioned the value of their work and the regard in which it was held. Wives of foreign service officers did not seek careers of their own. They devoted themselves to their husbands and enjoyed travelling and living in foreign lands and learning about foreign cultures.

Because Ottawa did not exercise much direct control over relations with other countries, and communication was slower than it is now, diplomats at posts abroad found their work more satisfying than it is today. In the early 1960s, personal and local initiative was encouraged and accepted, and views from abroad were given more credence than they were to receive twenty years later. McDougall said;

> Too little attention, however, was paid in those days to
> defining objectives, establishing priorities, planning for

possible changes in Canadian interests. As a result, some posts floated with little sense of direction or of leadership, either on the ground or from Ottawa. A strong head of post made all the difference. And personnel policies were the old hit-and-miss, throw-a-dart-at-the-board type of approach which has plagued the foreign service for years. I wish I could say there has been a lot of improvement.

Her inspection tour finished, McDougall was posted to the Canadian High Commission in New Delhi from 1961 to 1963, as first secretary and later counsellor. She handled internal and external political reporting and supervised the office's information section. On her return to Ottawa, she was made deputy head of External's Far Eastern division and head of its China section.

Having established herself as something of a specialist in Far Eastern matters, it was no surprise that McDougall's first (and only) ambassadorial posting was to Warsaw. The assignment simply reinforced a cynical and common quip in diplomatic circles everywhere. It goes something like this: if you want a posting to Brasilia, become fluent in Arabic.

McDougall arrived in Poland in January 1968. Almost immediately she felt the negative fallout which the Six Day War between Israel and Egypt had on internal Polish politics.

I was met at the airport by the chief of protocol, a Polish Jew – he was one of the ones who had gone out to Russia and come back at the end of the war. Within three weeks he was gone from the Foreign Office. I called on the foreign minister and within a month he was gone. I then presented my credentials to the President of Poland, Edward Ochab, and within three weeks he was gone. Then I went to call on the senior woman in the Foreign Office, she was a vice-minister, she was gone. The head of the Canadian-American section was gone, and there were others. All of them either were Jewish or had taken a particular position during the Six-Day War. I began to think that I had the kiss of death. And then it was an extremely difficult time in terms of knowing who was in a sensitive position, who you could feel was relaxed and would talk to you, or whether they were looking over their shoulder. These people were not being taken away and put into camps or something, they were just simply relieved of their jobs. Most of them had to leave the country because they couldn't get a job. The older men were pensioned off but the younger people were really in a terrible situation.

The aftermath of the Six Day War was not the only international event that made it difficult for McDougall to function efficiently in Poland. There was the Soviet invasion of Czechoslovakia in August 1968. It "cast a terrible gloom on the situation," McDougall said. "I don't know how the Poles felt but they went along with the Russians and kept a stiff upper lip. You couldn't talk to them about the Czech invasion. So the atmosphere was bad because of these really essentially external events for a good part of the time when I was in Poland."

McDougall was actually out of Poland when the invasion occurred, on a holiday motor trip that took her and a Canadian friend through the Polish countryside and into Czechoslovakia, Hungary, and Austria. McDougall described the trip in a 1 September 1968 letter to her mother in Ottawa. The letter, in clearly legible, closely spaced handwriting, takes up seventeen pages of blue airmail flimsy.

Strolling in a park in an Austrian village on 21 August 1968, McDougall overheard a fragment of a broadcast as she passed a couple sitting on a park bench listening to a portable radio. "I caught someone reporting from Warsaw in German about western broadcasts being jammed. So that was my first indication of what was going on," she wrote.

McDougall and her friend promptly left for Vienna. The Austrians could not ignore what was happening less than 100 miles from their border. Radio and television carried nothing but the dreadful news. While her friend made plans to fly to London, McDougall consulted Ottawa about the advisability of driving back to Warsaw. The letter continues:

> Finally decided discretion was better part of valour. Just as well because the border was definitely closed that night by Soviet troops asserting their control. My plane left at 5.30 p.m., L. got away at 1.30, spent time in between tucking my car, with a sad and affectionate pat, away in an empty garage space belonging to a kind-hearted embassy stenographer and then getting out to the airport carrying my precious transistor in my hand ...

We flew to Warsaw by going right across Hungary to the Soviet border and going around unhappy Czechoslovakia ... As you can imagine, there were many stranded or who left their cars in Vienna. I'm very lucky that Jan (the embassy driver), who took the official car out to Vienna for servicing the day I left, got back safe and sound complete with my cleaning a few days before the invasion. It was his first and probably his last trip so it was nice that he had it without worry. Both the British and American official cars are stranded in Vienna. The Americans are driving theirs back via Sweden. Which reminds me, I got back to find to my surprise that my new military attaché was stranded in Nuremberg with his wife whom he had happily driven out to have her tooth fixed. I think they will turn up via Sweden one of these fine days.

As you can well imagine, it was depressing coming back here in the midst of all this ... I suppose I must assume that the climate will eventually improve. Certainly it has done nothing but get steadily worse since I arrived and has now reached the stage where it's not only impossible but probably inappropriate to try to widen one's contacts with the Poles.

The effects of international politics aside, McDougall enjoyed her assignment in Poland and found the Poles even-handed in their attitude toward female diplomats.

They were extremely polite, they could also be quietly sticking a knife in your back and turning it quietly and sometimes you were aware of that and that was fairly irritating. On the whole they were good people to deal with, you had to be patient, you couldn't expect miracles.

Returning from Warsaw in 1971, McDougall was loaned to the Privy Council Office as assistant secretary to the cabinet for External policy and defence and senior assistant secretary to the cabinet for government operations. In 1974, she returned to External to become director general of the bureau of economic and scientific affairs; from 1973 to 1976, she also served as chairman of the personnel management commission.

In 1976, for family reasons that prevented her going abroad, she asked to be transferred to the domestic public service. She was appointed chairman of the Tariff Board.

In August 1979, Pamela McDougall became deputy minister of National Health and Welfare. She was the first female foreign service officer to be promoted to deputy minister, but the promotion was not a high point in her career. McDougall commented:

> To be very frank with you, why anybody ever appointed me as deputy minister of National Health and Welfare will always remain to me the mystery of the universe, just utter nonsense. I had absolutely no experience whatsoever in any of the areas of National Health and Welfare. The only thing I did have was a science degree so at least I understood what people were talking about when they got into technical matters, understood perhaps more than somebody who didn't have that background.

Yet it was an offer she could not refuse. It was made by the clerk of the Privy Council on the telephone at eight o'clock one morning while McDougall was on holidays. How could she say no when told that the prime minister, Joe Clark, had approved the appointment, that it was going through cabinet that very morning, and that her answer had to be immediate? "It had nothing to do with common sense," McDougall recalled. "Even the minister didn't know until after the appointment was made."

But if her year as a deputy minister was the nadir of her public service career, what followed was the apex. In September 1980, Prime Minister Pierre Trudeau asked McDougall to conduct a Royal Commission on Conditions of Foreign Service. In his letter of transmittal, Trudeau gave McDougall a framework for the inquiry:

> Some of the factors which come to mind here are the climate of violence which prevails in far too many places, the aspirations of women in Canadian society, the growing recognition of the need to provide full equality for both partners in Canadian marriages and how foreign service can stand in the way of this, and the pressures of foreign service on family life and the disruptions to that life which such service can cause and which fewer Canadians are willing to accept.

McDougall's experience as a foreign service officer, in Ottawa and abroad, her easy manner, and her rapprochement with everyone from the lowliest embassy security guard to the most eminent national personage, made her an inspired choice to head the royal commission. And her inspection tour of all Canada's posts abroad twenty years earlier had been an unwitting preparation.

McDougall travelled 121,600 kilometres and interviewed over 60 percent of the 1,800 employees and the 1,100 spouses at Canada's 119 foreign posts. Her report, delivered in 1981, was lively, thoughtful, and made sensible recommendations. It contains one of the most succinct descriptions of diplomatic work ever written. McDougall wrote:

> It has been said elsewhere in this report that much of what the foreign service does abroad today concerns operations, but by itself this is a pretty sterile term. "Operations" means helping get an aid project off the ground and ensuring that it is implemented; it means finding out what markets exist for Canadian products and exposing Canadian businessmen to them; it means negotiating with governments on behalf of Canadian businesses; it means learning about a country's agricultural and horticultural bases and relating them to Canadian possibilities; it means providing liaison with foreign governments on complex subjects like energy or the law of the sea or communications and broadcasting; it means to a large extent being all things to all men and never ruffling feathers in the process. It also means working in countries with very different ethical standards from ours without running afoul of our own values ...
>
> Unlike the domestic service, the foreign service lives with the employer twenty-four hours a day, seven days a week. In many cases the government is not just the employer but the landlord and the fount of whatever amenities are available to make life easier. The foreign service is quite literally on the job or affected by the job twenty-four hours a day. Its members live not according to local time but in response to clocks set back in Ottawa. Finally, they live within an environment dictated by international diplomatic protocol and practices that determine their status in society, often down to where they may or may not sit at a dinner table.

The summer 1982 issue of *International Journal* published a commentary on McDougall's report by Sir Geoffrey Jackson, of the United Kingdom Foreign and Commonwealth Office, and a review by Lord Garner, former British high commissioner to Canada. Jackson described McDougall as "popular and rightly respected" and said that the report "bears the stamp of Miss McDougall's lively and concerned approach to her assignment." Garner said, "this report was presented in little less than a year, is written in a brisk, down-to-earth style, punches home clear recommendations with no reservations, and concentrates on people. Can it be doubted that many of the qualities in the report derive from the fact that there was a single commissioner and that she was a woman?"

After thirty-five years of service, Pamela McDougall retired from the government in December 1981. For nine years she was a member of the board of governors of Carleton University, and for five years she was trustee and vice-chairman of the board of the Royal Ottawa hospital. That kept her busy until 1987 when, in her own words, she "resigned from these retirement activities to start an entirely new career as the wife of Lt. Col. Paul Mayer, Canadian Army retired (whom I first met in Vietnam almost 30 years before)."

Interviewed in Ottawa in 1992, McDougall reflected on the difficulties of trying to combine family life with a career in the foreign service:

> If you're saddled with a family that are having troubles,
> and you're not being promoted, and you're being sent to
> all the horror spots of the world, and you see some of
> your colleagues rapidly climbing the ladder, sitting in
> Ottawa a good part of the time, then you're not having a
> satisfying career, you can't get away from it.
>
> I think from that point of view it was really a lot
> easier to be a single foreign service officer. You could roll
> with the punches, you could try to get an interesting
> job, but if you didn't get the one you wanted, it really
> didn't matter. I think when you are dragging your family
> around with you it's a very different kettle of fish.

McDougall and her husband divide their time between their home in North Carolina and another in Ottawa. She has not entirely severed her ties with External. She is on the editorial board overseeing production of an official history of the department, the first volume of which was published in 1990. Many present-day female foreign service officers continue to regard her as a role model for their own careers.

CHAPTER SIX

TAKING THE INITIATIVE
JANICE SUTTON

In the mid-1950s, Janice L. Sutton, born and raised in Ponoka, Alberta, was working at her first job as a secretary in Edmonton and dreaming of seeing the world. A bright young woman who had won a governor-general's medal in grade nine at high school, she had gone to work after only one year at university. The world beyond her office desk seemed far away, completely unreachable, until her mother told her of a newspaper advertisement that caught her eye.

The Department of External Affairs sought secretaries; Sutton applied, was accepted, and left for Ottawa in the fall of 1956. It was that simple. Buoyed by the thought of living and working in foreign countries and making her travel dreams come true, it never crossed Sutton's mind that someday she would be a diplomat and not just a diplomat's secretary.

Of course, by the 1950s, there were women diplomats. But the basic requirement for a foreign service officer was a university degree, and Sutton did not have one. She was initially quite content to work as a secretary. She said, "That was my role, and in the '50s what were the career options? You could be a nurse, a secretary, a teacher. And so I burbled along doing that job for a number of years, having a good time in life, going on postings, to New York for four years ... But the career possibilities in External, the possibility of crossing over into the officer ranks, were just nil in that era of the department's life and so my ambition was just to get promoted, get through the secretarial ranks, which I did."

She was on her third posting, to Bogota, Colombia, when her ambition soared beyond typewriter, filing cabinet, and steno pad. Bogota had one of Canada's smaller embassies and Sutton, by this time a senior secre-

Courtesy of Janice Sutton

Janice Sutton is greeted by Prime Minister Indira Gandhi during the visit of a Canadian
Parliamentary Delegation to India in April 1984.

tary and learning Spanish, found herself doing a great deal of consular
work, in particular preparing the documents needed before visas could be
issued for travel or immigration to Canada. Once the paperwork was
completed, an officer would sign the visas. In addition, an astute embassy
clerk spotted her potential and gave her a chance to do the mission's
accounts, and the ambassador, Ormond Dier, supported her attempts to
broaden her skills and experience.

Back in Ottawa and working for the second time in the office of the
undersecretary – the staff called it "killers' row" – Sutton started to look
carefully at the papers coming across the officer's desk. She knew that she
could do the work; that she had the requisite intelligence; and that given
the proper training and a more comprehensive knowledge of the structure
and process of the department, she would be able to perform an officer's
duties.

Sutton was taking night classes at the University of Ottawa when she
learned about a departmental competition for administrative services officers. Working late was an occupational hazard in the undersecretary's
office. The men were at meetings all day, came back to the office at

5 p.m., and then worked until 7:30 or 8 p.m. Consequently, the secretaries often had time on their hands during the day. It was during one of those lulls that Sutton picked up a poster announcing the competition for administrative officers. She had the grade 12 diploma and the number of years' experience in the public service that the position demanded. She – and hundreds of others – wrote the examination in Ottawa's Glebe Collegiate. Having passed the written test, Sutton was called for an interview. She knew that she had succeeded in the competition when she was summoned to be fingerprinted – a security requirement of all officers in the foreign service.

Before she was officially informed of her promotion, however, she was posted to Saigon. It was an assignment that she had long sought. She went to Vietnam in the spring of 1968 as secretary to the Canadian commissioner on the International Control Commission. Sutton recalled some of her experiences:

> It was the height of the American involvement in the war. When I arrived in Saigon there was a 6 p.m. to 7 a.m. curfew. We lived in the Continental Palace hotel right on the main street of Saigon. The first night I arrived I woke up in the middle of the night sitting bolt upright in bed. It was like broad daylight in my room; looking around all hell was breaking loose around me, I didn't know what on earth it was. Just at the end of the street where the hotel was situated was the Saigon river and on the other side of the river was Viet Cong territory and the Americans dropped flares all night long over that territory to keep them from coming across the river. And that's what that was; it was the light of the flares coming right in my window.
>
> One night about two o'clock I was awakened by a loud "whoosh, bang." The Viet Cong had launched a rocket attack on the Vietnamese parliament which was next door to the hotel. Several rockets hit the building. By this time all the hotel residents were clustered together in the lobby watching the rockets zoom in and pieces of the building fall off in flames while the Vietnamese firefighters ran around in the dark.

The knowledge that death and destruction were going on all around them pervaded even the restricted social life among commission members. Sutton had no television set in her room. She and the other Canadians made do with old National Film Board movies enlivened by the sound of real gunfire and rocket attacks. Parties on weekends had to be held in the afternoon because of the 6 p.m. curfew. Sutton vividly remembers the table just inside the door of the party room where all the men parked their sidearms.

Her Vietnam tour over, Sutton returned to Ottawa in the winter of 1969 and took up her new duties as an administrative services officer. Secretarial work was behind her. Purely diplomatic assignments were still in the future and not immediately foreseeable. She worked in the consular and information divisions of the department and then in the personnel division where she was in charge of the secretaries. It was at this time that External instituted a new program to make it possible for qualified members of the department's support staff to attend university.

Janice Sutton was one of the first three staff members to be chosen. She enrolled in an arts course at the University of Ottawa, made the dean's honours list, and graduated in 1974. External kept her on full salary during her two years at university, paid her tuition fees and gave her a $250 allowance to buy books. During summer breaks, she worked in the personnel division. Her graduation coincided with the department's decision to convert administrative officers to foreign service officers. Sutton became a full-fledged diplomat.

But External at first did not know what to do with this former secretary and administrative officer, and newly minted female university graduate. In due course, she went to the Latin American division of the department, partly because of her knowledge of Spanish and her experience in Bogota and partly because male officers in the Latin American division were thought to be less chauvinistic than their counterparts elsewhere.

The foreign service union, called the Professional Association of Foreign Service Officers, was formed in 1968, soon after Canadian public servants had obtained collective bargaining rights. By 1974, the association was looking for a woman and a former administrative officer to sit on its board. Janice met both requirements and became the first woman on the PAFSO board, serving two years.

At one board meeting, Sutton acquired an insight into how other women in the department operated. Her account of the meeting also shows how she generated her own success:

> The first thing that came up was, how do you get the good jobs? I said, "The good jobs?" To them, those were

economic jobs, in the economic stream in the department. The focus for several women at this meeting was
on getting themselves into the good jobs. I said, "But
you can make any job a good job. What you do is look
at your job package and if there's no content you pull in
strands and make it into a good job. Which is what men
do."

And I've thought about that very often since. Just a
different approach to careers; if I can get into a good job
then I'm okay and I'll be in the right stream and get promoted. But you have to take the initiative.

Janice Sutton, an effervescent, self-confident woman whose sometimes prickly manner masks a genuine warmth, practised what she
preached. She seized opportunities, worked hard at what she undertook,
and succeeded so well that on two occasions in her career, when she left
Delhi and later the Middle East division, her work load was given to two
people.

It has a lot to do with confidence. For the first little
while you can't believe that you're an officer in the
Department of External Affairs. And then you're afraid
that somebody's going to find out that you were just a
secretary. So you have to say to yourself, "Well, I'm just
as smart as the guy across the desk, I'm a hard worker
and I know that I can do it."

At about the same time as she joined the Latin American division,
Janice Sutton met Franklin Wiebe, who also had made the transition
from administrative officer to foreign service officer. Offered a posting to
Buenos Aires, Sutton informed personnel division that she and Wiebe
planned to marry. Personnel immediately assumed that Sutton was leaving the department, an assumption she quickly dispelled. "You're not
going to deny me my right to work," Sutton told a somewhat startled
personnel official, who drew a line through Argentina and began looking
for a post that would take a married couple. It turned out to be Jakarta.

A grade one foreign service officer (FS1), Janice Sutton started off at
the Canadian embassy in Jakarta "doing the melange that FS1s do – consular work, public affairs, some aid, NGO work" until she was promoted
to FS2 and took on the more interesting and intellectually challenging
task of reporting and analysing political and economic developments in

Indonesia. Then a new ambassador arrived, and Sutton and Wiebe's plans to spend a third year in Jakarta went askew.

A new, young, male foreign service officer had arrived at the embassy. Even though he was junior to Sutton, the new ambassador decided to reassign the duties, giving the young man the political tasks and sending Sutton back to consular and public affairs. Despite her protests and those of her husband and the ambassador's wife, the male neophyte got the political work. So Sutton and Wiebe left Indonesia.

Sutton saw the proposed reassignment as a direct insult to her and as an example of overt discrimination against women. Her experience offers a glimpse into the snobbish caste system that has persisted in External since its early days as the elite of government departments.

> In the departmental hierarchy of duties an FS2 does not do consular/information work – that falls to FS1s who are learning the ropes. Political work has some sort of cachet which the other categories of duty do not. Presumably this is because on becoming an FS2 we are suddenly wiser, better analysts and reporters and closer to god than we were as a lowly FS1.

Before leaving Jakarta, they raised the possibility of being posted directly to another country instead of first going back to Canada. Recalled Sutton:

> Lagos, one of the most difficult and least popular posts in the foreign service, was offered. We accepted and then waited three months for word from the department. Finally, we were told it was off – the high commissioner had not wanted a couple (and a couple without African experience). How he thought you get African experience without serving in Africa is beyond me. He would have been lucky to have us – Frank as one of the best admin-istrators in the department, and flexible, adaptable me, eager to learn and make a contribution.

They reluctantly returned to Ottawa in 1978. They were on holidays in Napanee when External telephoned to ask Sutton to go on a two-year course at the National Defence College in Kingston. Initially excited at the prospect, she quickly realized that it would mean living apart from her husband and having a commuter's marriage between Ottawa and

Kingston. She turned it down because her marriage was more important to her than accepting an assignment, however challenging, from which Wiebe would be excluded.

Janice Sutton's decision to keep her own name after marriage raised some eyebrows among conventional women and diplomats' wives. One ambassador's wife confronted her and refused to accept Sutton's usual explanation that she liked her name, that it was her professional name, and that keeping it saved her all the bother of changing charge cards and bank accounts. Sutton finally had to say, "Look, it's my business. I made that decision and I really don't want to discuss it." But she found that some women seemed to feel threatened by the fact that she had not taken her husband's name.

Home from Jakarta, Sutton undertook one of the more interesting assignments of her career in the department's Middle East division. As desk officer responsible for Lebanon, Syria, Saudi Arabia, Kuwait and Iraq, Sutton expected problems as a female but encountered none. Because a number of students from Saudi Arabia and Iraq were coming to Canada to study, Sutton found herself sorting out problems with the provinces when international matters concerning education crossed into provincial jurisdiction. She also had to tell the Saudis, diplomatically but firmly, that they could not buy a Canadian university, a request they had made in all seriousness because they were in desperate need of doctors, scientists and engineers. They thought that the quickest way to produce them would be to buy a university in Canada.

> I took a trip around the Middle East as part of my responsibilities and was the first female to enter the Saudi ministry of foreign affairs. I was garbed appropriately; that is, I had a dress with long sleeves but nothing on my head and no long skirt. I had an escort officer from the embassy and we rolled up to the Saudi ministry, which was quite an imposing building with wide steps leading up to the portals, and there were a couple of guards standing there – big, fat, moustachioed guys – with AK-47s they held across the entrance as I approached. But the embassy officer just said, "Canadian embassy, we have an appointment with so and so," and in we went.
>
> As we walked down the corridor, I can remember a tea boy coming along with a tea tray and cups rattling and he had his head down and he saw my feet and legs –

> I was watching his eyes – his eyes just ran up me, he was
> just pop-eyed when he saw me in those hallowed halls.

On that same trip, Sutton also went to Lebanon, Syria, and Kuwait. Accompanied by a United Nations official and a representative of the Palestine Liberation Organization, she toured a Palestinian refugee camp in Lebanon. Next she visited the headquarters of the United Nations Interim Force in Lebanon (UNIFIL) to obtain a first-hand report of the fighting from there. In both Syria and Kuwait, she discussed the Lebanese situation with foreign ministry officials and was on the receiving end of some criticism. The Arab states found Canada insufficiently sympathetic to the plight of the Palestinians.

While in the Middle East division, Sutton also prepared notes and produced a briefing book for Prime Minister Pierre Trudeau's trip to Saudi Arabia.

In 1982, it was time for another overseas posting. Sutton and her husband were offered New Delhi. It was not high on their list of preferences, she said.

> I think we had both served quite a lot in the Far East;
> my husband had been in Malaysia, I'd been in Saigon.
> We also knew it was a very, very social posting. It has a
> reputation in the department of being one of the most
> party postings that there is, and by that stage in our lives
> we weren't very interested in partying.

But it is not easy for External to find posts for married couples where both officers will have satisfying, challenging work to do without encountering a conflict of interest. At that time, Delhi was a suitable post: the high commission needed an administrator with Frank Weibe's talent and acumen, and there was an opening as a political counsellor for Janice Sutton. So they went to India on a two-year posting that became three and was to prove, in Sutton's words, "difficult but very rewarding."

She was overwhelmed by India's enormous contrasts. In the world's largest democracy with a politically sophisticated population, she was startled to see that some people still bent to touch the feet of former maharajahs, and that the caste system had not been abolished completely. Millions of people lived in primitive conditions, but hundreds of millions belonged to the middle class. Many farmers still worked their fields with old-fashioned ploughs, but India put satellites into space, sent scientific explorers to the Antarctic, supported a flourishing film industry in several languages, and built its own computers.

Sutton observed that while cleanliness and a reverence for life are part of the religion and culture of India, men urinate in the streets, everyone litters, and thousands of people are killed each year in religious wars.

Sutton's work at the high commission involved research and analysis of political and economic developments in India and sending regular reports on these developments to Ottawa. She identified and outlined alternative policy options for Canada's relations with India. She made written and oral representations to the Indian government on bilateral concerns, and on matters affecting the United Nations, the Commonwealth, the International Monetary Fund, and other multilateral organizations.

Her ability to act quickly and decisively was put to the test when Indian Prime Minister Indira Gandhi was assassinated by members of her Sikh bodyguard in October 1984. William Warden, the high commissioner, was in Katmandu when Gandhi was shot; his second-in-command, the minister-counsellor, was also away from Delhi. Sutton proceeded to do what was necessary:

> Such things as secure the high commission, which meant closing the front gates, putting on extra guards and alerting all staff to the situation that was developing in the country. The Canada-India relationship was difficult at that time because of the agitation in Canada by Sikhs for Khalistan, a separate state in the Punjab. The Indian government wanted us to crack down on the agitators but in this land of freedom of speech and assembly it couldn't be done. As a result I was quite concerned that if a Canadian-Sikh connection showed up in the Gandhi assassination we would have demonstrations or worse outside the high commission.
>
> I sent local staff home as we heard of rioting and burning of Sikh homes and businesses; phoned immediately the director in Ottawa of our home division, got him out of bed to alert him to what had happened – it was 1 a.m. his time – so he could brief the minister and the prime minister and start writing condolence messages, getting replies to questions in the House ready, in short so he could be on top of the situation. I sent off telegraphic reports as the situation evolved and took

steps to prepare for what I knew would be a hectic and unpredictable few days thereafter.

When the high commissioner arrived back in Delhi that evening I took a high commission car and driver at nine o'clock, after the curfew hour, and drove to the residence to brief him. Deserted, eerie streets – all the Sikh taxi drivers gone from the taxi ranks en route, army patrolling the streets. Not a word of thanks or commendation from the high commissioner when I arrived at the residence and briefed him on my actions. I had several pages of notes.

It was not the first time that Sutton had run things. When her first high commissioner in New Delhi, John Hadwen, returned to Ottawa, he left her in charge for the two months before Warden arrived although she was not the senior counsellor at the time. Hadwen, though, had a high regard for her ability. Now retired and living in Ottawa, Hadwen remembered Sutton as a political officer adept at collecting information, absorbing and analysing it, with a talent for managing staff and creating a good atmosphere in the workplace. He added that her fine performance in running the high commission in the aftermath of the Gandhi assassination demonstrated that she had all the qualities an officer needed to respond to an emergency.

Janice Sutton did not spend all her time in Delhi on diplomatic duties. She did a study of the six Moghul kings, wrote two articles on Moghul culture and one on her visits to monuments and historic sites, which were published in *India Magazine,* and joined an organization for the mentally handicapped called Samadhan. It was an unusual initiative for a foreign diplomat.

I just had to do something on a personal basis in that country. I just could not live in that country and not make some kind of contribution, using my skills to help a little as best I could. At that point what I could do was write a newsletter and I had the time and skills to do that and so I did. And then I was asked to sit on the board.

When she left New Delhi, the members of Samadhan gave a tea party for Sutton and told her that they had been very suspicious of her when she first joined the board. They could not fathom why a foreign diplomat wanted to get involved with an Indian organization. "It soon became obvious that I just was sincere in what I wanted to do and they forgot that I was a diplomat, forgot my skin colour," she said. "So I worked with them most of the time I was there."

Six months before Sutton returned to Canada, her spouse retired from the foreign service. His action caused some consternation at diplomatic functions where men always are introduced before their wives. Whenever Wiebe was connected to the Canadian high commission, someone inevitably would ask what he did there. His reply, "Oh, I don't do anything, I'm retired, I play golf," would be followed by a stunned silence. His next remark, "But my wife is the political officer at the high commission," broke the silence and caused the entire party to rearrange itself.

When they came back to Canada in the summer of 1985, Sutton went to the Canadian International Development Agency (CIDA). External now allowed foreign service officers to transfer to the aid stream. For a long time Sutton had been interested in international development. She was qualified and was told that her transfer would take effect on her return from Delhi. From 1985 to 1987, she was a CIDA project officer managing Canadian development programs in the Caribbean islands of Barbados, St. Kitts, Grenada, Nevis, and Antigua.

Although Sutton was based in Ottawa, she made frequent trips to the Caribbean to inspect the projects. While planning one of those trips, Sutton encountered a not-infrequent male attitude that women simply were incapable of undertaking complex assignments.

> The work in CIDA was immensely stressful and difficult, especially for someone who was parachuted in and didn't know the routine. I was under a lot of pressure and I was leaving (in a few days) for a trip to my projects and I had so much on my plate that it was getting to the point where I had to make some choices, I had to establish priorities. And one of the things I thought was that I might not take the trip, that I just couldn't do it.
>
> So at this meeting my director was sitting there and I said to him, "I'm not sure I'm going to be able to take this trip." And he said, in a big, loud voice so all the people around the table could hear, "Well, isn't that just like a woman. Can't get your life organized. You just can't get your life organized so you can take a trip." And I said, "I beg your pardon ... it has nothing to do with my organizational ability. I've got too much work." And I did go on the trip.

She also took a good look at what the future might have in store for her and did not like what she saw.

> At that stage it was very obvious to me that my next posting was going to be in a developing country because I was in the aid stream. I had already had five postings in developing countries; my husband had retired and was having a wonderful time. I would not be head of an aid section in any post I went to because I was still new in the aid field. Although I was counsellor rank, CIDA wasn't about to let a newcomer like me come in and be a head of section.

After thirty-one years at External, Sutton decided to collect her pension and join her husband in retirement. She never regretted her decision. Nor was she bitter about never having been made an ambassador or head of a section or division in Ottawa.

> So why would you want to be an ambassador? Prestige? Yes, a little bit of prestige, but not at the price of having an ulcer or a heart attack. And anyway I've always had a lot of personal, outside interests, other things I wanted to do with my life, and we know people in the department whose life was the department.
>
> Well, it's very foolish to put your whole life into an institution. The institution doesn't care about you; you're gone, it closes, folds over, and you're forgotten.
>
> And if you've given your heart and soul and body to the department, I think that's very foolish. So why fight and struggle? And it also gets demeaning, fighting and struggling for promotions and not being promoted, knowing you're just as good as the next guy.

An outspoken, forthright individual, Janice Sutton did not back away from necessary confrontations. She took issue with one of her directors about an appraisal of her work in which he had written that her days were too short.

> I made him take that out since I never missed a deadline and my work required few changes by him or others up the line. I guess he was bemused by the fact that I came

in on time in the morning, took no coffee breaks, took a lunch hour most days (except when there was a crisis, which happens frequently in the department), and left at five o'clock. I had other things to do with my life.

It has always been common practice in External to come in late, read the *Globe and Mail* for awhile, take a coffee break and a long lunch break, then get to work in the afternoon and work until seven or later at night. I had seen a great deal of this when I was a secretary. It was not my style. I got in, worked hard and fast and went home to my music or writing or whatever else I was involved in.

She also took issue with leaders of her professional association during a round of collective bargaining. In a letter from Jakarta in January 1977 to the PAFSO executive director in Ottawa, Sutton wrote:

My understanding of a professional is someone who chose his career and who is concerned about quality of performance of a job which he likes doing and which is an integral part of his life. To demand more and more benefits for doing a job which the employee chose to do and which he enjoys seems to me to be missing the point – given the remuneration already paid.

In my view, members of the public service, and especially of the foreign service, which are, after all, services and not welfare schemes, have an obligation to serve and not to keep demanding more and more pay and benefits for less and less input. Service doesn't mean being poorly paid but suggests a commitment to the job and the employer ...

The members of the foreign service, and particularly the members of PAFSO, who regard themselves as the elite of the public service should, I believe, be taking a lead in trying to moderate the greedy, unthinking and (in the long run) destructive demands they make of their employer, ultimately, the people of Canada.

Janice Sutton and Franklin Wiebe live in the country near Kingston and spend part of each winter in New Zealand. While pursuing a second career as a freelance writer, she also serves on the boards of Interval House in Kingston and of the Lennox and Addington Historical Society and edits the latter organization's newsletter. She takes pains to correct a misconception often encountered by former female diplomats who are married. People who do not know the couple invariably assume that it is the man who was the diplomat. Sutton makes sure that everyone she meets knows that she was one too and not just "wife of." Sutton is also doing something almost unheard-of among female foreign service officers: she is writing her memoirs.

PART TWO

The Achievers

High Commissioner Marion Macpherson with President Sirimavo Bandaranaike of Sri Lanka at a Canada Day reception in Colombo.

CHAPTER SEVEN

OLD-SCHOOL DIPLOMAT
MARION MACPHERSON

The first woman to join the department of External Affairs as a foreign service officer, without sidling in sideways through the clerical ranks, was a slim, soft-spoken, somewhat shy graduate student from the University of Toronto. Marion Macpherson was twenty-four years old when she wrote the tough, six-hour examinations in 1947, the first time women were allowed to enter an External competition. She was accepted into Canada's diplomatic service the following year. It became her life's work for the next forty years.

Born in Moose Jaw, Saskatchewan, Marion Macpherson earned a BA in history and economics at the University of Saskatchewan in Saskatoon and an MA in economics at the University of Toronto. She initially thought of teaching history. But university broadened her perspective to include more current international affairs, sparking a special interest in the United Nations. Then she read an article about a Winnipeg woman who was in the British foreign service and a light went on. "I thought, that sounds just what I'd like to do," Macpherson recalled during an interview.

One of her university professors was not particularly encouraging. He reminded her that External had not hitherto employed women as officers, and he cautioned her that although women were being allowed to write the 1947 examination, a great many men discharged from the armed forces following the Second World War would be writing them too. Those men would be at the head of the line because it was government policy in the postwar period to give veterans preference in public service employment. Macpherson ignored the warnings. Confident and determined, she wrote the examination in Toronto, where she was work-ing at a summer job as a researcher at the university, and sat for the orals later in the summer. A November telegram told her that she had been successful.

Like all young officers, Macpherson began her career with a two-year, Ottawa-based training period. She worked in the United Nations, European, and economic divisions, found everyone helpful, and encoun-tered no discrimination. In 1950, she was posted to the Canadian embassy in Washington as "the most junior officer." Her duties included continuing discussions with American officials on economic and social issues facing the United Nations, and on civil aviation and territorial waters affecting Canada-U.S. relations.

The atmosphere at the Canadian embassy in Washington was excit-ing and stimulating for a young officer on her first posting. Hume Wrong was an unforgettable ambassador and mentor. Macpherson described him as "austere but warm and brilliant." She remarked that his friendship with Secretary of State Dean Acheson and his personal acquaintance with many members of the U.S. Congress provided him with sources of information that were very useful to Canada and Canadian interests.

On the embassy staff were representatives from the departments of trade and commerce, agriculture, and finance, as well as people from External and the armed forces. The weekly meetings at which Wrong presided were well attended, and the subject matter was wide-ranging as each officer reported on the week's work. For Macpherson, though, the most interesting and instructive reports were those given by the ambas-sador himself; they were like post-graduate seminars to a young diplomat still learning her trade.

Macpherson was also the embassy's protocol officer and was responsi-ble for organizing official functions, visits, and state occasions. Twice dur-ing her term, following the deaths of King George VI and then Queen Mary, the Queen Mother, the staff were required to wear mourning clothes. "And they meant it back then," Macpherson said. "Well, Mrs. Wrong said I could wear a white blouse with a black suit." An earlier, more festive occasion for the young protocol officer was the reception given by the Commonwealth representatives in Washington for Princess Elizabeth and Prince Philip in 1951.

Although Macpherson loved living in Washington and liked work-ing at the embassy, she found it a strange time to be in the U.S. capital. McCarthyism was at its height. The senator conducted a massive witch-hunt for communists, in the process curtailing the civil liberties of many

Americans, especially artists and writers. There were disagreements between President Harry Truman and General Douglas MacArthur about the conduct of the Korean War (MacArthur wanted to bomb China) that Truman finally resolved by firing the general. Macpherson thought that Truman was entirely justified.

Returning to Ottawa with a promotion in 1954, Macpherson broadened her departmental experience with assignments to the defence liaison and European divisions before chalking up another first in her career. She was the first female diplomatic officer to serve on the International Commission for Supervision and Control (ICSC), which was trying to keep the lid on the conflict between North and South Vietnam.

The commission, with representatives from India, Poland, and Canada, was established in 1954 by the Geneva Conference chaired by the Soviet Union and Britain. The commission's task was to supervise the implementation of the cease-fire between North and South Vietnam, the regroupment of forces, and the exchange of prisoners. Macpherson recalled that by 1956, when she went to Hanoi, most of the military matters had been resolved. However, the cease-fire agreement also had political provisions. Two in particular were intended to guarantee the freedom of movement of refugees between North and South and to assure that neither side would take reprisals against individuals for their activities during the war. Macpherson devoted most of her time on the commission to issues concerning the no-reprisals section of the agreement and often found the assignment frustrating.

> By 1956 the commission had become swamped by the number of allegations that political reprisals had been taken by the South Vietnamese government against former members of the resistance against the French. The sheer number of these complaints, as well as the attitude of the authorities in both North and South Vietnam, made it impossible for the ICSC to conduct impartial investigations. I believe the Viet Minh were well aware this would be so and flooded the commission with complaints in a propaganda effort to the South.

After eleven months in Hanoi and another promotion, Macpherson went to Ghana in 1958 as first secretary at the Canadian high commission in Accra. The former Gold Coast had just become independent from Britain; Kwame Nkrumah was prime minister; and a number of notable foreigners were on hand to help ease the new state's transition from colony to nation. Arthur Lewis, the economist from St. Lucia who won the Nobel prize in 1979, was an economic advisor to Nkrumah. Robert Jackson gave advice on development, and his wife, the famous writer Barbara Ward, was often in Accra giving lectures and meeting people. It was a small city, with a tiny diplomatic and international community; so everybody got to know everybody else.

Macpherson witnessed two important historical events during her stay in Accra. One was the first conference of independent African states, minus South Africa, at which Nkrumah was host. The second was the All-Africa People's Conference of 1958, attended by all the leaders of the English-speaking African colonies then seeking independence. Again, Nkrumah was the host. Tom Mboya and Kenneth Kaunda, who later became well known in the African independence movement and in the Commonwealth, took part in the meeting. Macpherson did not meet Kaunda on that occasion. The two became good friends later, when he was president of Zambia, and she was Canada's high commissioner in Lusaka.

Back in Ottawa for four years, Macpherson worked in the economic, information, African, and Middle East divisions. She did the first of two tours in the department's inspection service, travelling with representatives of other departments to Canada's posts abroad to ensure that they were functioning properly.

Although she had studied economics at university, Macpherson did not see herself as an economist. Her most challenging work in the economics division was implementing a scholarship program that had been set up at a meeting of Commonwealth leaders.

> The scholarship fund was supposed to be more of an exchange of intellectuals but it never really did that because of course the underdeveloped countries needed more graduates such as engineers who would be useful in development. But it was still quite an interesting thing to work on. When I was in the African division people used to come up before their countries were independent – Tom Mboya was here before Kenya was independent and Mr. [Julius] Nyerere and some of the others. They would come just to talk to Canadians about being an independent country.

In 1963, Macpherson finally was able to put her abiding interest in the United Nations to practical use when she was sent as counsellor to

Canada's permanent mission in New York. Canada was on the U.N. Security Council near the end of her stay. Altogether, it was a busy time at the U.N. with the 1967 war between Israel and Egypt, Ian Smith's unilateral declaration of independence for Rhodesia, the General Assembly's termination of South Africa's mandate over Southwest Africa, and the beginning of the U.N. involvement in Cyprus.

> We worked very hard. I think probably that was the most fascinating five years, the most interesting work. You were proud to be a Canadian down there. When the oil was cut off to Zambia after Rhodesian independence ... we had Hercules planes going in there with oil and years later, when in Zambia, I can remember some of the officials saying how wonderful it was to see that plane come in with the oil. In Cyprus we had troops out there very shortly after the Security Council decided to go in.

Macpherson continued her involvement in U.N. affairs following her return to Ottawa. After short stints in a career assignment program and as director of the personnel planning and development division, she became director of the U.N. political and institutional affairs division. The division's major preoccupation was to foster the recognition of the People's Republic of China by the U.N. and to put the People's Republic in China's seat at the U.N. and its various bodies, including the Security Council of which China is a permanent member. At the time, the Chinese seat was occupied by Taiwan, and the United States was adamantly opposed to yielding it to Beijing.

The evening China was admitted, Macpherson had gone to bed early but was still awake at 10 p.m. when a colleague telephoned from the Far East division to say that a popular television program had been interrupted with the news of the U.N. vote. "And then Godfrey Hearne phoned me and Yvon Beaulne, we had a great conversation about 11 o'clock at night," Macpherson said. "Godfrey went through the whole, very complicated, series of votes that they had before they came to the recognition."

Marion Macpherson got her first head-of-post assignment in 1973 when she went to Sri Lanka as Canadian high commissioner. She was one of three female heads of diplomatic missions when Sri Lanka was led by the world's first female prime minister, Sirimavo Bandaranaike. Macpherson found Bandaranaike a very strong and approachable woman, one who was even-handed in her treatment of male and female ambassadors.

Sri Lanka was a peaceful country in the 1970s, and Macpherson had many opportunities to see a large part of it. The Canadian International Development Agency was financing a number of aid projects, including a dam, agricultural programs, and forestry and paper developments. As high commissioner, Macpherson had some responsibility to make sure that the programs were functioning appropriately and to inform Ottawa of their progress.

She also fulfilled many speaking engagements. Colombo had its full complement of service clubs and voluntary organizations. Foreign envoys were in demand as speakers at their meetings, and Macpherson dutifully took her turn.

From Sri Lanka Marion Macpherson went to Boston as consul-general. She enjoyed the city and its amenities and New England generally – her territory took in most of the New England states except Connecticut. However, she found the work less than satisfying, partly because consular work involves business and trade more than international politics but mainly because foreign missions cannot have direct political dealings with state governments. Macpherson exploited the social role of a diplomat to meet important people, such as Michael Dukakis, Tip O'Neill, and Henry Cabot Lodge. From them she gained an insider's knowledge of political developments in the U.S. to transmit to Ottawa. She also tried to inform Americans about Canada by making public speeches, which are an inevitable, and sometimes tiresome, part of a diplomat's duties abroad.

Returning to Ottawa for a year, Macpherson did another stint in External's inspection services, this time as inspector-general. Then she went to Copenhagen as Canadian ambassador to Denmark. Female envoys were no rarity in the Danish capital; at one point, Macpherson was one of seven female heads of mission.

Official visits to Greenland were a memorable part of her tour in Denmark. She found that the premier of Greenland was very interested in Canada and that Greenland was much closer to Canada than she realized. In the lobby of a hotel in Godthab, now Nuuk, she saw a travel sign advertising shopping trips to Toronto.

On her return to Canada in 1983, Macpherson was made deputy commandant at the National Defence College in Kingston. It was an unusual assignment for a woman.

The college had been established after the Second World War to maintain co-operation between the military and civilian branches of government which began and then flourished in wartime. When she was appointed, Macpherson recalled, "There were about 40-45 students, half civilian and half military, usually at the rank of colonel, and fairly senior civilians too, but they all looked very young." The students began the course by studying Canadian security, defence, and politics. There were speakers from Parliament, the government, the military, and the academic world. Next they travelled throughout the country, including the North, and finally they made international trips – to the U.S., Latin America, Europe or Asia – usually about three for each class. Macpherson remembered the international journeys as especially stimulating.

Canadian embassies helped arrange the programs. To ensure free and candid discussion, the meetings were private, closed to the press, and proceedings were not published. Macpherson recalled that at the sessions which she attended senior officials and government ministers talked openly, with one exception. At one meeting the Czechoslovakians were less forthcoming than their western counterparts. But to have them there at all when the Cold War still prevailed was a considerable accomplishment. Czechoslovakia aside, Macpherson observed that participants "really do talk quite frankly about the problems of their own countries and their relations with their neighbours and their place in the world."

As deputy commandant, her responsibilities included helping plan the courses, assessing year-end student papers, and taking her turn entertaining the college's guests.

Marion Macpherson returned to Africa for the final posting of her foreign service career. She was Canada's high commissioner to Zambia and Malawi.

A highlight of her stay in Lusaka was a visit from the Eminent Persons Group established by Commonwealth leaders to investigate apartheid in South Africa and to recommend measures Commonwealth countries could take to persuade Pretoria to abandon apartheid and extend full civil and political rights to its black majority. When South Africa bombed a refugee camp near Lusaka even after a United Nations official had testified that there were no South Africans in the camp, Macpherson got a first-hand view of how the violence generated by apartheid spilled over into Zambia and the other nations of Southern Africa.

A more peaceful but equally moving moment occurred during an official trip to Zambia's Copper Belt. Driving from Ndola to Kitwe, where she was to give a reception, she asked her driver to show her the spot where U.N. Secretary General Dag Hammarskjold had been killed in an airplane crash in 1961. They stopped briefly at a monument to him set in a small open space in the middle of a pine forest off the main highway.

Retired from the foreign service since 1988, Marion Macpherson lives quietly in a cosy house on a modest residential street in Ottawa.

Asked to reflect on her four decades of diplomacy, she was characteristically self-effacing. "There are lots of things that Canada did that I was pleased about and had something to do with but it wasn't something I did." Pressed for specifics, she mentioned recognition of China at the United Nations, Canadian peacekeeping efforts, and preliminary discussions on Southwest Africa – now Namibia – held when she was Canadian representative on the U.N.'s fourth committee in the 1960s.

Even after five years of retirement, Macpherson still has the air of a diplomat of the old school. Her soft voice, warm smile, and calm friendliness put people at ease but tell them nothing she does not choose to reveal.

CHAPTER EIGHT

HERITAGE HOUSES AND HOCKEY
DOROTHY ARMSTRONG

From the earliest days of Sir Joseph Pope and O.D. Skelton, the External Affairs department has cultivated an officer corps of generalists. Even specialists were expected to be generalists. The reason behind this policy went like this: a Canadian diplomat, whether he had a degree in law or economics or was an expert in a particular region of the world, should have an education, interests, and knowledge broad enough to handle any assignment or solve any problem that came along.

An incident in the career of Dorothy Armstrong is a perfect illustration of this time honoured principle. A "thirty something" foreign service officer in External's European division in the 1960s, Armstrong was called from her desk one day and given a curious assignment. She recalls:

> There was some distress in the European bureau in the mid-'60s because the Canadian national amateur hockey team was behaving badly abroad as well as losing games; we got letters from five or six ambassadors in Europe all saying, in essence, "Please don't send the national team any more. When they come they undo at least five years of diplomatic work."
>
> I was asked to take a few weeks off and do a study on why the team was making such a mess of things and what we could do about it. It didn't take me long to discover why.
>
> This team was essentially a pick-up selection of part-time college students coached by a very well-mean-

ing priest, Father David Bauer. Now they were true amateurs but they were the only true amateurs on the world circuit. Like the Soviet hockey team made up of Red Army professionals, the other European teams were in similar situations, at least semi-pro.

So I recommended that until we could field a hockey team that would reflect our true abilities as seen in the National Hockey League's professional standards we should get out of international hockey altogether, which was a pretty drastic recommendation. Specifically, I recommended that we withdraw from international hockey competition until we could field a team that would include at least some professionals so that we'd be on a more equal footing with the other teams. Otherwise, we were wasting our time, spoiling our reputation – not only our hockey reputation but somehow our political reputation as well because our image was so connected with hockey.

Courtesy of Dorothy Armstrong

Ambassador Dorothy Armstrong introduces External Affairs Minister Mark MacGuigan, right, to Hungarian Foreign Minister Frigyes Puja on MacGuigan's visit to Hungary in March 1981.

The report was so well-received that Dorothy Armstrong became an informal adviser to the Canadian Amateur Hockey Association. Moreover, Canada did withdraw from international competition until new rules permitted NHL professional players – at least those who were not needed for the Stanley Cup playoffs – to join their national teams. The exercise also "deeply impressed upon me the importance of sport in international diplomacy," Armstrong added.

Her most vivid memory of the assignment concerns the reaction of then prime minister Lester B. Pearson:

> I got a message that the prime minister wanted to talk to me about it, he wanted to talk to the person who had done the report. He was a great hockey fan, of course. So I duly went over to his office and was standing outside when I heard him say to his aide, "I'm really looking forward to meeting the young man who wrote that report." The aide came out and saw me and said, "Here he is, sir." I walked into the room, Mr. Pearson looked at me and threw back his head and laughed. This was the best moment of all, particularly in view of his known scepticism about women in External.

Pearson was not the only sceptic on that subject. The dean of arts and sciences at the University of Toronto, where Armstrong studied for a master's degree in political economy, did his best to discourage her from pursuing a diplomatic career. In 1955, Vincent Bladon told her that it was almost impossible for women to get into External and that she should not break her heart over it. Instead of dampening her enthusiasm, however, the dean's advice made her more determined. After all, she had been thinking of the foreign service as a career since she was eighteen years old.

Born in Elva, Manitoba, in 1931, Dorothy Armstrong devoured historical novels as a teenager, was absorbed in history as a high school student, and took an honours BA in the subject at Mount Allison University in New Brunswick. Along the way, she concluded that international affairs were "history in the making," and that a career in diplomacy would not only maintain her interest but also satisfy her growing curiosity about other countries, cultures and societies.

Even before she had received Bladon's cautionary counsel, Armstrong knew that she would have to be better qualified than the young men if she wanted to be on an equal footing with them in the foreign service examinations. After completing her MA at Toronto, she went to Paris to do doctoral work at the Institute of Political Studies. It was there that she wrote the examinations in 1956, shortly after the beginning of the Suez crisis. The memory of those days gives Armstrong the shivers:

> Oil supplies were cut off to France for some time from the Middle East and, on the basis of very restricted supplies from other sources, only certain public buildings in Paris were heated. This did not include the residences at the Cité Universitaire where I was living and I can remember preparing for the exam – as much as you can prepare – bundled up, gloves and so on. In fact, we almost had to sleep that way, it was so cold. We were allowed one hot shower a week, I recall.
>
> Then when I wrote the exam – it was at the Canadian embassy, the old Avenue Foch address – I actually wrote in gloves because of the lack of heat. There were five or six of us writing at the time and I expect none of us will forget the extreme discomfort of that exercise.
>
> It was a long exam … a lot of essays, précis and so on, and it went on for hours. The exam today is, it seems to me, a much lighter affair compared to that. I can remember one major question: we had to choose one out of four topics on which to write for three hours. They were really trying to see if we could do analysis, one of the most basic skills required in the foreign service. This was presumably supposed to weed out people who couldn't. Nowadays, the exam may not be tough enough in that department.

Having succeeded in the written examinations, Armstrong was summoned to appear for a rigorous interview conducted at the Paris embassy by a panel of ambassadors chaired by Norman Robertson, the high commissioner in London. (Armstrong called him "one of the department's legendary 'greats.'") She tried to prepare herself for the grilling by memorizing the United Nations Charter and studying other important international documents. She failed to read the morning papers, however, and muffed the panel's first question about an overnight crisis in the Algerian war that was all over that day's front pages. She was also disconcerted when Robertson asked her for her view of marriage.

I knew this was a heavy question meant not only to find out what I thought but to put me off stride a little. That is one of the purposes of the oral interview, to see how unflappable you might be in a tight spot. I thought about it for a few seconds and told the truth: "Marriage is fine for those who are interested in it." At that time, I certainly wasn't. So many years of my life had been invested in preparing for the foreign service that was the big thing. I think I was also dimly aware of the strictures against marriage for women officers then in the department. Thus the commitment had to be strong.

When Armstrong joined External in 1957, she found considerable ambivalence about women officers and their determination to stay the course. A number of women had married and left the department after five or six years because their husbands were unwilling or unable to give up their professions to follow their wives around the world. "There was that kind of reluctance about us and a certain sense that we were not serious," Armstrong remembered. "We truly had to prove ourselves, over and over, as professionals in those early years of the '50s and '60s."

John W. Holmes, who had had a distinguished career in External from 1943 to 1960 before joining the Canadian Institute of International Affairs in Toronto, unwittingly revealed the kind of doubt and condescension encountered by Armstrong and her female colleagues. Speaking at Ladies' Night at the Toronto Board of Trade in February 1965, Holmes said:

> Although there are few women in the service, that is because fewer apply. The competition is open to them on equal terms in spite of the fact that they are a risk no insurance company would take. I needn't tell you on Ladies' Night that they are all attractive and marvelous diplomats to boot, but they have a habit of getting themselves attached by marriage to someone else's diplomatic service. It is a particularly lamentable form of dame-drain.

Nobody could say that Dorothy Armstrong was not serious about her diplomatic career. From her very first assignment in the department's economic division, she displayed the same determination that had got her into External in the first place. Her first posting abroad, as third secretary and vice-consul at the Canadian high commission in New Delhi, was part of her career plan. "Twice I waited an extra year or two to get posts I wanted, including New Delhi. The department's posting policy isn't entirely random; there are 'wish lists' that people submit and personnel will use them if they can ... I always let people know what I wanted and it often worked out."

The year's delay in her departure for Delhi was due to the fact that she was a woman. The head of personnel had been in India when a female staff officer was in a traffic accident and lay pinned beneath her car, undiscovered, for several hours in the intense heat. The incident led him to conclude that India was too dangerous for women. So Armstrong was not posted to New Delhi until a new man took over at personnel. Soon after she arrived in India, she had an adventure that inadvertently seemed to prove that the country was indeed a dangerous place for women in motor vehicles.

Armstrong liked to travel during India's so-called cool season – November, December, January – when the weather resembled early fall in Canada. With a car and driver, bottled water, tinned food, and a bedroll, she visited many parts of India, writing reports and meeting people, including Canadian doctors and teachers in remote areas. She stayed in bungalows that had accommodated British district commissioners in the days of the Raj and were subsequently maintained by the Indian government as lodgings for official visitors.

> One day in the Punjab, we got mired down in a river which I thought was shallow enough to ford though it turned out not to be. But just as we were sinking, the upholstery was getting wet, and tears of rage were welling into my eyes because my car was getting damaged – the driver was saying, "Miss Sahib, chalk it all up to experience;" I remember saying, "Experience for what?, this is it" – just at that moment, luckily, a unit from the Indian Army went by on manoeuvres and they fished us out with ropes.

On another trip into the Himalayas, Armstrong met the Dalai Lama, who was living in a former district commissioner's house in Dharmsala. Armstrong stayed in town overnight and next morning trekked a mile or two on foot up the mountain. A group of Tibetan pilgrims made the ascent with her; to them the Dalai Lama was a holy person. "To me, he was a very intelligent and charming young man of my own age, interested in photography and tennis, and we had an enjoyable conversation. He could speak enough English then to manage and was kind enough later to autograph some rather good photos I took of him."

Many years later, when Armstrong was Canada's ambassador in Denmark, she met the Dalai Lama again. She had kept track of his efforts to achieve some sort of independence for Tibet. However, when he came to Copenhagen, the Danish government refused to receive him officially because it did not want to offend the Chinese government. A private organization sponsored the Dalai Lama's speech in a large auditorium. The Chinese embassy in Copenhagen let it be known among the diplomatic corps that it would frown on any diplomat who went to hear the speech. Armstrong went anyway.

> I very much wanted to hear his ideas on how Tibet might be governed, rather like Greenland, with a form of home rule. It was a very conciliatory proposal he was offering and a compromise: not complete independence for Tibet but local autonomy, with the Chinese maintaining responsibility for defence and foreign relations. That's the formula in Greenland, which is a province of Denmark; they have domestic home rule and it works well for the Inuit population. So he was suggesting this as a solution for Tibet and I thought it was a good idea and creative though the Chinese certainly haven't taken him up on it yet.
>
> I spoke to the Dalai Lama afterwards and took the picture that he had autographed for me earlier – he appeared to remember my long-ago visit.

As it turned out, Armstrong's attendance at the Dalai Lama's talk had no adverse effect her relations with the Chinese ambassador in Copenhagen.

In New Delhi, Armstrong did the usual consular work assigned to junior officers at posts abroad. She and a senior officer supervised the various Canadian aid and development projects underway in India. She administered the Canada-India reactor project, some major hydroelectric developments, and technical assistance programs. On visits to the hydroelectric sites, the engineers always seemed surprised that a young woman came to do inspections.

On a trip to Chandigarh Armstrong was pleasantly surprised to come upon the famous French architect, Le Corbusier, who was designing the new capital building for the Punjab. She found him "perched on a stool before a drafting table in his signature polka-dot bow tie," she recalled.

> I suppose he was equally surprised to see a young woman and one ready to speak French, so we embarked on a long, rambling conversation that lasted most of the morning while he explained to me how he first hit upon the idea of putting buildings on stilts (with sketches which I still cherish) and how, in India, he was reversing the principles he had used in Europe to maximize the sun. Here, he was containing and minimizing. "Le Corbu" had the reputation of being difficult but on this occasion he was like a patient and charming professor.

After four years in India, where she received her first promotion, Armstrong went to Paris as second secretary with the Canadian delegation to the Organization for Economic Cooperation and Development (OECD). She was the first female officer to be a member on any country's permanent delegation to that international body. She immediately encountered the kind of irritations experienced by every professional woman who walks into a man's world.

> I asked about a washroom, for example, in the Chateau de la Muette which was where all our meetings were held. I was told that I would have to go three blocks down the street. I could hardly believe my ears but made it my business to ensure that there was a women's washroom in the delegates' area of the building before very long. It seemed somehow symbolic.

Armstrong recalled how other OECD delegates were reluctant to accept a woman in their midst. In the minds of many delegates, her graduate degree in economics and politics meant very little.

> There were three distinct types of reaction. There was a group of conservative West Europeans who showed their disapproval by sometimes ignoring my presence at the table. Others would send notes showering me with compliments. Both were upsetting but typical of the time, 1962. Fortunately, there were delegations who treated me as a fellow-professional, as I wished, and *that* was

progressive for the time. Would it be a surprise if I mentioned that among these were the Americans and the Nordic countries? And some others, too. I remember them with gratitude.

Armstrong came home to Ottawa in 1964 and spent the next nine years immersed in German affairs. For four of those years she was desk officer for Germany and Austria in the European division. Then, having been promoted again, she spent the next five years as counsellor at the Canadian embassy in Bonn.

The German posting was particularly memorable because it coincided with Chancellor Willy Brandt's "Ostpolitik" – Germany's first opening and overtures to the U.S.S.R. and East Europe since World War II. It was a national effort at reconciliation and it was not easy for Brandt because not all Germans were behind it. But this courageous policy paved the way for the peaceful revolutions ending Communism in 1989-90.

Armstrong had a trying experience when she was chargé d'affaires at the Bonn embassy, on the Easter weekend of 1969. Word came from Ottawa that Canada was unilaterally withdrawing two-thirds of its German-based NATO forces from Europe. It was, said Armstrong, "An unpopular decision that it was my duty to convey at the highest level. Sometimes you have to do something you privately think is unwise but still be very convincing about it. That's diplomacy."

Back in Ottawa from 1973 to 1978, Armstrong was deputy head of the department's policy analysis group and then director of the Northwestern Europe division. In October 1978, she was appointed Canadian ambassador to Hungary. It was her first head-of-post assignment, and she was only the fourth Canadian woman to reach that level in the diplomatic service.

Budapest was a beautiful city, rich in history and culture, but it was a difficult place for Westerners during the days of Janos Kadar's communist government. In its dealings with the representatives of foreign countries, the Hungarian government had a priority list. Fellow-communists – the Soviet bloc, Cuba, Vietnam and China – were at the top, the developing world came next, followed by the countries of the Common Market. The NATO countries were last.

> This had a strong effect on our daily lives.
> Administratively, we couldn't do anything except
> through the so-called Diplomatic Service Board. We
> had to go to them for everything – repairs to the house
> or repairs to the telephone and staffing – every last
> thing. And of course we Westerners had to wait
> because we were not of the right political persuasion.
> Sometimes this was an inconvenience. My personal
> relations with the head of the Diplomatic Service
> Board were good and their innate courtesy did take off
> the rough edges. But because of the policy we often
> had to wait and our lives were therefore sometimes
> quite difficult.

Life was doubly difficult for Armstrong because she had to oversee
the complete renovation of the embassy's new headquarters. When she
arrived, the offices were located temporarily in an unprepossessing apartment block; her predecessor had chosen the new building but had not
completed negotiations for its acquisition. Armstrong described the
building as "a classical villa in pleasant grounds, that had been empty for
many years. Although it had a great deal of potential, in its present state
it was little more than a decaying shell."

Complicating the renovation project was the need to engage a special
Hungarian contractor experienced in working on heritage buildings. The
villa may have been thoroughly dilapidated, but it had been designed by a
famous architect, Josef Hild, and consequently had been given a heritage
designation by the Hungarian government. Just as the contractor seemed
ready to begin, a more important project came along – renovation of the
Budapest opera house.

> This set us back a year and a half. He just dropped us,
> because we were definitely a lower priority than the
> opera. Now I liked all these people personally and they
> liked me and they would come to me and apologize for
> having to do this. They'd say the decision was the gov-
> ernment's; the opera house comes first. It was really very
> disappointing for me.

At one point, Armstrong also was at odds with Ottawa, which wanted to
turn the villa's small grassy area into a parking lot. Armstrong won: the
area remains a lawn. But the interminable delays meant that it was her

successor who was the first to occupy the ambassador's office in the reno-
vated building.

Despite the fact that she was the only female ambassador in Budapest
during her four-year stay there, Armstrong experienced few of the difficulties which she had encountered previously in Paris. The Hungarians
accepted her at once; the Western Europeans took a little longer. She
recalled:

> The NATO ambassadors met fairly regularly because it
> was the time of the Solidarity crisis in Poland and there
> were at that time indications that the Soviets might move
> into Warsaw and put an end to the fun, and other tense
> moments, so we would meet often to exchange informa-
> tion, usually weekly. It was at these meetings which we
> chaired alternately, leading the discussions, that I came to
> be fully accepted as a professional who knew the field,
> and this early scepticism disappeared. By this time, I had
> been a diplomat for twenty-two years, as long as most of
> them.

In 1981, Armstrong arranged Mark MacGuigan's trip to Hungary.
He was the first Canadian foreign minister to pay an official visit to that
country. His appearance helped relieve long standing Canadian-
Hungarian tensions created by the 1956 revolution. The main purpose of
his visit, though, was to promote bilateral trade in manufactured goods
and agriculture. Recalling a later visit to a state farm producing herds of
cattle by artificial insemination from Canadian stock, Armstrong said,
"One of the more philosophical experiences of my life was to be given a
bowl full of slim glass vials and to be told it was a future herd I held in
my hands."

In addition to arranging MacGuigan's trip, Armstrong also persuaded
the Hungarian government to agree to a visit from the National Defence
College. It would be the first time Budapest had received a group of western military and government officials. Hungary was unknown territory to
the Canadians.

> They had never been there before. It was an interesting
> country among the Warsaw Pact group, being the most
> economically liberal, although not necessarily the most
> politically liberal. There was great interest but they'd
> never been able to penetrate it before. It was a particu-

larly interesting visit because it was just before the Afghanistan invasion and the détente of the 1970s was at its height.

For the final reception I organized a buffet on one of the pleasure boats on the Danube and we went sailing down the river one lovely June evening with floodlit Budapest on either side. We had invited military attachés from not only NATO countries but from Warsaw Pact countries as well and it was a wonderful, convivial occasion; the last hurrah, really, before the curtain went down. After Afghanistan, relations were severely curtailed with Warsaw Pact countries and the Soviet Union in particular. So we all remember that last evening with special pleasure. Not until the Gorbachev period did things begin to thaw again.

Armstrong remembered a country in transition:

It was an interesting time in Hungary – the late Kadar period, when much of the old bitterness over the events of 1956 had been forgotten or at least submerged. This was mainly because cautious economic reforms had produced enough consumer goods to make life reasonably comfortable; censorship in the media was there but much less intrusive – more like self-censorship; some private property and entrepreneurial activity was tolerated. Hungary was, by the late '70s, moving to a borderline area, not yet a free market, not yet an open society though the standing parliamentary committees were embryonic democratic forms, but on the way in both instances ... It used to be said when I was there that he [Janos Kadar] was the only East European leader who could have won a free election.

In 1980, while she was still ambassador to Budapest, Armstrong's alma mater, Mount Allison, gave her an honorary doctorate of laws. On her return to Canada in 1982, she spent a year as diplomatic visitor at the University of New Brunswick and three years as director of External's Commonwealth division. In 1986, she was appointed ambassador to Denmark.

Like Marion Macpherson before her, Dorothy Armstrong found trips to Greenland a particularly rewarding part of a posting in Copenhagen. After Canada decided to open a consulate in Nuuk, to recognize the increasingly close relations between the Inuit of Greenland and those of the Northwest Territories and both nations' growing interest in the Arctic generally, Armstrong presided at a Canada Week in 1989. Canadians showed off their commercial, cultural, and technological achievements. In addition to exhibits by thirty Canadian companies, most of whom came from the Maritimes, there was something for practically everyone: a state-of-the art Canadian icebreaker, the ubiquitous Mounties, speeches in high schools and gifts to Greenland's university, and entertainment by the Throat Singers from the Northwest Territories and guitarist Liona Boyd from southern Canada.

Despite the derisive but popular image of the diplomat as cookie-pusher, the social functions that are an important part of a diplomat's life are work, not play. A diplomat's social life is not always easy for an unmarried woman. Armstrong articulated the difficulties most clearly:

> It's something that our own personnel people sometimes forget, that when you're a single head of mission you have a double job. You are required to organize the residence, the residence staff, and all the representational activities which are sometimes very heavy. These are duties normally assumed by a spouse. They were very heavy indeed in Copenhagen, as they are in all Western European posts.
>
> Of course, your most important job is the embassy, the work at the embassy, and the supervision of the staff there; then you have all this extra at the residence as well. There's often decorating, maintenance and other problems, particularly if you live in an old house. I found that I was spending many of my rare free evenings and weekends planning, organizing some event or carrying out domestic duties like inventories and so on. I didn't really have very much private free time. I found that to be true at both my posts, although the entertaining was heavier in Copenhagen.
>
> And if you weren't entertaining, you were being a guest, which is also hard work – this is not like being a guest in private life. You have to be on the alert at all times because it's really an extension of the office; you're talking shop, you're trying to get things done and very

often in languages other than your maternal tongue. I can remember dinner parties in Germany, I was speaking one language on my right and one language on my left and another one across the table. Those were truly strenuous evenings, English, French and German constantly back and forth.

Having completed thirty-five years in External, Armstrong did not expect another posting abroad; on her return from Copenhagen she joined the department's policy planning staff and undertook some major policy studies. It was a fitting way to end her diplomatic career. She said, "It's people like myself who have had a lot of experience in the field who can really help doing studies like this."

Dorothy Armstrong retired from the public service in March 1993 but continued to accept assignments on contract from External Affairs. She has kept a Hungarian connection as a member of the board of a foundation dedicated to restoring castles in Hungary, and she maintains a lifelong interest in the arts.

CHAPTER NINE

ON THE CREST OF A WAVE
MARGARET CATLEY-CARLSON

Two women – Flora MacDonald and Barbara McDougall – have been minister of External Affairs. They are unusual if not unique in the worlds of diplomacy and politics. In contrast, there has never been a female deputy minister at External.

Margaret Catley-Carlson might have been. She certainly had the credentials; she was enormously popular among her colleagues; she was also very ambitious.

But her fast-tracked career at External, which began in 1966, almost immediately upon graduation from the University of British Columbia, got side-tracked. In 1989 she occupied a large corner office in the Jeanne Mance building, in Ottawa's Tunney's Pasture, instead of quarters in the Pearson building on Sussex Drive. Like Pamela McDougall before her, Catley-Carlson was appointed deputy minister of Health and Welfare.

Born in Regina, Saskatchewan, in 1942, Margaret Catley spent most of her childhood years in Nelson, British Columbia. She developed an early interest in foreign countries through an aunt who taught at an Armed Forces base overseas and travelled extensively. She brought tales of her adventures home to her young niece, which left a lasting impression that women could have a career at an international level. At university, Catley expanded her youthful horizons by taking courses in international relations, political science, and economics.

She wrote the foreign service examinations for two rather practical reasons. "I wanted to use it as a lever," she said during a sprightly inter-

Margaret Catley-Carlson performs a ceremonial brick-laying at a village clinic in Rwanda in 1985.

view in her Ottawa office. "I wanted my then boyfriend to propose marriage and I wanted my then faculty head to propose paying my way through a master's and a Ph.D. program."

The plan worked. Catley was accepted by External and got the two proposals she wanted. By then, however, she had become so intrigued by the idea of a foreign service career that, instead of marriage and graduate studies, she went to Ottawa and spent her first three months in the department learning French.

> And then, I think, the single happiest day of my life still, was the day that I was told I was going to New York for the General Assembly. I just couldn't imagine anything more wonderful than to be twenty-four years old, out of university, and the government was going to send me to New York to the General Assembly for eight weeks.

To add to her happiness, the man she married four years later – Stanley Carlson – was also a member of the Canadian delegation to that U.N. assembly session.

After the session ended, Catley returned to Ottawa and worked in External's African and Middle East division. In 1967, as desk officer for Ethiopia, she organized the official visit of Emperor Haile Selassie to Canada. Selassie was the first of many heads of state to come to Canada during centennial year; because Catley worked on that first visit, she became something of an expert. Others turned to her for advice on how to plan subsequent events.

Catley was posted to Sri Lanka in 1968 and spent two years working as a junior officer at the Canadian high commission in Colombo, before returning home to join External's economic division. It was then that she and Stan Carlson decided to marry. "I became the first woman in External Affairs to get married and not to resign, so that was my little niche in history," Catley-Carlson said.

From the time women were first admitted as officers in 1947, it had been External Affairs policy to require their resignation if they married. The presumption was that married women officers could not be posted abroad because their husbands would be unwilling or unable to accompany them. At the same time, it was simply taken for granted that the spouses of male officers would move anywhere with their husbands and would undertake representational roles that made them a valuable but unpaid part of the diplomatic service. Young women officers from the mid-1950s onward, who argued that this was an unfair double standard and that at the very least the decision to resign should be up to the individuals themselves, got short shrift from male department heads.

External's policy on women and marriage persisted into the 1970s, even though the Royal Commission on the Status of Women in Canada had just finished extensive public hearings and was about to present a report containing wide-ranging recommendations to end discrimination against women in all areas of their lives.

When Stan Carlson and Margaret Catley decided to marry, she decided to do battle. According to Catley, "You were not fired the day you got married but when the first baby came along, or when your husband was posted. It was understood that you would move away from active foreign service and go and be a supportive wife in the field." Carlson was posted in Trinidad at the time. They decided to keep their marriage plans secret in order for Catley to receive the retroactive pay all civil servants had won recently in a collective-bargaining agreement. She might need the money for lawyers' fees and other expenses if she had to take her battle, as she vowed, all the way to Parliament. Moreover, only those actually employed on the date the agreement was signed were entitled to the pay. Catley was afraid that if the department knew her marriage plans, it would assume that she had resigned and refuse to forward the extra money.

So I hadn't told anybody. I had to get this back pay settlement business in hand so I would have the money to take on this battle. If they just fired me, I'd be bereft of resources. I was too young, I didn't know anybody I could borrow money from, and I didn't have any connections with the women's movement or anything.

She waited it out, got her retroactive pay, and, in her characteristically breathless fashion, went to see her immediate supervisor. She told him that she was getting married and that she had no intention of resigning. He expressed pleasure at her marriage plans but sent her to the division head to discuss her determination to stay in the foreign service. That official sent her to Bruce Williams, who was then the assistant undersecretary for personnel and administration.

> I walked in with great timorousness, said, "Hello, Mr. Williams." And he said, "Hello, Maggie." I said, "I am going to get married, I am not going to resign, and I am prepared to take it all the way up to Parliament if necessary." He sat up, looked at me, and said, "It's probably time we changed that rule, isn't it?"
>
> So that was my great fight for women's rights. It collapsed absolutely bloodlessly, I'm delighted to say, because I wasn't the least bit looking forward to the fight. I was not the least bit keen on being a martyr for this cause because you can fight City Hall and you win the battle but you personally usually end up fairly damaged by the exercise.

Having decided to change the policy on married women officers, the department made a gracious gesture. So that the newlyweds could be in Trinidad together, Williams suggested bringing an officer back from there and sending Catley in his place. With an early instinct for administrative niceties that was to serve her well later in her career, she replied, "Heavens, no, that's no way to start a policy. Why don't I go on educational leave?" Williams agreed and the new Mrs. Catley-Carlson spent a year doing post-graduate work at the University of the West Indies, Trinidad and Tobago.

In 1975, after a stint back in Ottawa, the couple went to Canada House in London, Carlson as political officer and Catley-Carlson as economic counselor. The Canadian high commission in London is an ideal post for a foreign service couple. The staff is large enough that spouses do not have to report to each other and thus are able to avoid conflicts of interest. While they were in London, Margaret Catley-Carlson's foreign service career took off in an entirely new direction.

Bruce Williams, who by this time was a senior vice-president of the Canadian International Development Agency (CIDA), called Catley-Carlson and offered her a vice-presidency with the agency. She was incredulous.

> I couldn't imagine who in their right mind would invite me to be a vice-president – that's the equivalent of an assistant deputy minister. I was thirty-four, I had never been a director-general, I had never been a director. You don't go around skipping two levels in the service, all the skills and stuff you acquire there. But of course I accepted. The department counter-offered and said that they would put my name forward to the prime minister to be an ambassador and I would have been one of the youngest ambassadors ever appointed, if not the youngest.

Catley-Carlson grasped the bird in the hand and became vice-president (multilateral) at CIDA. She worked with the World Bank and the InterAmerican Development Bank and administered a budget of $350 million. Although she found her new responsibilities "quite scary," she carried them out with such ability and verve that eighteen months later she was promoted to senior vice-president. Shortly afterward, when CIDA's new president became ill and had to spend four months in hospital, Maggie Catley-Carlson became acting president of the aid agency. "It was meteoric: from counselor in London with no actual managerial experience up to being acting president of the agency for four months, in the period of three years, was a fairly substantial leap."

During those three years with CIDA, Catley-Carlson remained an External Affairs officer. When the department invited her back, she accepted, out of a sense of loyalty and belonging. As she recalled, it turned out badly. Although she was given the title of assistant undersecretary, she was really a director-general. As a result, External's hierarchy failed to recognize that she had managed a whole other department of government when she was at CIDA. Her talent, experience, and ability were being wasted. In her view, External's professional career structure prevented her superiors from recognizing a person's productive time in another department.

> Having been, through an accident of fate, acting presi-
> dent for three or four months but substantively the
> number two in CIDA, I came back and sort of disap-
> peared into the labyrinth of External Affairs and was,
> therefore, profoundly unhappy and realized that I had
> made a terrible mistake, that you can't go backwards,
> you can't go from running a sizable operation down to
> being on a medium branch of a division tree ...
>
> That's a problem External has, it's a structural prob-
> lem, and I understand it because I come from there. It's
> a problem that relates to the fact that if you are going to
> run a professional career stream, you can't let people go
> out, shoot up, and drift back. You have to protect the
> interests of people who are posted far and wide, and you
> can't just let people bounce out and then come back in.

To remedy matters, Catley-Carlson went to New York as an assistant
secretary-general of the United Nations with the specific task of deputy
executive director (operations) of the United Nations International
Children's Fund (UNICEF). In 1983, she returned to Canada to become
president of CIDA in her own right. It was then that her husband, who
had remained in External while his wife's career veered down other roads,
left the department. They agreed that since her work kept her in Ottawa,
he would give up the rotational life of a foreign service officer. Carlson
stayed in the public service; by 1992 he was a senior bureaucrat in the
Privy Council Office.

Despite the unhappy parting, Catley-Carlson gives External credit for
accelerating her ambitions.

> My image of being in External when I was, was that I
> got to ride the crest of a wave, that managers in the pub-
> lic service were under increasing pressure to promote
> women and to diversify their managerial cadres with
> more women, and that I was able to ride that wave. I
> never felt External Affairs was giving me trivial and/or
> offside assignments, other than my first ten weeks in the
> department, and you hardly judge things on that basis.

Catley-Carlson left CIDA in 1989 to become deputy minister of
Health and Welfare, Canada. She was the second female foreign service
officer to be appointed a deputy at health and welfare; McDougall was

the first. Both women consider the appointments a coincidence. They were not the result of some strange mindset in the prime minister's office that reasoned if women were going to be deputy ministers, they would have to run nurturing departments. Of Health and Welfare, Catley-Carlson said:

> There are a lot of women over here and I think that it's probably seen as a place where a woman will not have extraordinary difficulties because she is a woman. It's a damned difficult department to run but it isn't any more or less difficult because you are female.
>
> I suppose there are still some people who would feel that running Energy, Mines and Resources or running Industry, Trade and Commerce would, at least in the minds of some of the people you are meeting, cause issues to be raised. I don't think like that, most of the male colleagues I have don't think like that, but it is still out there as a form of thinking. I suppose that's a factor in who they send to Health and Welfare.

She is equally philosophical about the prospect of a female deputy in External:

> Until a fairly short time ago there probably wasn't an eligible range of candidates because there weren't that many women deputy ministers. They do try to assign somebody who's had some External Affairs experience; it is not a department like the others. Around about now, or the next time, or the next time after, is the time that there will be women who will be very reasonable contenders for the job.
>
> I would have been one of the very reasonable candidates to go to External Affairs when Reid Morden went there, but I had been in my job only for two years, I had absolutely no desire to be moved. Huguette Labelle could have been another one who could have been a good candidate but after that you get no woman at the appropriate level.

Catley-Carlson had no regrets about being a deputy at Health and Welfare. On the contrary, she saw her days there as a challenge and an opportunity to sharpen her managerial skills in a domestic department, after having devoted all her career until then to international affairs.

> It's not a plum, going to External Affairs. It may have been twenty years ago, but how do you ever judge what things were really like before? It's a very tough managerial job. Canadians basically do not understand the foreign service. Canadians are looking more and more inward or continentally, there is not a lot of understanding for a department that lives its life abroad in exotic circumstances and the only time people notice something that's done in External Affairs is usually something that has gone wrong rather than something that has gone right.

Canadians have a very different attitude to Health and Welfare, and Catley-Carlson sounded passionate as she talked about it:

> There isn't a person in Canada who isn't touched by Health and Welfare. If you have children, you get a family allowance cheque; if you are old, you will be getting an old-age pension cheque; if you are working, you'll be part of the Canada Pension Plan; if you ever take a pill, we have certified it. We help inspect the food, we tell people not to smoke, we advise on the drug strategy, we reach into everybody's life.
>
> We need to have 2,400 people running the Canada Pension Plan and Old Age Security and Family Allowance. This is an understood fact. Canadians see the relevance to themselves and accept it.
>
> External Affairs is abroad, it's living abroad, the media do it the great favour of only showing up swimming pools and clubs and consular cases that raise questions. The routine good service that is offered by External Affairs to businessmen, to stranded Canadians, to ministers, to the internal ministry, is never, ever highlighted, and so therefore you are constantly battling against the odds of public perception as to how you are spending Canadian taxpayers' resources, what it is you do.
>
> Policy issues are very badly understood by the public, whereas people have a working understanding of

family allowances, the Canada Pension Plan, and drugs
and bugs, and all the things that we deal with here.

The woman who knocked down the already shaky barrier against
marriage for female officers in External argued that married couples now
have an easier time than single officers in the department.

Even though it's hectic and difficult to get posted with
your spouse and to get everything set up and arranged,
because there are two of you moving, at least when you
get to a posting there are two of you. You are not alone
and you've also got a spouse who understands the obligations. You don't have to spend a lot of time explaining
why you're not coming home that evening or what's
happening. You know what each other is up to and
about so you've got a support system, you share duties
like entertaining, you travel together. I think that it is
much easier.

I know that a lot of the single women in External
Affairs really feel that they are used as the kind of glue to
make the system work, that if a post suddenly becomes
vacant there is an assumption that a single woman's life
can often be disrupted in a way that a man with two
kids in school can't be, or a couple is unlikely to be.

I never minded being used as the glue in the system.
I think you get more interesting jobs if you're the glue in
the system, but anyway I know that that's the source of
aggrievement.

Catley-Carlson has no children. She said that she did not know how
career women, wherever they worked, managed with children. "I take my
hat off to them."

During her career in External, whether in Ottawa or abroad,
Margaret Catley-Carlson encountered only minor incidents of discrimination, which she peremptorily dismissed as insignificant specks of foam
on the wave that propelled her upward. She also had the somewhat
unusual attitude that discrimination is in the eye of the beholder:

Probably one of the reasons that I don't think I had any
discrimination is that I decided a long time ago that I
wouldn't see any. And if you don't see it – other than

two or three very small examples from very early times – it really doesn't exist. So you find another explanation which causes you to try and do better. It can be very motivating and it doesn't allow you to sit there saying, "Well, it's obvious that they haven't done this because I am a woman." That immediately takes all the blame away. "Isn't that wonderful, I have somebody else to blame, I didn't get that job because I am a woman, it's clear, absolutely clear." Well, that's too easy an out so I just have never let myself do it and I really don't want other people around me to do it either because it is the quickest way to stop the momentum.

On 1 January 1993, Catley-Carlson left Ottawa for New York to become the first woman, and the first non-American, president of the Population Council. The council's board of trustees chose her from among 300 candidates. The board chairman, McGeorge Bundy, said of the decision, "We didn't set out to elect a woman, but the best possible person turned out to be a woman and there are some real advantages. The problem of population inescapably engages a broad range of questions about the role and rights of women, and this appointment will reinforce our effort to give full attention to that reality."

Appointment to the Population Council took Margaret Catley-Carlson back to the international arena. John D. Rockefeller III established the non-profit council in 1952. It is a leader in contraceptive research and assists over fifty developing countries in family planning.

Stan Carlson gave up his civil service post in Ottawa and joined Margaret in New York, proving that there are some men willing to go where their wives' careers take them.

CHAPTER TEN

HAVING IT ALL
INGRID HALL

Adecade after women were first admitted to the rank of foreign service officer, conventional wisdom in the Department of External Affairs held that they could not be posted to Muslim, Latin or so-called backward countries and that their usefulness ended when they married. A 1957 memo to External Affairs Minister Lester B. Pearson from the undersecretary, Jules Léger, was blunt: "By the voluntary act of marriage, a female FSO really disqualifies herself for service abroad ... What we must avoid is having married women block the entry of new recruits, whether male or female."

Ingrid Hall, Canada's ambassador in Jakarta from 1989 to 1992, shattered External's conventional wisdom concerning women in the foreign service. Married and the mother of two daughters, Hall was the first woman from any country to become an ambassador to Indonesia, a state not only Muslim but military and male-dominated. This dark-haired, forthright woman with the engaging smile was so effective at her post that Indonesians treated her as a celebrity. Other diplomatic missions saw her as a role model and started promoting the women on their staffs.

Hall did not set out to be an iconoclast. As she said in an interview in her Ottawa office, shortly after her return from Jakarta, she became a diplomat almost by accident. A bilingual student at McGill University in Montreal, Hall decided to settle for a master's degree in political and economic theory and not pursue the doctorate that had been her original intention. On the afternoon of her decision, a group of fellow-students was scheduled to write the foreign service examinations and invited Hall

Ambassador Ingrid Hall with a Muslim market woman in Palankaraya, Indonesia.

to join them. Ever ready for a challenge, off she went. "The thought of going into the foreign service really hadn't entered my head," she remembered. "This was in the late '60s, there weren't really women in the foreign service, women were not recruited on campuses, there was no advertising that the foreign service could be a career for women."

Hall joined External in 1968 when it was still the rule that officers – male and female – had to get the department's permission to marry (usually granted once prospective spouses were cleared for security) and female officers were expected to resign. It was not until 1971, after Margaret Catley-Carlson vowed to take the issue all the way to Parliament, that the resignation rule was rescinded.

Following an assignment at the United Nations General Assembly in New York, Ingrid Hall's first posting was as third secretary at the Canadian embassy in Washington, reporting on economic issues. There she met her future husband. They had what she called "a modern relationship" until 1976 when they decided to marry because they wanted to have a family. By this time, Hall was back in Ottawa while her prospective husband was still in Washington.

> We supported the bus and the airlines. But because I had already been in the foreign service, at that point we decided jointly that we wanted to continue on in the foreign service. We always felt that there must be flexibility on all sides, that the flexibility does not fall to the government employer only but also to the couple. We have always been extremely imaginative in the way we organize our own lives.

Hall remained in the foreign service after their marriage, and her husband moved to Ottawa and went to work with the International Development Research Centre. According to Hall, she set out to demonstrate "that women did get pregnant, were quite capable of continuing to work, and that provisions had to be established to enable not just officers but support staff – secretaries and clerks – women and not only men to have a family."

She made the point with subtlety and humour. Pregnant with her first child, she was working on air-rights negotiations with an assistant deputy minister whose office was directly across from that of another assistant deputy minister, who was in charge of personnel. She was six and a half months pregnant when the personnel ADM deigned to notice and to acknowledge that he would have to do something. "And from then on," she said, "every second day I stood in profile at his door, displaying my rapid expansion in full view, and smiled, 'Good morning.'"

Hall finally was granted leave without pay. When she returned to work, she had to make double contributions to the civil service pension fund and to maintain her own health insurance coverage. "But I won the right to return to a job," she said.

She incurred a similar penalty when she had her second child. Changes, however, were made in 1984 to provide seventeen weeks' maternity leave at 93 percent of salary and ten weeks of parenting leave with unemployment insurance benefits that could be drawn by either parent. Taking advantage of maternity leave provisions, though, may jeopardize an officer's chances for promotion. In the foreign service, promotions are made annually on the basis of four performance reviews, each of which is written after an employee has been in a job for at least six months. Someone on maternity leave might not serve for that length of time in one particular job. One woman commented to the 1990 Task Force on Barriers to Women in the Public Service that "The only way to avoid this problem is to time your deliveries for August 1, so maternity leave extends over the first half of the assignment year!"

Ingrid Hall claimed some credit for creating the climate that made change possible.

> It became much easier financially and more and more women are having families. But what's important is that it is not just officers, it's all the women in the foreign service, and I think that's good. Married, unmarried, I'm a firm believer that it is all possible.
>
> What happens, of course, is that you do take time off and one cannot expect to be promoted when one is not in the office. But what often happens is you go through a change, a very normal change, and in many cases you return to the office considerably more organized, considerably better thought-out, and your career zooms.

Marriage and motherhood certainly did not hinder Hall's career. In 1979, she was posted to the Philippines where she was responsible for five different programs, including Canada's aid program, and began developing a new perspective on Islam that was to be useful when she later became ambassador to Jakarta. Travel throughout the Philippines, from the communist areas in the north to the Muslim regions of the south, enlarged her perspective.

I had been socialized and educated, like many western women, to think that Islam was a constraint for the progressive development of women. I began to understand, through these visits, that very often the key catalyst in a small community was a woman, a strong person between the ages of twenty-three and twenty-seven, and I saw this pattern repeated time after time after time.

I began to feel that one of the greatest challenges that we would have in the world ahead was the mutual misunderstanding between the Christian-Hebraic and the Islamic worlds. I wanted to understand Islam much more deeply, to understand the decision-making in particular, and so I began to think about the countries in which I could do this.

Hall set her sights on Pakistan and Indonesia and then narrowed her choice to the latter country. She also wanted to be head of post the next time she went abroad.

Back in Ottawa from Manila, Hall spent two years as deputy senior adviser to the Canada/U.S.A. trade task force and another two years as director of the Western European Relations division in External. In 1989, she achieved her goal and became ambassador to Indonesia. It did not come automatically.

She knew that there would be resistance, in both Jakarta and Ottawa, to the notion of a woman head of post in a country that was at once Muslim, military, and male-dominated. So she set about working to change the way people thought about the prospect of a female ambassador to Indonesia. Her appointment proved the success of her campaign.

Her three years in Jakarta met all Hall's expectations:

It was an extremely positive experience for myself and for Indonesians. It put me in a public profile that is enjoyed by very few people. At times it was rather sensitive and I would have extensive media coverage but it enabled me to get access to individuals that it would be extremely difficult for most people to see.

Curiosity opened the doors. How is it that a woman can do a job such as this? Thereafter, of course, you had to be three times as good as anybody else. It's the same the world over and it's no different in Indonesian culture than anywhere else.

It was a very high-profile assignment, intentionally so, designed to raise the profile of the work and the Canadian government, Canadian business, Canadian NGOs [non-governmental organizations], to raise the presence of Canada considerably.

After I had been in Jakarta for about three or four months and had shown everyone that the job could easily be done by a woman, women in other embassies started to become chargés. It had a demonstration effect and a very important one in staff assignments.

It was very fruitful. What quite struck Indonesians was that at the Canadian embassy a woman was country director, running Canada's third largest aid program in the world, reporting to a woman ambassador, reporting at that point to an assistant deputy minister – a woman – who in turn reported to a minister who was a woman.

Her posting to Jakarta also furthered Hall's personal goal of learning more about Islam and the influential role of women in Islamic societies:

It is a little bit more difficult to identify the way in which your personal thinking evolves. I have a much deeper understanding of the various forms of Islam, a deeper conviction that, yes indeed, there is a fundamental misunderstanding between the two traditions – the Christian-Hebraic and Islam. And these are ones that will challenge us in world affairs and economic affairs in the next ten or fifteen years.

It was also fascinating for me to look at the various forms of Islam. What exists in Indonesia is a harmonious form of Islam which recognizes and respects other religions. And the other religions, though they are most definitely the minority, live side-by-side with Islam.

The changing role of women suggests how Canada in women-in-development assistance programs can assist the integration of women in the socio-economic evolution of their own countries.

Like many professional people, Hall guarded her children's privacy. In interviews with journalists in Jakarta – Canadian, foreign or Indonesian – she would limit her remarks about them to the fact that she had two daughters who were fourteen and nine (in 1992). But toward the end of her term in Indonesia, Hall finally broke her self-imposed rule and gave a series of interviews, answering the questions everyone had always wanted to ask. In Ottawa, she volunteered to talk about how her children liked having an ambassador for a mother:

> I was in the media at least every week, on television frequently, giving public speeches sometimes on a weekly basis, always on a monthly basis. If I went into a store in Jakarta, I was recognized. I was an extremely public figure.
>
> The children found that a bit difficult, as I'm sure children also find political parents a bit difficult. I was constantly in the press but particularly in the Indonesian press. Their teachers would come in with the articles every second or third morning. Not the easiest for the children to cope with.
>
> When we went out to Indonesia it was most difficult for the youngest one and easiest for the oldest. It's the reverse here.
>
> On the other hand, the very interesting thing is they would both like me to go out as an ambassador again and they would both like to come. And for my oldest daughter that would be unlikely because she should go to university in Canada.
>
> My husband and I made the decision to put them into the Lycée ... to give them a school system that they could follow wherever we were in the world. It does present a challenge because we are an anglophone family and their schooling is in French. And so Mom does a lot of homework.

Hall expressed the firm belief that couples striving to sustain dual careers, when one of them is in the foreign service and required to serve abroad, must take most of the responsibility themselves.

> I've said to so many people that to insist on a prearranged job from Ottawa may work if you are a dual-career couple in the government but if you are not – and that's a personal decision – it limits the size of the chess board and very often there are so many professional

opportunities available in a country that you only learn about once you arrive there.

She also has no doubt that women can have it all – a career, marriage, family life:

> You have to be very organized. I have a fundamental belief that girls start to learn managerial and organizational skills at a young age by looking after their siblings and then, on the financial side, helping out with the shopping and doing the household chores. These are fundamental managerial skills that, when translated into the business environment, work very well.
>
> A woman who is married with children tends to be a highly organized individual because time has a monetary value. You simply accomplish a lot on a daily basis and this becomes a way of life.

Other female foreign service officers see Hall as a role model and give her credit for setting up an informal women's network within External. Asserting that "the diplomatic profession is networking," Hall did express satisfaction that women ten years her junior are "beginning to have much better career opportunities, wider career opportunities, and this I see as a very positive development."

It is nevertheless a slow process. No female foreign service officer has been ambassador in Washington, Paris, or Tokyo, or undersecretary in Ottawa. This is the result of what Hall called the Golda Meir syndrome:

> There has been, not only in the Canadian foreign service, not only in Canadian society, but in the rest of the world, a tendency to espouse the Golda Meir phenomenon. You appoint one woman and sit back and don't have to do anything for another ten years. The result is that one woman is highlighted and featured and no others, and it goes in ten-year cycles.

Discrimination is also a factor, Hall said.

> Any woman who says that there haven't been instances of discrimination is not being honest with herself. I think the key question is, is there more or less discrimi-

nation now in a systemic sense rather than individual instances of discrimination? And there is most definitely less.

What I do find is that managers who are most comfortable with women managers are those who have succeeded in their own right in their own careers. This is not unique to the foreign service; I think it is just the business environment, be it private sector or public sector.

Where there really are the most sensitivities to assertive women managers are in the middle ranks where the middle-ranking manager is a high flyer, is very keen on moving himself or herself ahead, and less adept at accepting the intellectual challenges of a high-powered woman. That's where the very sensitive phase is.

For women who find themselves in such situations, Hall has some advice:

I just say to everybody, be well prepared before you go into your meetings. Know your dossiers. Be prepared to argue your point of view. You will win some, you will lose some. Simply show that you are fully able to do the job and to do the job very well, not only your own role but across the board. You can deal with routine questions, with crises, with policies, not just in your own unit but several units together, to ensure that results are achieved.

That she followed her own advice is evident from Hall's record: first female ambassador to Indonesia and first woman to hold the position of director-general of the foreign assessments bureau in External, supervising a staff of sixty and working in an almost totally male environment.

Ingrid Hall described herself as "a natural networker, not just among women but among men. I've always had a proclivity to challenge the way people think, never to accept a shibboleth, to wonder, to ask, to query."

That last sentence would not be out of place in a job description for any country's diplomatic service.

CHAPTER ELEVEN

DEPUTY-IN-WAITING
LOUISE FRÉCHETTE

May 1992 was a typically hectic month at the United Nations. Violence in the former Yugoslavia preoccupied the Security Council: Canadian peacekeepers in Sarajevo faced sniper fire as they tried to evacuate a hospital; the president of Bosnia-Herzegovina appealed to the U.N. for help in lifting road and rail blockades and opening the airport. Planning for a global summit on the environment to be held in Rio de Janeiro in June was almost complete; about 100 heads of state and government were expected to attend, though there still remained some question whether U.S. President George Bush would be among them. U.N. officials were concerned about refugees in the Middle East, especially Kurds fleeing Iraq, and there were on-again, off-again peace talks between Israel and her Arab neighbours.

At the weekly staff meeting of the Permanent Mission of Canada to the United Nations in New York, these and other issues were discussed by Ambassador Louise Fréchette and her ten member staff, two women and eight men. It was an informal meeting held at the mission's offices in a high-rise complex just across the street from the imposing U.N. head-quarters in Manhattan. The diplomats, carrying mugs or plastic cups of early-morning coffee, seated themselves along two sides of a long table in a book-lined conference room that was also a library and an informal reception room.

Fréchette, Canada's first female ambassador to the U.N., neither chaired nor dominated the meeting. She did not sit at the head of the table but to one side with colleagues flanking and facing her. Her deputy, Philippe Kirsch, was chairman. Yet there was no doubting who was in

Louise Fréchette

charge; as each officer reported on his or her activities, Fréchette asked penetrating questions, made light-hearted interventions when they were appropriate, and was firm but never arrogant in making decisions. Although the officers addressed her formally as "ambassador," Fréchette exuded such an air of confidence as both a diplomat and a woman that she created an atmosphere of easy camaraderie around the conference table.

Louise Fréchette, who joined the department of External Affairs in 1971 and became ambassador to the U.N. in January 1992, occupied the most important diplomatic post ever held by a female career officer in Canada's foreign service. No other woman has risen that high in External's pecking order. Yet she became a diplomat almost by accident.

Born in Montreal in 1946, Fréchette attended the Collège Basil Moreau and studied history at the University of Montreal. In her final year there, still harbouring fond memories of a three-month trip to Europe, she saw a notice informing students that foreign service examinations were being conducted on campus. Having nothing more tantalizing to do that October evening in 1970, she and a friend wrote the examinations.

Interviewed during lunch in the elegant Park Avenue apartment that is home to Canada's U.N. ambassadors, Fréchette recalled her impulsive decision. The European holiday had given her a taste for living abroad, and she saw the examination as offering a way to do that while working for the government.

> I had not made the connection in my mind that this was a diplomatic career that was awaiting. It was out of curiosity for foreign countries. I'd always been interested in foreign affairs; I took history in university and through history I guess I had a fairly broad knowledge and a definite interest in what was happening outside of Canada.
>
> But to say that I planned a diplomatic career from age twelve, like some of my colleagues have, certainly not. It was only when I finally joined External that I realized that I had taken that step. It goes to prove that your instinct sometimes serves you very well because it is a career that has given me every satisfaction.

Her career zoomed from the start. After spending an initial nineteen months getting acquainted with External's Western European and personnel divisions, Fréchette was first exposed to United Nations' affairs in 1972, when she went to New York for four months as an adviser to the Canadian delegation to the U.N. General Assembly. In March 1973, she was posted to Athens for two years as second secretary at the Canadian embassy. She recalled the excitement and the sense of discovery which she experienced there, and she inadvertently revealed the self-sufficiency and adaptability that continue to be invaluable assets in her career:

> One of my biggest thrills was when I arrived in Greece, my very first post, my first time by myself in a foreign country. On the first day, I went to a little supermarket next to my hotel to buy eggs and milk. When I walked out of that store I was so proud of myself, just to know I had done it on my own and had found my way around. I told myself, "I'm going to make this city, this little area, mine, and I'm going to feel comfortable here."
>
> And I remember during that same posting, a young immigration officer and his wife had been sent to Athens for the summer to help out. They were living in ideal conditions, they stayed in a hotel and had all expenses paid. But his wife couldn't stand it and they decided to leave the foreign service after that summer because she felt that this was too strange. She needed her house, her street corner and her neighbours, and she just could not stand it. Whereas there's no place that I wouldn't go at least for a few weeks.
>
> I guess you do need a certain type of personality to be happy in the foreign service.

Home from Athens in April 1975, Fréchette spent two more years in External's Western European division with responsibility for Spain and Portugal. The Iberian peninsula's economic situation was a major concern at the time, and Fréchette found herself on shaky ground. Aside from a few university classes in economics, she had little background in the dismal science. Aware of the importance of economic issues in Canadian foreign policy, Fréchette asked External to consider giving her an assignment with considerable economic content in order that she could remedy her deficiencies in that particular subject.

> Within a few weeks personnel phoned me back and said, "Well, how would you like to go to the College of

Europe?" This is a post-graduate institution situated in
Bruges that focuses on European Community affairs.
One of their specialties is economic affairs. So I took one
year in Belgium, doing economic topics of all kinds, and
that gave me the kind of theoretical grounding I needed.

I never quite mastered the jargon but I came out of
it with better economic credentials. Throughout my
career afterwards I was given various assignments that
had a high economic content.

After Bruges and a short time back in Canada, External's rising star
found herself once more in Europe, as first secretary at the Canadian mission to the United Nations office in Geneva, where she worked on trade
policy, sharpened her economic skills, and learned something about the
General Agreement on Tariffs and Trade. She recalled that most of her
time in Geneva was spent on East-West economic relations that were not
exactly flourishing during the Cold War. Both sides were suspicious of
any overtures toward normal exchanges of business or trade. She drafted
proposals on ways to increase Canada's trade with Eastern Europe, and
she learned a great deal about shipping, the United Nations Commission
on Trade and Development, and similar esoteric subjects that are a diplomat's stock-in-trade as well as cocktail-party small talk.

From November 1980 to July 1981, Fréchette was also the Canadian
representative to the Madrid meeting of the Conference on Security and
Co-operation in Europe. The CSCE, as it was popularly known, was a
loose association of thirty-five countries from Eastern and Western
Europe plus Canada and the United States. It was formed to foster human
rights, develop democratic institutions, and build bridges in order to ease
tensions and reduce suspicions between NATO and the Warsaw Pact.

Returning to Ottawa at the beginning of 1982, Louise Fréchette took
on many high level responsibilities. At one time or another, she was
deputy director of her old Western European division, deputy director of
the trade policy division, and director of the European summit countries
division. Those were important positions for any officer to occupy; that
Fréchette, a woman, held them when she was still in her thirties proved
not only that she had the requisite ability and competence but also that
External recognized her gifts and talents. Fréchette claimed that personal
ambition had little to do with her rapid advancement:

The challenges were offered to me before I had any time
to ask for them. In a sense, the system was very support-

ive of me. I guess they decided early on in my career that I had potential and, through a combination of circumstances and the action of people in positions of authority who gave me challenging responsibilities, the system was very supportive and I never felt I had to prove myself. I thought the progression was natural, if faster than average.

External Affairs is a place where you have to "do your time" before you move up to the next level, so I moved up reasonably fast in relative terms but I never felt that I was being tested as a woman. I think I was being tested as an officer and after a while, when you realize that you have passed the tests one after another, you acquire a certain amount of self-confidence. I don't know whether people have looked at me as a test case; I don't think so. Maybe they have, but that is not the way I look at myself.

I always say I am not ambitious but people don't believe me. They say, "How can you go so far so fast without being ambitious?"

To be very honest with you, I was offered challenges without my asking for them and sometimes they have offered me challenges that I wasn't even sure I was ready for. I remember when I was named director for Europe – that was going to be my first director's job. There were two European divisions at the time, one that dealt with the four major countries of Europe and one that dealt with all the other Western European countries. My instinct was to go for the smaller countries, thinking that the other package was too big, and I remember the assistant deputy minister at the time said, "No, I want you for the bigger countries, you are capable, you are ready."

So if seeking bigger jobs, more responsibility, and being dissatisfied with what you are offered – thinking you are worth more – is a measure of ambition, I don't think I am that ambitious. I've moved as fast as I think was possible given my experience and my abilities. I am very happy with what I have achieved but I am not looking into the future and saying, "So what is the next bigger job that I can get?" For one thing, I've come to learn that, especially in the foreign service, the best plans fall apart because the world is moving all the time. You can be disappointed if you set your sights on something that may not be achievable, for all kinds of circumstances. I have been a little relaxed about where I was going to go next and so far it has turned out well.

In June 1985, Louise Fréchette, fluent in Spanish, English, and French, was given her first head-of-post assignment as ambassador to Argentina. At age thirty-eight, she was among the youngest officers, male or female, to become an ambassador. Some of her friends were worried about how a young and single woman would survive as head of post in a macho, Latin country. Fréchette dismissed their concerns:

> I was very, very pleased when they offered me Buenos Aires and I did not hesitate. I did not give much thought to how they would react to me as a woman. In fact, that's never been much of a pre-occupation for me. My career developed normally; I occupied all kinds of jobs and never thought that the fact that I was a woman was a negative factor. Therefore I was quite fearless when I went to Argentina. And I was right to be fearless because I was very well received.
>
> Of course, there was a lot of curiosity about me because I was maybe the second woman who had ever been named ambassador to Argentina. Some of the people I met there vaguely remembered that maybe 10 years earlier the Danes had had a woman ambassador for a short time. But I was very much a novelty in Buenos Aires. It turned out to be a very great advantage to me because everybody I met was curious and wanted to get to know me. But it wasn't in an unpleasant way, quite the contrary. I found great openness. I established myself professionally, and I know I was highly respected as a professional as well as being well-known because I was a woman. So it played very much in my favour in that sense.

During her time in Buenos Aires, Louise Fréchette began to think that Canada should have a larger, more influential role in Latin America. Returning to Ottawa in October 1988 as assistant deputy minister in External's Latin American and Caribbean branch, she set about redefining Canada's Latin American policy. The result – Canadian membership in the Organization of American States – created considerable public controversy in Canada at the time. But Fréchette considered it a very important diplomatic accomplishment. "It was a rather ambitious project in the sense that it was really taking the whole of the relationship of Canada and Latin America and trying to redefine what our interests in that region are." She put particular emphasis on the importance of Canada's economic relations with Latin America, hoping to expand trade and take co-operative action to ameliorate the debt crisis plaguing many of that continent's countries. She felt strongly that Canada's long-term interests in the region were inadequately served by our country's observer status at the Organization of American States, at a time when Central and South American leaders were urging Canadian membership in the OAS and lobbying the Canadian government to participate more actively in the affairs of the southern hemisphere.

Acting from deep conviction, Fréchette led the process of changing Canadian policy, a process that resulted in Cabinet approval for entry into the Organization of American States.

> I'm very proud of having done that. Time is confirming that it was the right thing to do at the right time. If there is one place where I left my personal mark it is probably in our relations with Latin America. I was excited about it but others around me were not so sure it was the right thing for me to do, maybe I was taking too many chances, maybe there would be too many obstacles. I never saw it that way.

Her work eventually drew her back to economics. Appointed assistant deputy minister of the department's economic policy and trade competitiveness branch in 1990, she was a leading member of the team planning Canada's participation in the 1991 London summit meeting of the world's seven leading industrial countries, commonly called the G-7. It was a satisfying exercise. Fréchette recalls:

> The economic summit pulls together all the big issues in foreign policy. Of course, I was involved at a time of great challenge. The biggest theme for the summit was economic assistance to the Soviet Union. [Mikhail] Gorbachev came to London as a guest at the end of the summit. I felt I was living a little piece of history.

Fréchette found that being a female ambassador at the United Nations in New York was almost as rare as being one in Argentina. In November 1992, there were only six women ambassadors among the permanent representatives of 179 U.N. member-nations. Also, the multicultural nature of U.N. membership is a complication for female diplomats.

> The fact that you are dealing with the entire world at the U.N. means that you do encounter all the cultures and in some cultures women don't have the same role as in our country. I started with Latin America where, although women don't have exactly the same role in society as they do in Canada, there are a lot of similarities between Latin American countries and Canada or other western countries. There are religious roots that are the same and therefore it's not that foreign.
>
> Here you meet all kinds of cultures and some representatives may find it less natural for them to deal with a woman than others, but I would say they are a very, very small minority. What I find is that people are used to thinking of a permanent representative as a man and therefore there are all kinds of little protocol mistakes that are made.
>
> I will every once in a while receive an invitation to the Ambassador of Canada and Madame Louise Fréchette. It's not because my colleagues have forgotten that I am a woman. It's just that, in the routine of writing 179 invitations, the social secretary thinks, "If it's a permanent representative, it's a man." I don't think that is a strike against me, it's just machinery that cranks up "Mr." when it's a permanent representative. The machinery will adapt; I'm sure it will.

The female ambassador, who is a relative rarity at the U.N., does have one distinct advantage over her male colleagues. She is seen as a novelty, an object of curiosity. Consequently, she is invited to more functions than her male colleagues (if only, sometimes, to balance a dinner table) and has access to more information and to more contacts without having to work as hard as some men do. In U.N. circles, it is said of Fréchette that her ability and intelligence enable her to exploit her easy access and gain an advantage in informing herself and Canada of current international issues and policies.

Fréchette acknowledged that because diplomacy is a twenty-four-hour-a-day vocation, in which entertaining is part of the job description, it is often difficult and lonely for single persons.

> Our world relies on couples or involves a couple. This kind of job, more than many other jobs, involves your whole life. When you are abroad it's morning, noon and night; your evenings, your social life, are part of your job. In the evenings, there are couples and you're an oddity if you're not married. But it has never stood in the way.
>
> I will admit that, when you first start at a post, it's easier to be with someone else to walk into a dinner party or a reception where you don't know anybody. I am sure that my male single colleagues would feel the same way.
>
> But that is a temporary difficulty. There is a bit of an added pressure on single people because you really are on your own. You have to discover a city on your own until you make friends. But in terms of running an operation as an ambassador, you have to trust your staff and, frankly, they respond very well.
>
> One of the challenges, of course, for single people who are heads of mission is to run a residence. There's only one way to do it. Trust your staff, get out of their hair, you can't be in their hair anyway. Try to know your mind, be clear in what you expect, and then trust them.

Her management style is the same in the office as at home. She runs a tight ship and makes sure that everyone knows where she stands and what she expects of her staff. But she is not arrogant or aloof.

> I get to like the people I work with very much. I grow fond of them personally so I have fun listening to the staff. My door is always open and people come in for a chat. In a mission like this one it's easier because it's not that large (about thirty-five people altogether). You can really get to know your team.

At the time Louise Fréchette joined External, in 1971, everyone thought that Margaret Catley-Carlson was the rising star in the female firmament. But Catley-Carlson's career veered away from diplomacy. Now Fréchette is seen as the primary role model for women in the department. But she never sought such a distinction.

> When I was named here [to the U.N.], the number of congratulations I received from women from within the foreign service and outside was remarkable. I could feel that there were sincere expressions of joy and support from women from all walks of life. That was very touching.
>
> There is a certain solidarity among women in the foreign service. Not that it's organic, although there have been attempts on various occasions to form women's groups and networks. This came a bit after my time – by then I had already reached management levels – but I don't think they were very important phenomena in External. They were occasional.
>
> But I think there is a network of solidarity or at least of special interest among women in the department. For the longest time, I knew all the women in the department. I certainly knew the women from my generation and the ones that joined in the following ten years. I followed their careers more closely than I have those of most men. Now, of course, I've reached a level where there is a large number of people I don't know – the newcomers – but I suspect it continues in the same way.

Louise Fréchette brushes aside incidents and remarks that might be construed as discrimination. Instead, she accentuates all the positive aspects of her highly successful career.

> In all honesty, I don't recall that I have ever perceived any discrimination. If anything, I've always found that my seniors in the department as a whole were supportive of me and my career. They have given me good breaks and in my relationship with individuals around the department I have not felt that there was a bias against me.
>
> I am trying to remember if there were incidents that bothered me very much. Not really. I don't see it, I refuse to see it, so if it is there I just ignore it. I would be hard put to say, "Oh, so and so has been patronizing." I

have seen patronizing individuals in the department or in other departments but they are patronizing with everybody. I can think of a few people who are unpleasant – they are very patronizing and they think they are smart – but it is not directed at me in particular.

Not everybody is perfect in the world. There are a lot of people who are not perfect, who are not pleasant, who have an attitude that I don't relate to particularly well but it's just the way they are with everybody they deal with. I guess the secret in all of this is you have to be very self-confident; you have to know what you are worth and carry on.

Fréchette was both perceptive and philosophical about the prospect of women being appointed undersecretary in the department or head of post in Washington, London, Paris or Tokyo:

I have no doubt it will come about but I think to have women heading the most senior posts you have to have the numbers and we don't have the numbers yet. Having one Maggie Catley-Carlson does not make a pool of senior women. It's only now that we are starting to have a significant number of experienced female officers. I think I am the most senior woman in the department and I have moved as fast as is possible to move in the External Affairs system.

You have to have the numbers to choose from. Maggie could have had any of these posts but she was also very much in demand to be president of CIDA, deputy minister of health. I also think assessing the performance of women in External by looking only at how many become head of post is a mistake. There are many other jobs that are less visible but are very important and should be looked at to determine whether women are making a breakthrough: assistant deputy minister jobs, director-general jobs.

Sometimes it's not even the title that makes a difference. When you look at lower levels, a deputy director job in a marginal division may be far less important and far less symptomatic of the degree of women's success than a really key desk job in one of the hot divisions.

You have to have a very detailed knowledge of the structure in the department and what are the up-and-coming areas and what are the sleepers. You can tell whether a woman is doing well and is getting a fair shake in terms of the assignments that she is getting. In my case, for instance, I was given Spain and Portugal when I came back from my first posting. I don't know to what extent it was by design but it was the best two years to be on Spain and Portugal. That's the time when everything changed, when the old regimes disappeared and the new ones came in. This had been a sleepy area for decades and then there were two years of intense activity. It was a fantastic job; it was the perfect challenge.

So when you are trying to assess when I had a good break, I was given a good break when I got Spain and Portugal. In that case, I don't know if it was really by design already. I know all the other jobs I had after that one were by design, they were meant to give me new challenges, to broaden my horizons.

Being an ambassador can be lonely sometimes, but Fréchette waxes almost lyrical about a diplomatic career:

It's a very funny type of job yet I think its greatest attraction is that you have guaranteed change without major risks. If you were to have the same kind of change in any other profession you would have to take huge risks. You would have to leave your company or start on your own all over again. In our case, the change is built in; it's normal that every three or every four years you move on to something else. Yet you have the same employer and there are certain things that you find from job to job. Your embassy is your little piece of Canada. So we are a bit addicted to change.

Fréchette's future has been the subject of considerable speculation in the corridors of the Pearson building and even in the daily press. Toward the end of 1992, after the announcement that Derek Burney was leaving his post as Canadian ambassador to Washington, press reports had Fréchette's name on a list of possible successors to Burney. As it turned out, the press and the pundits got it wrong. In January 1993, Prime Minister Brian Mulroney appointed the former chief of the defence staff, General John de Chastelain, Canada's envoy to Washington.

Fréchette's tour of duty in New York ended in November 1994. She returned to Ottawa, was named associate deputy minister in the finance department, and supervised arrangements for the June 1995 G7 meeting in Halifax. Later in the month, the summit over, Fréchette, who was regarded among her Canadian diplomatic colleagues as having the ability, intelligence, and drive to be External's first female deputy minister, became deputy minister in the Department of National Defence.

CHAPTER TWELVE

MISS BRIDGES
JULIE LORANGER

Established in 1909, External Affairs has sought university-educated applicants who were proficient in languages. In 1947, a public service commission advertisement announcing forthcoming examinations for grade two officers specified the following qualifications:

> Graduation from a university of recognized standing; preferably with post-graduate training in political science, history, economics or law; several years of experience as an FSO in the next junior rank or in work of equivalent character and standard; a knowledge of international relations; preferably a good knowledge of modern office practice; preferably command of a modern language additional to English or French; integrity, tact, perception, good judgment and good address.

The educational requirements put women at a disadvantage and assured an already reluctant department that not many of them would qualify. As Louise Reynolds observed in a study for John Hilliker's official history of External's beginnings, few female university students took the required courses and fewer still went on to do graduate work.

Julie Loranger, a Queen's Counsel and member of the Quebec bar, had the qualifications in spades. Born in Montreal in 1937, Loranger earned a BA from the University of Paris, a degree in civil law at McGill University, an MA in international law from the Institut des Hautes Études Internationales in Paris, and a doctorate from the University of

Courtesy of Julie Loranger

Ambassador Julie Loranger, in the garden of the Canadian embassy in Havana, with Cuban President Fidel Castro and former prime minister Pierre Trudeau in the summer of 1992 when the CBC was filming a TV series on Trudeau.

Navarra in Spain. She is fluent in Spanish, French, and English, and she has experience in several government departments in Ottawa and Quebec City.

Yet to this day Loranger is considered something of an outsider in External. She came to the foreign service by a circuitous route.

Admitted to the bar in 1960 and having finished her university studies in Spain, the young lawyer went to work for the Quebec department of education in 1965. It was the time of Quebec's Quiet Revolution. She was involved in drafting legislation pertaining to education, while reflecting on the whole field of public law. By 1970, her desire to work in constitutional law and international jurisprudence took her to Ottawa.

Any thought of joining the foreign service immediately had to be put on hold. Like many single professional women, then and now, Loranger had to look after her elderly mother. Her parents were divorced, and her mother lived in Montreal, restricting Loranger's freedom of movement. She went to work in the constitutional review section of the Privy Council Office in Ottawa and spent two and a half fascinating years helping plan the reform proposals which Ottawa presented to the provinces at the Victoria Conference in 1972.

Assigned the task of determining which level of government – federal or provincial – has responsibility for various aspects of Canada's international relations, Loranger had many meetings with officials from External and made friends among them. The meetings and the friendships kept her interest in a diplomatic career simmering on a back burner.

When the Victoria Conference foundered and constitutional reform was abandoned, at least temporarily, Loranger was out of work. Of course, she was still a public servant and not unemployed, but she needed a place in government where her knowledge of law and international affairs would be the most productive. External Affairs seemed the logical choice.

However, Loranger was disinclined to write the examinations and join External at the grade one level. She would have had to compete with recent university graduates; her six years of government service might not count for much; she was still financially responsible for her mother; and moreover, entering at the grade one level would mean a drastic cut in salary. Instead, she explored the possibility of transferring to External from the Privy Council Office. Supported by people in the department who had come to know her and her work, Loranger was seconded to External in 1972, as a desk officer in the United States relations division.

> I dealt with all the boundary waters between Canada and the United States, from the Columbia river at one end to the Great Lakes at the other end, and it was the period when the governments of the two countries were getting into the whole question of cleaning the Great Lakes. So it was a big issue. It was the beginning, really, of the talk about the environment in a real national sense.
>
> I also, in that job, was responsible for a peculiar file which is international bridges. Who would ever know that someone has to look after international bridges? But of course, international bridges – and there are lots on this long border – are half in one country and half in another.

Indeed, questions about transborder bridges were often important and contentious enough to be raised at cabinet meetings, and Loranger showed up at those meetings so frequently that ministers came to call her "Miss Bridges."

The International Joint Commission, dealing with boundary issues and disputes between Canada and the U.S., was another of Loranger's responsibilities, She later became legal counsel for Canada at the commission.

As varied and stimulating as the work was, it seemed to be leading Loranger into a dead end on her career path. Because she was only on loan to External, she could not get a pay increase or a promotion. She said, "There were limits to how long I could take this financially." People in External were pleased with her work and wanted her to stay in the department, but the idea of lateral entry from another ministry was still frowned upon. In 1974, Loranger joined the international telecommunications branch of the Department of Communications.

"I went from the dirty waters between Canada and the U.S. to issues concerning satellites and hardware in the sky and the peaceful uses of outer space," Loranger said. She was concerned specifically with direct broadcast satellites and the effect that they might have on national sovereignty when they beamed their powerful messages willy-nilly across international boundaries. Those same issues also were being discussed at the United Nations. Loranger travelled frequently to New York and Geneva whenever international telecommunications issues were on the agenda. At those U.N. meetings, Loranger worked closely with the legal branch of the External Affairs department, which was examining the same subjects from the viewpoint of their effect on Canada's foreign relations.

In 1976, just as Loranger had become "tired of dealing with hardware and things of that nature" and had decided that she wanted to work on social issues, Marc Lalonde, then minister of health and welfare and responsible for the status of women, made her an attractive offer.

Five years earlier, the Royal Commission on the Status of Women in Canada had recommended that the federal government establish an agency to coordinate all the activities affecting women in all its departments and agencies. Lalonde intended to implement that recommendation, and he invited Loranger to become the first Coordinator for the Status of Women. It gave her the rank, though not the title or the pay, of a deputy minister. It also broadened her horizons.

> It brought me into an issue that I hadn't personally been directly involved in an activist way but obviously, as a woman professional doing my own thing, I was involved in it. I think I could say I was a feminist without necessarily having the name.
>
> So I had a hard time, actually, being accepted in this

world of status of women, precisely because I wasn't considered to have the proper credentials by the women
who were involved previously. But anyway, I did my
thing and I did it well and, of course, eventually made
my little place and became accepted.

Being coordinator for the status of women within the federal government in Ottawa brought Julie Loranger back to the international arena. It
was the U.N. decade for women, and she found herself once again at
U.N. meetings, this time dealing with human rights and women's issues
from a global perspective.

I really became quite knowledgeable in U.N. affairs.
That's what, in fact, had always attracted me when I was
studying international law and then when it came into
reality turned out that I really did like it.
 It's a very special world, what we call a multilateral
world, requires a lot of patience and a special type of
personality. It's not everybody who has the hang of it. In
any case, I managed to find it interesting.

Loranger's mother died in 1976, the year Loranger took the status of
women post. She was free to consider a foreign service career. But there
remained a taboo on lateral entry into External, and it was doubly difficult for Loranger because by then she had reached a senior management
level in the public service. She started scouting international organizations and was attracted to a management post in the legal branch of the
United Nations Educational, Scientific and Cultural Organization
(UNESCO) in Paris.
 One day while discussing status of women matters with Allan
Gotlieb, then External's undersecretary, Loranger mentioned that she was
interested in the UNESCO job and might need a reference. His reaction
was encouraging. A few days later she was called by the director-general
of External's personnel division and informed that he was coming to see
her in her office. Loranger was somewhat taken aback by the call.
Personnel division directors usually summoned people to their offices.
The upshot of his unusual visit was the suggestion that instead of going
to work for UNESCO, she continue to work for the government of
Canada in one of its posts abroad. That was how she entered External
Affairs. She is one of very few career public servants to arrive by such an
indirect route, and she did not feel entirely welcome at first.

> To some people inside this is anathema, I never acquired legitimacy. But for most people they've seen me so much for so many years that I don't think they realize the difference between when I was in and when I was out. I didn't suffer very much from the outsiders' syndrome. External Affairs can be very fierce on outsiders. But I was an outsider who had been inside so much – I knew the department so much – that for me it was a natural fit.

In 1978, Loranger became Canadian consul general in Strasbourg. The post had been opened only recently – she was its second chief – and some setting-up was still required. (It was later closed during a government economy wave.) During her four years in Strasbourg, Loranger's expertise in multilateral affairs was useful in her work with the Council of Europe.

On Loranger's return to Ottawa in 1982, insiders at External finally accepted her as an officer who had earned her epaulettes. She was appointed director of the department's United Nations social and humanitarian affairs division. "Which brought me back," she said, "to women's issues, human rights, and all sorts of other issues I dealt with in Vienna and Geneva in the United Nations."

About a year later, while on summer holidays, she telephoned her office to discover that her entire division had vanished during one of External's regular spurts of re-organization.

> My division disappeared and my job disappeared. They had amalgamated two divisions. Well, first I was offered one of the jobs as head of a small division that had been hived off and I refused. They had taken it for granted that Julie would just say "yes." After pleading with me two years before, now they were putting me down a notch. So I refused.
>
> Anyway, I put up a little fight and the end of the story is that I ended up becoming director of one of the two western European divisions, the one that dealt with northern and southern Europe, the non-Group of Seven countries – not France, Germany, Italy, but the rest of Europe. And so that was interesting for me because it was the first time I was given what we call a bilateral responsibility, in other words, relations between Canada

and a country or countries, whereas before I'd always
been doing multilateral work.

So that lasted another couple of years and then, to
my great pleasure, I was offered the position of director
general of United Nations affairs which was always my
favorite area.

Loranger succeeded to the U.N. affairs post in 1985, by which time
she had been back in Ottawa nearly four years and was hankering for
another posting abroad. In fact, she was on the list to become high commissioner to Kenya when she suddenly became ill.

I had cancer – serious breast cancer – so that, of course,
took me off the list. It was reasonably advanced but I
continued to work throughout '86. This happened in the
spring of '86 and I stayed in External, I stayed in my job,
I went through chemotherapy, I lived through the whole
works. My colleagues supported me well. I was present in
the office except a day or two every two or three weeks.
As difficult as it was, it was easier that way.

In December of that traumatic year there came an unexpected vacancy for the post of ambassador to Spain. External was looking for a candidate who spoke Spanish and was immediately available; Joe Clark, then
External Affairs minister, wanted to appoint a woman, all else being
equal. Julie Loranger's name turned up on the short list.

By then I had finished my chemotherapy. I consulted
the doctors and they said yes, if I am going to a country
that has reasonable medical care and is not too far from
Canada. There was nothing more they could do for me.

So, as I say, I didn't have any hair on my head and I
was selected to be appointed ambassador to Madrid.

Loranger took a long holiday and then left for Spain in the early spring of
1987 for a normal four-year tour of duty. She enjoyed the tour immensely. "It's a stimulating country," she said, "one that was coming back into
respectability and so they were making all sorts of efforts to relate to
other countries."

Julie Loranger was not keen to return to Ottawa at the end of her
term in Madrid. Her health was fine, but she did not want to risk the

stress of a desk job at External. She left Madrid and went straight to Cuba as ambassador in 1992.

Interviewed in Ottawa during a trip home for a holiday and a medical check-up, Julie Loranger talked about the differences and the similarities she found during her postings to the two Spanish-speaking countries.

> The Cubans were colonized by the Spanish until virtually 1900. So a lot of the people who are there, their parents were Spanish, and they have cousins. There's a lot more exchange in the case of Cuba with Spain than there would be between Argentina or Peru or any of these other countries that were colonized in the 15th or 16th century. So it's peculiar in that sense.
>
> There are many similarities. Fortunately, I don't have the same schedule for eating and things like that; in Spain you have dinner at ten o'clock at night.
>
> Of course, the main differences are the type of government which needs no explanation. But I'm finding it quite stimulating and in fact probably the big difference for me, and one that people might not think of, is that in Havana the Canadian embassy is a very important embassy whereas in Madrid we're just one of many embassies with whom the Spanish have good relations.
>
> But in Cuba we're a big wheel because we practically feed the country. I don't mean in the sense of giving them food but they buy a lot of things in Canada. We have a lot of business going on between our two countries and therefore they work on maintaining the relationship in good condition and so, in that sense, it's different and quite fascinating at the same time.

Loranger found that being a female ambassador was no handicap in Havana.

> I suppose it's the Cuban revolution but they really treat women on a very equal footing. I've never felt in Cuba, as I had sometimes in Spain though less than I had anticipated when I went there, people looking through you or looking at the wall or at the person next door while they're talking to you. No, the Cubans treat this

very, very normally and naturally. You still get the eternal comment, I mean that happens around the world, "Oh, how sweet to have a woman ambassador, you are the fifth one, isn't that nice, and maybe someday we'll have a woman ambassador." These are ridiculous things that I now just don't bother about any more. They used to make me nervous and sometimes I would bite back but I've decided let them be the way they are.

I think it's fair to say that throughout my career I have not suffered, if that's the right word, from being a woman in a professional field. I've done all sorts of things, most of them at my own initiative.

I like to change, I like to get new stimulus, and in this sense External Affairs is perfect for me because change is inherent in the system.

I can say that I have managed to control my career to a certain extent and haven't, in any serious way, felt hampered personally by the fact of being a woman. Indeed I would say that, in some instances, probably the fact of being a woman has helped me. I'm thinking of appointments as head of mission. Joe Clark was definitely making a very specific effort to increase the representation of women abroad and he would insist on getting lists with women on them. Now in my case I was of the proper rank and I was going to places that also made sense, I was not favoured in the sense of being pulled up or asked to do something that was out of sync with my normal career progression but I suppose – I don't really know these things, of course, because you never get to know how the process works – but I suppose it means my name was put on lists if only to be looked at.

And I had done so many varied things that I'm moveable to a lot of places. In my case, the things were sensible and they worked all right. I think I benefited from a general atmosphere that made it easier, let's say, to appoint women to various positions than it might have been ten years earlier. Now that being said, I don't mean that the department is a place where life is made easy for women. It isn't. If you appear, in any way, to try to displace somebody, they can make life very difficult for you. In other words, if the appointment appears to be forced a little bit, either because you're of a lower rank, you're occupying a senior position or you're being sent to deal with a totally new field where you haven't proven your credentials, if you're a woman they'll give you a hard time. They'll put you in an impossible position and they'll make it difficult for you to prove yourself.

We've always said of any woman of our generation that she would have to be more competent. When I got involved in status of women I used to say that we would have reached equality when as many women in visible positions as men could be as mediocre as men. Now, if one woman slides on a banana peel, all of womanhood goes down the drain. Until we get rid of that syndrome, and I suppose we are making strides, we will not have reached equality.

Loranger said that a foreign service career is particularly difficult for women. It requires mobility, and many female foreign service officers give up marriage and children in order to be mobile. "It's objectively difficult to move with a husband across the world," Loranger continued, "and our society still attaches more importance to the jobs the husbands will be leaving behind than it does to the ones so many wives have left behind."

Being a single female head of post sometimes resembles a juggling act. Loranger single-handedly takes on both the social and the professional responsibilities of a diplomat. It can be funny, too. Loranger recalled a day in Madrid when a visiting Canadian cabinet minister was coming to lunch at the ambassador's residence. Before collecting the minister, Loranger had to pick up the bread and flowers for the luncheon party, a chore usually performed by a spouse.

It really requires a lot of organization. But once you get used to it, it is possible to manage, and we have staff, fortunately, and there is paid help to do it whereas the spouses in the old days, well, they just had to do it whether they liked it or not. More and more of them now decline to get involved too much.

Julie Loranger reflected on her future. "I've sort of attained my goals in External Affairs," she said. "Having had that illness a few years ago cut my ambition a little bit and I'm not anxious to come back to Ottawa in any responsible position. I'm more likely to leave for the private sector or do my own thing or something like that. I find government very hard to work in now."

CHAPTER THIRTEEN

REVELATION IN A HURRICANE
KATHRYN McCALLION

International trade has been the cornerstone of Canadian foreign policy since before Canada became a nation. The fur traders were sending pelts to Europe when the top half of North America still fit Voltaire's 1759 description of it as *quelques arpents de neige*. Indeed, the fur trade flourished until the animal-welfare movement of the late twentieth century persuaded Europeans that wearing furs was politically incorrect, if not downright unfashionable. By then, a modern industrial Canada was trading in all the goods and services befitting a signatory to the General Agreement on Tariffs and Trade and a member of the Group of Seven leading industrial nations. The major foreign policy achievement of the Progressive Conservative government of Prime Minister Brian Mulroney was the conclusion of the Canada-U.S. Free Trade Agreement and the negotiation of the North American Free Trade Agreement designed to bring Mexico into the continental bazaar.

From Confederation in 1867 to the outbreak of the First World War in 1914, Britain managed Canadian foreign policy. The rationale was that the British Empire, that far-flung collection of colonies and dominions coloured red on the map of the world, had to present a united front to those outside the imperial domain. Independent-minded Canadians began to chafe at this one remaining bond of colonialism. Tensions rose following the American Civil War when negotiations on east coast fishing were conducted by a British delegation on Canada's behalf. Although Prime Minister John A. Macdonald was a member of the British delegation on a joint high commission discussing cross-border problems in 1871, he could not persuade his colleagues to accept his argument that

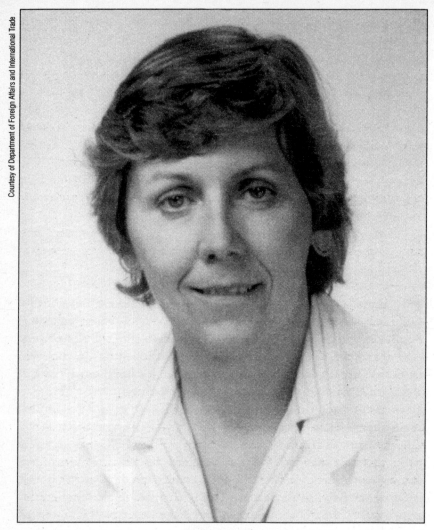

Kathryn McCallion

reciprocity in trade with the U.S., which had been in existence between 1854 and 1866, should be restored in return for concessions on fisheries. Before the Department of External Affairs was established in 1909, it often seemed that the governor-general, who was appointed by the British government and who reported to the colonial office in London, exerted more influence on Canadian foreign policy than did the elected politicians in Ottawa.

The one area where Canada did have considerable jurisdiction was foreign trade. Our first diplomats, so to speak, were really trade agents.

Shortly after returning to office in 1878, Macdonald sent former finance minister Alexander Galt to Spain and France for commercial and trade talks. In 1880, Galt became Canada's first high commissioner to London. (The title was chosen to avoid any supposition that its holder possessed diplomatic status, which the British had no intention of granting to envoys from countries of the empire. It persists today among Commonwealth countries, partly as a relic of history and partly as one of those quirks of diplomatic protocol which holds that the Queen, head of state in Canada and head of the Commonwealth, cannot send representatives to herself.) Galt's task, Macdonald told the House of Commons, was to give "a higher status to Canadian commerce and more direct means of communication with the various nations."

Sending trade representatives abroad became more formal and routine when the Department of Trade and Commerce was established in 1892. Two years later, a trade agent was dispatched to cover Norway, Sweden, and Denmark. The first full-time trade commissioner was John Short Larke, who went to Sydney, Australia, in 1895. By 1911, when the title Trade Commissioner Service had been formally adopted, there were twenty-one full-time commissioners and five part-time agents representing Canada in South Africa, Australasia, the United Kingdom, continental Europe, Japan, China, Newfoundland, the West Indies, the Bahamas, and Latin America.

Because trade commissioners were the first diplomats to be sent abroad, they regarded themselves as having pride of place as the senior foreign service. A certain amount of rivalry, even jealousy, was generated when diplomats from the upstart Department of External Affairs started arriving on the scene after 1909. The rivalry persisted, to a greater or lesser degree, until the two departments were integrated in 1982 and became External Affairs and International Trade Canada. It has two ministers who occupy separate grand suites of offices in the Pearson building overlooking the Ottawa River on Sussex Drive.

However, there was no rivalry when it came to the recruitment of women. External Affairs certainly dragged its feet by not admitting women officers until 1947, but it was decades ahead of Trade and Commerce. There were no female trade commissioners until Patricia Marsden-Dole became one in 1969. (By 1992, she was Canada's high commissioner in Tanzania.) Marsden-Dole was a minority of one until Kathryn Elizabeth McCallion, a tall, athletic, forthright woman, arrived in the department from the University of Waterloo in 1972.

Like many other female officers, McCallion initially did not have the foreign service on her list of career choices. Born in Toronto in 1945,

McCallion had an honours BA in political science. She also had taken courses in economics and had started graduate studies with a view to following in her father's professorial footsteps. Her timing was off.

In the early 1970s, Canadian universities experienced an extraordinary period of growth and expansion and had reached a plateau. Senior men had tenure; few new faculty members were being hired; women were at the bottom of everybody's short list. "The universities were not yet ready to select women," McCallion said. "They were still selecting men – men with families over just single men. All the old prejudices were there." Her academic adviser suggested she try the foreign service examination.

It was more in the nature of a dare. I really thought, well, I could or I couldn't. In those days, you had to try the public service exam first and then you took the foreign service exam, as a separate exam. I took them mostly on the basis of leaving doors open, not closing any. I had not actually decided, "I want to be in the foreign service, therefore I shall study to pass the exams." I'd already worked for the Ontario government at Expo '67 and public service seemed like an acceptable thing to do, a very secure type of job, but it didn't have any immediate sort of emotional attraction.

Because I am a bit of a sceptic, through the whole recruitment process I didn't think they'd ever actually recruit me, so I wasn't really worried about it. It was a very relaxed series of interviews. I was the only woman to be interviewed at the University of Waterloo and one of the few to be actually recruited; I believe that my success was because at that time it didn't matter to me so dreadfully, so there was more wooing on the government's part than on mine.

The only big question came: would I be interested in External Affairs or in Industry, Trade and Commerce? because at that time the two departments were quite separate. They were also recruiting for CEIC [Employment and Immigration Canada] but not the way they have been for the past ten years. It was more along the line that, if you weren't accepted by External or Trade, would you be interested in Immigration?

I chose Industry, Trade and Commerce because it was much more practical. I'm a rather practical person;

it seemed to me to be a more result- and goal-oriented department. To me, a very strong basis for Canada being a multilaterally oriented nation is because we are a trading nation. It is imperative to our well-being. We have a very strong multilateral identity in the world; it's one way we survive, and it is based on our trade and economic relations.

McCallion arrived in Ottawa as one of three women in a group of fifteen new trade commissioners. In an overwhelmingly male department, the women were made very conscious of their rarity and of their slim chances of survival.

The first year was very interesting because the trade commissioner service had been required by the government to recruit women that year. They had recruited two women earlier in 1968; one is still in the service, the other had resigned at the end of her first year primarily as a result of the fact she was married and the government at the time refused to assist her husband in finding a job abroad. So the statistic we all heard when I joined TCS was that 50 percent of all the women ever hired had quit in the first year because of their marriage. Many of the women are now married but in those days it was very difficult and the system made it harder, not easier. The women who were married had to make some very difficult choices between career development and family.

In 1973, after a year learning the ropes in the department, McCallion was posted to Mexico City as second secretary (commercial) at the Canadian embassy. It was there, far more than in Ottawa, that the men's club mentality among trade commissioners made an impact on her.

I enjoyed Mexico and didn't have any difficulty with the Mexicans but I did with certain of my colleagues. There was definitely an existing mind set about women firmly entrenched in the trade commissioner service. It was virtually a men's club that had been started in 1895, preceding External. It is part of the little ongoing rivalries. It's sort of, "We were in existence before you therefore

we were really the true foreign service." They were very
much a men's club and they weren't prepared to handle
women as trade commissioners.

I got along very well with the Mexicans. My greatest
difficulty was my boss. He kept telling all the Mexicans,
"If Miss McCallion can't help you, just call me," and so
they did. You shouldn't do that to anyone, male or
female, it's just bad management.

In Mexico there have been, still are, and presumably
will continue to be, a number of extremely good female
graduates of the Colegio Nacional de Economia. They
have, in their own right, produced some very good
women. If you are aggressive enough, you can play a
bifunctional role or be a dual personality. I met a very
good group of Mexicans who were quite well-to-do and
so you got dressed up in the evening and were very feminine and they could accept that as a counterbalance to
being rather tough and aggressive during the daytime,
because then they could see it was related to your work
and achieving your goals. They needed to be reassured
that you were feminine as well as competent. They are a
very matriarchal society and they became uncomfortable
if you were too "masculine" in your attitudes.

After two years in Mexico, McCallion went to the consulate general
in Boston in 1975 as vice-consul and assistant trade commissioner. It was
there that she saw for the first time the shortcomings and timidity of
Canadian business in the international marketplace.

I found that the three years in Boston were quite interesting. I learned a lot about the strength and the weaknesses of Canadian business, particularly some in the
Maritimes. Because I have a Maritime background, it
was very hard on me in the sense that we worked very
hard and there was despair at the inability of the
Canadian businessman to do his job well in a very tough
market. The American market really is a very tough
market.

It was an interesting post and Boston's a great city. It
was a fun three years and I didn't have any real problems. I certainly learned a lot about the weaknesses of

the Canadian economy, weaknesses that are endemic to
the Canadian economy and have been compounded and
increased by certain government policies.

So it was a very strong learning post, definitely not
very foreign service, you know, consulate in Boston is
very much just across the border. One thing with the
Americans that disturbs me is they call you "Kathy"
right away and they condescend to you but I can't say it
was because I was female. If your name is Charles they
instinctively call you "Chuck" or something. It is quite
amusing to realize how different the cultures are when
you can't articulate it very clearly.

Being the most junior officer at the consulate and operating in a
man's world made McCallion realize very early in her career that she
always would be the odd person out. She also learned, as have her female
colleagues in the foreign service and women in other male-dominated
professions, that women have to work harder than men to achieve the
same successes.

I was never going to find myself in a room where there
were nine women and one guy and the women would be
tough on the guy. I was always going to be in a room
with nine guys and one woman and they were going to
be tough on me.

It reaffirmed my own personal views that if you are
really good at what you do, unless they are overtly
insulting, you sit in a very strong position. You have to
work harder and you have to know your subject better
and work longer hours at it, but once you have done
that, it gives you a very secure base and it allows you to
look outwards because you are better prepared than
most people, you're not protecting anything because you
are protecting yourself so thoroughly by being more
knowledgeable, that you're not as positioned or as self-
centred as some people in the room.

If you are talking to people or working with people
it gives you a funny kind of confidence because you
know you are going to be attacked before it ever starts so
you are never taken by surprise. Also, you're being
attacked for something you can't do anything about. So

all you can do is shift the area and keep shifting it. We are not discussing whether I am good at this, we are discussing whether this is good for Canada or we can do this together as a Canadian company with an American company.

So you stay goal-oriented and don't worry about it and the word spreads: "She seems to know her work and you can work with her." In the end it gives you more strength if you are prepared and you have to be prepared. So it was quite a good time in terms of adjusting my mental equipment.

Before she left Boston in 1978, McCallion had been promoted to consul and trade commissioner. On her return to Ottawa, she briefly served in the U.S. marketing and operations division of the trade department's western hemisphere bureau. The work was not particularly challenging, and she welcomed the chance, midway through the year, to become deputy chief of the commodity arrangements division in the department's office of general relations. She took part in formulating trade policy and conducting international trade negotiations.

It was my first exposure to the inter-departmental community in Ottawa and also to international negotiations. It turned out I was good at it and I enjoyed it very much.

I believe that certain personalities are attuned to negotiation. I'm not sure you can actually be trained to be a negotiator.

I spent quite a few years negotiating commodity arrangements, the sugar agreement, the rubber agreement, and those kinds of things. A lot of North-South dialogue issues, the developed world versus the developing world, learning to work with the inter-departmental community trying to formulate common goals. In some instances, the hardest negotiation was getting an agreed Canadian position. Geneva was easy after you had negotiated with sixteen people – all men – at an inter-departmental meeting in Ottawa.

I developed a lot of useful skills. I found it quite fascinating. I found I had a very good mind for negotiations. I could find medium-ground solutions. I also learned to be tricky; you have to be tricky to get solutions. It was a good couple of years, I was enjoying myself.

In 1980-1981, McCallion also served as the second woman president of the Professional Association of Foreign Service Officers (PAFSO). She moved into the deputy minister's office as his executive assistant in 1981. When the department merged with External Affairs the following year, she took on the additional duty of co-ordinator of international economic relations in External. She has good memories of that merger period.

It was an exhausting time but an interesting time. Part of what I found exciting at that point in my career was that I had certain administrative skills which I had never had to use before because I had never been a boss. I had always been a "one of" sort of thing. While you don't get to be an administrator when you're an executive assistant, you do get to influence certain parts of things.

I guess what I was busy with was structures, [devising] the best way of redesigning the new department so that it worked because just grafting the trade side onto the External side didn't work. After the first six months it was apparent to everybody it wasn't going to work. Again I was fortunate, I was learning a lot, sometimes just by watching.

In 1983, McCallion moved out of the deputy minister's office and became director of External's agriculture, fish, and food policy division. She held this post for a year.

By this time I was getting tired, I'd been back to Ottawa for quite some time and it is hard to believe you are in the foreign service if you're never abroad and all my friends were having wonderful careers off in exotic places. It was time to get posted so I went to Paris, to our mission to the OECD [Organization for Economic Co-operation and Development], and that was a continuation of trade policy and negotiations.

McCallion went to the Paris mission as a counsellor in 1984. She was working hard and enjoying herself when she got a telephone call from

Ottawa asking her if she would agree to have her name put forward for a head-of-post appointment. She had been in Paris for just two years and was reluctant to move for that and other reasons.

> I turned it down because I was working hard on agriculture at the OECD and we were making progress. I had quite a long agenda that I had yet to achieve. There was quite a bit of "to-ing and fro-ing" and quite a lot of pressure. You don't turn down an assignment easily, if ever. At the time I honestly didn't think I was ready to be a head of mission. I was still very junior, I was an EX-1 [first level in officers' executive ranks] and I didn't feel I had the proper training or qualifications for whatever job they were offering me.

Realizing that the department was anxious to appoint more women heads of post, McCallion was concerned that failure on her part – a possibility which she apparently took more seriously than her superiors did – would reflect badly on her and on all her female colleagues and could jeopardize opportunities for other women in the foreign service.

> After some heavy negotiations with personnel and senior management, it was agreed that I would put it off for a year. So because of being female I was offered a senior appointment very early on. It was potentially a great opportunity but risky without appropriate training or preparations.

True to the goal-oriented approach McCallion has taken throughout her career, she used the year's wait to give herself a crash course in how to be the "head honcho" at a Canadian embassy.

> I postponed the appointment for one year and approached my ambassador for some guidance and advice about what heads of mission actually do. Unfortunately, in terms of training the OECD is a very small mission, it's six officers plus a head of mission and no real administrative staff because it's all managed by the Paris embassy. You are managing issues, you are not managing people and events.
> Fortunately, he had been an ambassador elsewhere

and so we went into a kind of mini-training course from time to time where I would listen, he would point out my weaknesses and I would try and change them. One of my weaknesses is a very high level of impatience with people. I am quite a demanding person and he kept trying to tell me, "Listen to the other side, slow down, and be open." It sounds a bit trite but they were helpful comments so I kept my little notebook of things to do and, sure enough, one year later they offered me Jamaica.

Kathryn McCallion was Canadian high commissioner in Jamaica from 1987 to 1990. When she accepted the appointment, she had no idea that she would be on the hot seat or that her work in the mission would appear in Canadian newspaper headlines. The Canadian high commission in Jamaica is a large post. It keeps watch on a sizeable foreign aid program, screens large numbers of would-be immigrants to Canada, is very active in trade promotion, and has a small political-reporting requirement. McCallion recalled her time there:

It's important to Canada, you can blow it, but basically you also go there and not many people really notice, it's not a high profile post. So I thought, well, if I was going to be head of post for the first time, it might as well be something that develops my skills. It had a large staff but doesn't give you a profile that could get you into trouble. I was worried that I would be in over my head so I arranged to have a safety net that if I thought, "I am in trouble," I could call Ottawa and get the necessary support. In effect, I was trying to build a support network.

Despite her planning and precautions, McCallion found her first three months in Jamaica more difficult than she expected.

No real training, for a start. There's a training course for new heads of mission but it didn't seem to cover any of the things I needed to know. The course has been greatly improved since then.

At the beginning I felt very inadequate as a very young [forty-two], female, high commissioner for

Canada in Jamaica where they'd had mostly more senior diplomats who were older and more distinguished. And they got me – younger and undistinguished. The Jamaicans kept trying to find out why. I became a bit of a media star in the local community press and, with no media training, it was hard to avoid saying the wrong thing. But you learn fast.

There was also a measure of resentment by our own staff – "you are too junior and your only qualification is you are female" – plus they all thought that they could have done it better. You have to overcome that by a strong interest in their program and an expertise in their program plus helping them with contacts they don't have. I was lucky because, as a result of being an executive assistant for a deputy minister, I did have contacts. It was reassuring to them.

I also told people up front, "I'm here because I'm female. I'm not here because I'm not good but the little extra edge was being female. I know it so we don't have to hide it but it is not the only reason I am here and I am going to work hard and achieve things." I found that it helped me to get established but many of my female colleagues wouldn't do it that way. I am female but I also happen to be quite good at what I do so it didn't worry me but it took a little of the strain away because people said, "Well, at least she acknowledges why she was posted here."

Hurricane Gilbert tested McCallion's mettle and proved to herself, the staff, and even the Jamaicans that she was made for the world of diplomacy. Called "the mightiest hurricane of the century", Gilbert struck Jamaica with tremendous force on 12 September 1988, killing forty-five people, leaving thousands homeless, and causing an estimated $1 billion worth of damage. For McCallion, however, it was an ill wind that blew much good.

The hurricane turned out to be good for me. It turned out that I was very capable in crisis management, that people trusted me to do the right thing most of the time. I found team building fascinating and I enjoyed working with the Jamaican government, with my colleagues in the British high commission and the American embassy. It certainly helped my self-confidence particularly as I had to make quite a few important decisions on the spot. As a result, I really grew into that job very quickly, courtesy of the hurricane. I found it professionally and personally an extraordinarily rewarding experience. I learned a tremendous amount.

I went into the job knowing fairly clearly that I'd been asked to do it in order to have more women on the heads-of-post list and I came out of it thinking, "Thank the Lord I am female because a lot of my male colleagues have not yet had the chance and may never get it." So it all worked out very much to my benefit.

Unmarried, Kathryn McCallion has avoided having to choose between family and career. She has found that being single has its advantages and disadvantages. "I can come in earlier and stay later and I do," she said during an interview in the Pearson building, in a tidy corner office that has a superb view of the Ottawa skyline and the Gatineau hills. "I have worked very hard for a long time. I am in most mornings at 7:30 and I'm probably still here at 7:30 in the evening and that would be impossible if you have family and other commitments outside the office."

Like her counterparts, McCallion learned that the life of an unmarried head of a post abroad can be very lonely. She called it "The loneliest job in the world."

In the post-hurricane phase, there were twenty-seven Canadian-based staff plus their spouses and their children, there were a hundred and some Jamaican employees, and I was responsible for them and I didn't have anyone to talk to privately. It was, "How can I take this responsibility and do the best I can, what if I make a mistake and it hurts people, etc.?" So you miss having someone to talk to on a personal basis.

Now that's where the networking comes in. I have some very good friends in the service posted all over the world – other women, women who had already been head of post – so you phone them. Of course, the phones have to be working. Networking is part of the system – it doesn't have to be women, it can also be men. But sometimes it really is a female thing, you know, "I feel very responsible for the well-being of all these people, help! help!" and it's the need for a certain perspective. One key is to have friends outside the system who don't know anything about the foreign service.

McCallion returned to Ottawa from Jamaica in 1990 and spent her first year as a senior departmental assistant to then External Affairs Minister Joe Clark. In 1991, she was appointed director general of External's Western Europe bureau.

During our interview, McCallion reflected on the role and experiences of women in the still largely male world of diplomacy and international trade and on her own career in particular.

I've done very well, I don't feel that I could have done any better if I'd been male. Nor do I feel that I'm that much further ahead by being female. There are certainly some of my colleagues who joined either with me or after me further ahead at this point in our careers.

If you're keen on your career, being female – as long as it doesn't overwhelm you or preoccupy you or give you too many negative chips – is an asset. It's like speaking four languages, it's like having a good computer brain or something. It's one of your whole arsenal of attributes.

I think for a long time the foreign service was an old boys' club and prejudiced against women. But if you let it get to you, you are in effect keeping yourself down. I think in many instances we are our own worst enemies, imagining slights and quotas where there aren't any, for now being female is an asset. But it can't be the only reason you get ahead, it only gives you that extra edge. Our business is highly competitive, the promotion system, in getting assignments, in the way you are perceived by your peers.

The testing is constant, it's the down side of External Affairs, in my view. It's not easy; there are not very many comfortable slots. Therefore if you think, "I'm going to get ahead because I'm female," you'll take one step and stop. If that's your only attribute it's like being left-handed, you only get through the gate and that's the end of it. Therefore it can't be regarded as a

sole asset, it can only be part of your arsenal. From time
to time, in certain circumstances, it works against you.

Even though the trade commissioner service came late to recruiting
female officers and handled them badly at first, McCallion gave it credit
for improvements.

> Trade commissioners are very goal-oriented so if you
> were a high achiever your acceptance factor was higher,
> along the lines of, "Geez, she's actually good at this; she's
> still a woman but she seems to be able to do this job
> well." It was what all the women of my generation went
> through. You had to work twice as hard to stay even but
> you could actually see some results. It is the kind of
> career path that if you were doing a job well there was a
> measure of acknowledgment, primarily because the job
> package was easier to delineate and define.
>
> One of the things I found since the amalgamation
> of the trade commissioner service with External Affairs
> is that damage limitation exercises – working very hard
> to make sure nothing happens – are very hard to quanti-
> fy; whereas if you're a trade commissioner – trade went
> up, sales were made, contracts were signed, those kinds
> of things – it's easier to list off your successes.

The woman who built herself a telephone network to help steer her
over rough spots while she was high commissioner in Jamaica recalled
that the trade commissioner service once had a built-in network for new-
comers. McCallion has tried to establish a similar network in External.
Conscious of the fact that people have helped further her own career, she
has tried to do the same for some of her junior officers.

> The trade commissioner service had a better system
> when I first joined; they actually actively paired people.
> They asked senior officers if they would be willing to
> take on the guidance of a junior officer. It's not onerous.
> You take them out to lunch and you talk to them and
> you give them some hints and if they want to talk to
> somebody that is not their direct boss, they can come to
> you, that kind of thing.

So there are two or three people in the system that
were assigned to me and there are two or three others
that I've got my eye on and I just, if things are happening, say, "Well, this is a good person," and you mention
names and you guide them and push them a bit and it's
like any other system. People who don't acknowledge it
and don't use it, in my book, are fools.

How you actually get one for yourself is harder.
There weren't any women ahead of me and it made the
men a little uncomfortable. I wouldn't say I had a specific mentor all the way through but certainly the ambassador to the OECD gave me a helping hand.

Although Kathryn McCallion was one of the first female trade commissioners and the first one to be a head of post, such milestones do not
mean much to her.

I've never had benchmarks about being the first female
to do anything and it just doesn't motivate me. I am not
striving to be the first female at anything and part of the
burden – the social conscience type of burden – I have
carried all my life, through the foreign service and elsewhere, is being seen as a representative of all women.
The day I know that women have made it is the day I
am free from the burden of carrying the success of all
women with me but I don't think it's going to happen in
my lifetime.

Up until about three years ago, I thought maybe
someday I could get to the point where people would
say that I had done a bad job because I was not competent or had poor judgment but without the corollary
that if I didn't do well women are not suited to that job.
If we could only get there, for a lot of women it would
be the day we are free at last, and I honestly think my
generation is never going to get there and it's quite sad
because we have worked hard to make it as individuals.

The rules of diplomatic protocol, written when foreign service
women were either secretaries or spouses, do not make life easier for
career women. Of course, most hosts no longer send women to the drawing room while the men linger over post-prandial port and cigars.

However, McCallion said, "Most official protocol is very male-oriented, very outdated. It makes it very difficult for a female head of mission and even more difficult if you are single. It's the same with female ministers. They don't have an easy job either."

McCallion also found that it is tiring to have to protest all the time. "I wish I didn't have to protest any more but every time you pretend discrimination isn't there and it doesn't matter, it rears its head again. So you might as well acknowledge that it does matter." But Kathryn McCallion does not brood about the difficulties. As she proved during the hurricane in Jamaica, she has the ability to take everything in stride and to rise to every occasion, the test of a true diplomat.

CHAPTER FOURTEEN

ABOVE THE SALT
COLLEEN CUPPLES

There is a pecking order within the Canadian foreign service. External's political officers are intellectual aristocrats; trade commissioners are money-grubbing nouveau riche; and immigration counsellors are poor cousins who work hard but always sit below the salt at embassy tables. From the public's point of view, however, immigration is the most important component of Canada's foreign policy. It affects Canadians directly, in their homes, places of employment, communities, and neighbourhoods. Immigration always has been important. As early as 1854 – thirteen years before Confederation and fifty-five years before there was an External Affairs ministry – the Department of Agriculture sent its first agents to Britain and Europe to find settlers to populate the empty spaces in the Canadian hinterland.

Public concern about immigration from Asia is no new phenomenon. The 1907 race riots in British Columbia were triggered by discontent about immigration from China, Japan, and India. The government of Sir Wilfrid Laurier was reluctant to ban Japanese immigration, despite the riots and political pressure from the province. Laurier sent Postmaster General Rodolphe Lemieux to Tokyo to arrange a gentlemen's agreement to curb emigration voluntarily. (Eight decades later, Japan agreed to a voluntary quota on the export of Japanese cars to North America.) One of the first Canadian legations to be established, after the formation of the Department of External Affairs, was in Tokyo. It opened in 1929, primarily to promote trade and signal Canadian interest in the Pacific region. It was also intended to counter Conservative opposition demands on Prime

Colleen Cupples

Minister Mackenzie King to stop Japanese settlement in Canada. It was easier to control the flow of immigrants by having a Canadian official on the spot in Tokyo issuing (or refusing) visas. By putting the onus for approving or rejecting immigrant visas on posts abroad, the government kept the issue out of the Canadian media and the politicians out of hot water.

At the same time as immigration from Asia was creating public controversy and problems for politicians, Canadian officials were scouring

Europe for the kind of settlers described by Interior Minister Sir Clifford Sifton in 1922. "I think a stalwart peasant in a sheepskin coat, born on the soil, whose forefathers have been farmers for ten generations, with a stout wife and a half-dozen children, is good quality," Sifton said. The message that white European settlers were preferable to Asians or blacks was clear although never put into words.

Sifton's immigrants opened the prairies to the plough and turned Canada into the breadbasket of the world. Those who come today – still seeking a better life for themselves and their children – gather in cities and turn them into archetypal global villages. Because increasing numbers of people in every corner of the globe continue to see Canada as a land of freedom and opportunity as well as a place of refuge, immigration remains a major responsibility in nearly all of Canada's embassies, consulates, and high commissions.

The foreign service officer who handles immigration in a post abroad works with people more than with policy. The task is often onerous – processing all the documents Canadian law requires of prospective immigrants is not easy in countries that do not keep meticulous records – and turning down an application can take an emotional toll on an empathetic official. By the same token, seeing a family happily on its way to a new and prosperous life in Canada, or being reunited with loved ones, can be very satisfying. It is one reason why many women choose the immigration stream in Canada's foreign service.

Colleen Leora Cupples is one of them. A former Canadian ambassador to Burundi, Rwanda, and Zaire and most recently immigration counsellor at the Canadian embassy in Rome, Cupples was born in Port Arthur, Ontario. She began her public service career in 1967 as a twenty-two-year-old manpower counsellor in Toronto, after graduating from Lakehead University with a BA in English literature. She was Canada Manpower's student placement director at Ryerson Polytechnical Institute in 1971, when she learned of a competition for manpower counsellors to join the foreign service.

Interviewed in Ottawa, where she was director of External's Asia and Pacific programs division before being posted to Rome in 1992, Cupples recalled the beginning of her diplomatic career. She passed the written examination and was waiting for the results of her interview with the foreign service selection board when she was offered the job of registrar at Ryerson. She explained to Ryerson that she had applied to join the public service, and Ryerson paid Cupples the compliment of keeping its offer open until she had been accepted. During her encounter with the selection board, Cupples had an amusing experience that enlightened her on how ham-handed and condescending the men of the foreign service could be toward the women in their ranks.

> Those board members were all male and they asked me a question which I didn't understand. I thought they were suggesting that women were too emotional; I didn't understand what they were driving at. I said, "If you are talking about emotionalism, I know as many men as women that are emotional and I don't think one particular sex has a monopoly on it and I don't see what you are getting at."
>
> There was a nervous moment's pause and the three of them looked at one another to decide who was going to put the question. Finally this individual who shall remain nameless leaned forward and said, "Miss Cupples, we are saying that men can't get pregnant."

Once she recovered from her astonishment at the remark, she assured the interviewers that if she were hired and posted abroad she would not become pregnant.

After a ten-month training period in Ottawa, she was sent to Paris on her first posting in June 1972. Paris was naturally a francophone post where all the work – oral and written – was in French. Cupples was bilingual, but her mother tongue was English.

> They thought I could cope and, of course, I realized on going that it would reinforce my French ability. It was wonderful to have the opportunity at that time. There was, let's be honest, resistance from the post before I was sent because they thought that possibly this person was not going to be able to handle it. But handle it I did, and survived.

She handled it so well that when she was posted to London in the summer of 1973, the Paris embassy strove to keep her and even offered to send a francophone to London instead. But Cupples went to London. While there she decided to marry an American businessman whose company planned to send him to Kenya. Female foreign service officers who married were no longer required to resign – and Cupples had no intention of doing so voluntarily – but her marriage did pose a real problem.

There was an interdepartmental committee on external relations which co-ordinated policy issues that affected all of the departments, at the time, that had foreign services, and that group considered my case first, about what to do about this woman intending to marry.

They decided they would oblige me to the extent that they could and they would give me a leave of absence because the man I was marrying was moving to Nairobi. So a commitment was made to me that I would be posted to the first available vacancy that came up in Nairobi. In the meantime, I would be given a leave of absence to accommodate my waiting for that vacancy to occur.

So I married, left London, went to Nairobi and spent seven months on leave without pay waiting for a vacancy. Then on 1 April 1975 I was posted to Nairobi, stayed on for another three years and then was posted back to Ottawa.

Two years later, having been promoted from FS1 to FS2, Colleen Cupples went as consul to Los Angeles. She stayed only seven months before going to Buenos Aires in 1981. That year the immigration foreign service was integrated with External; so Cupples's name was on the diplomatic list as first secretary (immigration) and consul. Fluent in Spanish, she found Buenos Aires a fascinating city, enjoyed the countryside, loved the people, and found the work challenging.

My time during the military juntas in Argentina was a very interesting time because I was responsible for human rights reporting and we had a program for Argentina and worldwide political prisoners and so I was actively involved in following the cases of people where there was a Canadian interest, where they were imprisoned for their political beliefs in Uruguay and Argentina.

Unlike foreign service officers in the political stream, who usually spend a year or two at country desks in Ottawa between postings, Cupples has spent most of her twenty-one years of service abroad, at posts in eight different countries. There were three years in Argentina, two in Sri Lanka, and one in Syria as counsellor and consul. She counts her days in Damascus among the most memorable in her career.

I was there at a very interesting time. It was a very difficult time but it was a fascinating time and Syria is a
country key to any resolution of Middle East peace. So
in contemporary politics it's important, it's vital, it's
interesting.

You have also in Syria a very strong sense of our
Western history, our religious history – the Roman
Empire, the Crusader castles – so it was fascinating.

For four months, Cupples was chargé d'affaires at the embassy in
Damascus after the Canadian government recalled its ambassador,
Jacques Noiseux, in the wake of the Hindawi trial. Nezar Hindawi, a
Palestinian, was convicted in London, in October 1986, of attempting to
bomb an Israeli airliner the previous April. Following the conviction,
Britain broke off diplomatic relations with Syria, the U.S. withdrew its
ambassador, and Canada recalled Noiseux. "Our message to Syria at the
time, recalling the ambassador, was that we were obviously reflecting dis-
satisfaction at perceived Syrian support for terrorism and, in that regard,
we expected Syria to expel Abu Nidal's organization."

The timing of the recall left Cupples juggling a hot potato. After two
years of looking for new property for a chancery, embassy officials finally
found a suitable parcel of land, and they unwittingly asked the Syrian
government's permission to buy it just before Noiseux departed for
Ottawa.

Ottawa thought that it was impossible, that obviously
approval would not be given under the circumstances;
we were pointing a finger at Syria and wagging it. But
we knew that the foreign ministry had agreed with our
request and that it had gone from the foreign ministry
to the interior ministry, which had the final word.

About a month after Jacques's recall, I had occasion,
at a social function, to meet the interior minister. I indicated that I would like to come and see him and he
agreed to see me. Now this was somewhat of a surprise
because in a country like Syria it is not easy for a fully
accredited ambassador, at a time when the countries
have normal, happy relations, to be received by the interior minister, let alone a chargé of a country which has
expressed its displeasure.

She saw the minister shortly thereafter. His first question was "What about the recall of your ambassador; how could you do this?" It was not unexpected. Cupples gave the ritual response – that normal diplomatic relations would be restored as soon as Syria expelled Abu Nidal and renounced terrorism – and then changed the subject to the real reason for her visit. "'I am here to ask a favour of you. We have been trying to buy property and we found something and now I understand the only approval outstanding is yours and may we please have the approval?' To everyone's astonishment, a few days later we got it."

Cupples credits what she called "the novelty factor" – being a woman in a man's world – for the success of that particular undertaking as well as for other highlights in her career. Of her encounter with the Syrian minister, she said, "I think that he could not believe that this woman had the nerve on the one hand to deliver this severe message and on the other to say, 'Now, will you please do us a favour?'"

Cupples never found it a disadvantage being the only female chargé in a country that was both Muslim and politically secular. She recalled what happened immediately after Noiseux left for Ottawa.

> He had a number of outstanding invitations which he had accepted before being precipitously withdrawn and so, just to cover ourselves, I asked the secretary to phone each of the hosts and say, "As you may know, Monsieur Noiseux will not attend your function, do you wish to have the chargé instead?" One of the occasions he had accepted was a dinner or lunch being given by one of the Gulf state ambassadors. All the people who were called but the Gulf state ambassador said, "Of course, Madame will come instead of monsieur l'ambassadeur." The Gulf state ambassador said, "No, this is an occasion for men only."
>
> But even he, a month or two later, had turned around. He had a farewell lunch, which he hosted, for an outgoing ambassador and only two western representatives were invited to that lunch, the rest of them were Arab ambassadors or African ambassadors. I was one of the two exceptions and the other was the Papal Nuncio.

Having acquitted herself well as the temporary head of an embassy during a trying time, Cupples was posted to Kinshasa in September

1987, to become ambassador in her own right to Burundi, Rwanda, and Zaire. In 1988 she was also accredited to Congo (Brazzaville).

Colleen Cupples, a tall, slim, elegantly turned-out woman with a firm handshake, was the only woman head of mission during her term in Zaire. She said that her male diplomatic colleagues were "uniformly wonderful." One amusing incident involved protocol at the dinner table of the Zairean president.

> I used to be mildly irritated that they always, when they made addresses, began, "Messieurs les ambassadeurs," and I made a big point the first year of saying, "This isn't fair." When they thought about it they would say, "Messieurs et Madame les ambassadeurs," but they slid out of the habit very quickly. But that's an irrelevant, tiny point.
>
> I did once have a very amusing exchange with [President Joseph] Mobutu on the fact of being the female head of post because he invited me and a few other ambassadors to sit at his table at lunch on one occasion.
>
> There is an annual presentation of wishes on the occasion of the new year when the diplomatic corps get together with Mobutu and his wife and the cabinet. As I said, I was invited to join his table for lunch, which was a signal honour. It was January 1988 and the honour was bestowed because of Canada's forgiveness of their debt at the francophone summit in Quebec.
>
> Mobutu, of course, always controls everything. We were seated at our table at a buffet lunch and he said, "Now, ladies," and pointed to his wife and the wives of the other ambassadors at the table, and said, "Ladies, you will now go and serve yourselves first. Not you, Madame ambassador," to me. His wife and the other wives got up and served themselves. Just as they were coming back to the table he said, "It's your turn, Madame ambassador." I got up in a distinctive class of my own and then he said, "All right, gentlemen, now we will go."

Cupples returned to Ottawa in the fall of 1989 and spent a year as director of the Latin American and Caribbean programs division. She then moved to the Asia/Pacific division and finally to Rome.

In her office in the Pearson building in Ottawa, Colleen Cupples shared her thoughts on the changes which she has seen during the past two decades. One major change is the right of married women officers to continue their careers. Cupples has been married twice; neither marriage lasted. The main reason, she explained, was that in her early days in the foreign service female officers rarely even contemplated the possibility of marriage. Given access to her personnel file, in 1978, she found an appraisal that described her as one of the best trainees in her group but assumed that she would soon marry and leave the service. On seeing the remark, Cupples became quite indignant. She said, "I thought, how dare they make that presumption?"

Always determined to pursue her career, Cupples contrasted her experiences with those of younger women in the service.

> I think that at a sort of middle ground and a middle generation that I was trying to find a way to have a career and married life both and I did not succeed. I don't think there are very many people in my generation who have. But when I look behind me, at younger women foreign service officers, I see significant numbers of them being successful at it all in their careers – having marriages that are able to sustain the experience and the disadvantages of their careers to family life, and particularly family life for women officers, on top of it all having babies. So I think that's a big change, a big part of the evolution.
>
> I think for my generation, men of my age were less conditioned to expect to have a wife who had her own career interests which she would actively pursue and which, if necessary, would take her to the ends of the earth. To some extent, some of my problems exist to a lesser extent for the younger generation because men of the younger generation are far more likely to expect to have a wife who has a career which is of equal merit and value as his own. That's one important difference, I think.
>
> The other difference is that where they are career couples, there is now a stated policy to try and accommodate them to the extent that they can be accommodated. In my own case, in the instance of both my marriages, a problem which arose in each was that my hus-

band became unemployed and I continued to work. And so, I would argue that compounded the generational difficulty with having a spouse who had a career of equal importance. In the end, they were without employment ... so I was the "working person" in the family.

That's very difficult for people of my generation. Again, that situation I see behind me. I know female officers behind me who have house-husbands; their husband is the person who willingly assumes the role of looking after the other things while the wife brings home the bacon. But that was how they chose to start out or that was a matter of choice.

When Cupples and her colleagues in the immigration foreign service were integrated into External Affairs in 1981, they became members of the social affairs stream of the foreign service and took their place alongside the trade and political streams. In the decade that followed, the social affairs stream attracted a considerable number of women. In January 1992, for example, of 337 officers in the social affairs stream, 104, or 31 percent, were women. In contrast, women made up just 16 percent of the officers in the trade stream (85 of 519) and a slightly higher 18 per cent of officers in the political stream (98 of 458). In February 1992, the government decided to transfer the social affairs stream back to the Department of Employment and Immigration.

There was considerable consternation among women. Protests came swiftly. The president of the Professional Association of Foreign Service Officers argued that the transfer would diminish Canada's ability to coordinate the formulation and implementation of its foreign policy. In a letter to External Affairs Minister Barbara McDougall, on 2 March 1992, PAFSO president Donald R. Mackay said:

> The explanation that External Affairs "needs to get back to basics" is one that ignores a consistent theme of your government, that Canadian foreign policy must serve the broader national interest, including such important issues as national reconciliation, economic competitiveness and prosperity, the development of human rights and respect for ethnic or other minority groupings. To a large measure, the ability of External Affairs to deal with the diverse international agenda is dependent upon its minis-

ter having a pool of creative, diverse and multi-focused talent to draw upon. The men and women of the social affairs stream bring to this department unique skills, talents and experiences that are invaluable to this process ...

The "back to basics" philosophy is also troubling in the large context. It is symptomatic of an extremely narrow vision, that does not accord proper importance to the multitude of activities that have increasingly come to characterize state-to-state relations. Long gone are the days when the conduct of international relations could be limited to those "traditional" concerns of political/military relations and international trade.

The multilateral system in particular (i.e., the United Nations), has legitimized the view that nation states have authentic interests in a wider portfolio of issues. An illustrative listing of "non-traditional" issues that are dealt with internationally would include: the environment, women's issues, the development of science and technology, international co-ordination of monetary and fiscal policies and co-operative efforts in the areas of health (i.e., containing the AIDS epidemic and international trade in illegal drugs).

On 27 March 1992, a group of women officers in the department sent their own letter to McDougall, pointing out additional concerns not raised by Mackay. The letter said, in part:

We believe that the transfer to the Department of Employment and Immigration of the social affairs stream, with its substantial complement of women officers (31 per cent), represents a failure of this department to adhere to the principles of employment equity. The women officers of External Affairs have the education, skills, training and talent which equip them for senior management positions – yet, due to the transfer of the social affairs stream, the pool of skilled women officers in the department with the potential for advancement will be significantly reduced ... With the departure of the social affairs stream, the proportion of women officers in the Department of External Affairs will fall to 17 per cent.

This will complicate the department's ability to fulfill its stated five-year objective, as described in the 1991 report *Employment Equity: Where are We?* of reaching a proportion of women officers in management positions of 14.1 per cent by 1996 – seven years after the public service as a whole reached that level. At present, only 6.2 per cent of officers in the management category at External Affairs are women.

These facts are all the more disturbing when we consider the leading role Canada has played internationally in raising the issue of women's equality, particularly within the United Nations, where Canada strongly supported an international commitment to filling 35 per cent of professional posts with women by 1995, with 25 per cent of that number in management categories ...

There is an embarrassing gulf between our international exhortations and domestic reality. We should not be surprised, therefore, that among OECD countries, Canada ranks among the lowest in terms of numbers of women in public life.

The traditional male-oriented management style of External Affairs will thus be perpetuated, as the transfer of the social affairs stream jeopardizes the steady advancement of the last ten years towards the objective of attaining a more equitable female/male ratio.

The letter ended with a request that the transfer be suspended and further study be undertaken to ensure that any decisions about the composition of the department take into account its "commitment to the advancement of skilled and talented women."

The request and the protests fell on deaf ears, and the transfer is now a *fait accompli*. Colleen Cupples and her counterparts in Employment and Immigration's foreign service remain eligible for appointments abroad as heads of post, but they must feel, from time to time, that they are once again the poor cousins of the Canadian foreign service.

CHAPTER FIFTEEN

SWIMMING WITH SARDINES
ANNE LEAHY

In a staff paper prepared for Pamela McDougall's Royal Commission on Conditions of Foreign Service, there is an anonymous, plaintive observation about appointments to posts abroad. "It was felt that senior management or its favourite high flyers hopped between Ottawa, London, Paris and Washington, leaving the others 'toiling for years on end in the Third World.'"

The observation was made with both men and women in mind, of course, but it is especially applicable to female officers in the foreign service. By 1993, twenty-eight women had been Canadian ambassadors or high commissioners in twenty-eight countries – eighteen of them in Africa, Asia, Latin America, and the Caribbean. Only one woman – Jean Wadds, a former MP whose appointment was political – had been high commissioner in London. At the beginning of 1993, there were female ambassadors to the United Nations in New York and the United Nations Educational, Scientific and Cultural Organization (UNESCO) in Paris. Women have been heads of post in lower-profile European countries – Hungary, Denmark, Portugal, Spain, Poland, Sweden, Austria, and Finland – and in Israel and New Zealand. However, no woman has been an ambassador to any of the following capitals: Washington, Paris, Moscow, Rome, Tokyo or Bonn.

While statistics tend to validate the anonymous observation cited above, it has little resonance among women who have been in charge of Canadian embassies and high commissions in Third World countries. These women take a very practical, positive, and philosophical attitude to their appointments. Anne Leahy, who was Canada's ambassador to

Ambassador Anne Leahy at a CARE water pump project in the village of Esseng II in the Eastern Province of Cameroon in January 1990.

Cameroon, the Central African Republic, and Chad from 1989 to 1992, expressed it best. "When you're accredited to Italy, France, Germany, Britain, you can picture yourself as a 'medium fish' swimming alongside whales as well as sardines. You tend to have more impact in countries in which you can make a difference than in others where you're just one of many players."

A Canadian envoy's impact does not necessarily depend on whether the host country considers Canada important, Leahy observed.

> In Great Britain we're important, for example, with respect to the human dimension of our relationship. Deep and multi-faceted links between Britain and Canada have been forged through years of immigration. However, trade and investment patterns have evolved over the years and are not what they used to be. Over all, you feel you have greater weight and greater impact in a country which relies on you for development assistance and advice than in a country where you're just another representative.

Leahy's career began more by chance than by choice. Born in Quebec City in 1952 and fluently bilingual, she obtained an honours BA in economics at Queen's University and an MA at the University of Toronto. While pursuing post-graduate studies in economics, she wrote the foreign service examination.

> I happened to notice, as I was walking by the employment office, that the foreign service exam was being held shortly thereafter and I decided then that I would write it. It's not to say that I did not have an interest in international affairs or Canada's foreign policy but I had not made up my mind beforehand that I would join the foreign service. I say that because some people think that motivation is measured by wanting all your life to become a foreign service officer, implying thereby that those who haven't thought about it long ahead would not be good foreign service officers. And I obviously don't think that.

Arriving in Ottawa in June 1973, Leahy started out in External's U.S. relations division. She moved quickly to the commercial and economic relations division, where her academic specialty was put to good use, and within a year she had received her first posting. From 1974 to 1976, she was second secretary to the Canadian mission to the European Economic Community in Brussels. Her role was to facilitate negotiations for a precedent-setting framework agreement on commercial and economic co-operation between Canada and the European Community. "I arrived in 1974 two weeks before Prime Minister [Pierre] Trudeau visited the commission in Brussels to launch a series of pre-exploratory talks for the negotiations that followed the year after. It was the first agreement that the European Community signed with a developed country outside Europe." The agreement was signed in 1976. It reaffirmed Canada's interest in Europe as a trading partner and was intended as a counter-weight to reliance on trade with the United States.

Leahy returned to Ottawa in October 1976. She spent nearly two years in the department's press office, headed by Derek Burney when Don Jamieson was minister. The press office is exposed to the entire spectrum of issues affecting Canadian foreign policy and must provide timely answers to the media and House of Commons. Leahy's stint in the press office added considerably to her knowledge and experience, far beyond her specialty in economics.

She returned to economic issues in 1978 when she transferred to the trade relations division. Next she spent six months learning Russian in preparation for her 1980 posting as first secretary and consul at the Canadian embassy in Moscow.

As a political officer, Leahy's main task was to analyse and report on the internal political and economic affairs of the Soviet Union. That was easier said than done in the closed and suspicious society that existed before Mikhail Gorbachev introduced *glasnost*. Leahy found Moscow the most difficult yet the most rewarding of her assignments. "Rewarding in terms of relationships," she said. "I still stay in touch with Russians and colleagues of other embassies who were in Moscow 14 years ago."

After two years in Moscow, Leahy went to Paris as counsellor with the Canadian delegation to the Organization for Economic Co-operation and Development. Her experience there as the Canadian representative to the OECD's development aid committee, with its emphasis on development economics and aid policy, would serve her well when she became ambassador to Cameroon.

Before that posting, though, Anne Leahy returned to Ottawa and spent three and a half years in External's personnel division, first as deputy director and then as director. She took part in revising the foreign service examinations and the criteria for selecting new officers.

Candidates are still required to have a university degree and a broad base
of knowledge, but there is also considerable emphasis on personality.
Leahy said, "We look mostly for personality characteristics in a person,
good 'horse sense,' good judgment and an ability to get along with people
in trying and difficult circumstances. And this is harder than it seems."
Those years in personnel revealed to Leahy the department's patterns of
recruitment and promotion and the ways in which it accommodated its
female officers who were married and had children.

> When I joined the foreign service most women who
> joined as officers were single and now single women are
> the minority. There has been a tremendous change.
> Women foreign service officers who take a year off to
> have a child and continue their career are no longer odd-
> ities. It took a long time before it was accepted but a lot
> of progress has since occurred.
>
> A few years ago we worked on a policy of maternity
> leave and benefits for women abroad and we went from
> zero cases to at least two or three a year – women who
> are in the foreign service, who are having children, tak-
> ing several months off and coming back to work, not
> being penalized or otherwise disadvantaged. Now this is
> something which was unheard-of five years ago.

The department, which until 1971 required women officers to resign
when they married, has had to resign itself to the two-career couple,
Leahy observed.

> Today, families depend on two incomes, families are
> used to two incomes. So in a sense, it's no harder to post
> a married woman than to post a married man. The
> female spouse is as important a "factor" in determining
> an assignment for the officer as is the male spouse. And
> besides, why concentrate on the foreign service officers?
> A lot of women who are not officers are married and get
> posted. In 1988 we did some statistics and found the
> number of foreign service married couples – where both
> spouses were in the foreign service as clerks, administra-
> tive officers, et cetera – was over a hundred.
>
> Up to now we have tried to accommodate the
> couple at the same post, in the same city, or nearby

cities. It will be more difficult as the missions are down-
sized.

Leahy remarked that neither Sweden nor Britain takes family configura-
tion into account when posting members of its foreign service. "It can
happen that one foreign service officer ends up in London and the other
in Malawi."

A spouse's function as an unpaid social secretary in the ambassador's
residence also has changed.

> There are several heads of missions or heads of programs
> – large programs – whose spouse has his or her own
> working career and is not around to act in a support role
> to the other. It's a question of organization and availabil-
> ity of resources. The drawback is when you're working
> together as a unit you can network, you can see a lot
> more people, maybe do a bit more in functions than
> when you're alone, but in terms of preparation, all that,
> you work it out. I would think that today you find few
> spouses who confine themselves, or are happy, just to
> support their husbands.

Leahy's appointment as ambassador to Cameroon was more expedient than planned. She was ready to return to Moscow as minister/coun-
sellor in 1988 when Canada and the Soviet Union engaged in a round of
diplomatic expulsions. Canada sent nine Soviet diplomats packing when
evidence turned up that Soviet agents had been trying to penetrate the
Royal Canadian Mounted Police and the Canadian Security Intelligence
Service. They wanted access to classified military and industrial information. In a traditional diplomatic *quid pro quo*, Moscow replied by
expelling several Canadian diplomats. Leahy's second tour to the Soviet
Union was aborted. Instead, she went to Yaounde in September 1989.

Leahy's first venture as an ambassador turned out to be a happy experience. She enjoyed the work, the country, and the people. She soon realized how important Canada is to an African country. "The aid relationship was the major aspect of our bilateral relations with Cameroon, Chad
and the Central African Republic, although I was ultimately responsible
for all our programs, including our commercial interests in Cameroon."

Leahy travelled extensively, "particularly in Cameroon which is quite
a diversified country. Cameroon is said to be 'Africa in miniature.' You
therefore must travel to get to know the country. It's a bit like Canada;

not by sitting in Ottawa do you get a feeling for Quebec or Western Canada. In addition, I travelled twice a year to Chad and to the Central African Republic."

Leahy was thirty-six and female, and the beginning of her tour in Yaounde produced some initial awkwardness. She was unperturbed.

> Being a head of mission, especially in Cameroon which is very traditional, had its funny moments. As in many traditional societies, women are not accepted in the same way as in Canada. However, Cameroonians know that in Canada the status of women is fairly equal to men's and they accept it. It still is difficult for some to deal with a young woman in a position of authority. They are also uneasy about a woman without children since in most African societies – probably that's one generality that applies – women are meant to have children.

> On one occasion I welcomed a highly placed first-time visitor in the lobby of the chancery and accompanied him to my office where I invited him to sit down. It took him a few moments to realize this young woman was the ambassador – and it showed! He later laughed and admitted he had expected the ambassador to be a man.

> There were some awkward moments during my courtesy calls. I was asked bluntly – "How could you do this job?" – in a genuinely candid way. Anglophone Cameroonians (20 percent of the total population) tended to be more straightforward than the francophone ones. One government minister asked, "Look, how do you intend to manage?" I learned quickly to finesse personal questions. I said that I didn't think I'd have any problem given that we enjoyed a large bilateral relationship and, in particular, a number of co-operation projects in his area. He got the point that if he wanted to have continued good relations then he'd better accept me.

During a long conversation in Ottawa in April 1992, Leahy looked back on her time in Cameroon and observed:

> Africa is a continent everyone forgets about. Africans feel very marginalized. There is the perception that when

the G-7 countries get together they don't think of developing countries except in the sense of, "How much debt do we need to write off?" On the other hand, if you look at some issues that are important for Canadians, such as protection of the environment and respect for human rights, all of a sudden Africa becomes a lot more important. A major part of the tropical rain forest is in Africa and it is threatened by exploitation which we feel should be stopped. The Africans have their views about that, as forests are vital to their development, which we must listen to.

And secondly, on the protection of human rights, now that we've turned our attention away from Eastern Europe with the collapse of communism, we're looking more closely at other countries, such as in Latin America, China or Africa.

So, in a sense, although Cameroon may be a marginalized country over-all in terms of power politics, it isn't necessarily irrelevant in terms of Canadian foreign policy interests.

Leahy was optimistic about a Canadian role in protecting human rights in places such as Africa and China.

I think we can have some influence, in particular as we act in concert with other major donor nations. In Africa we can have an influence quite directly through quiet diplomacy.

We're known as a country which has probably one of the best records in the world in human rights. There are always people who complain about our own problems; these are usually Canadians who don't have much of an idea how bad things really are in some countries. Other countries know that Canada has a good record and that we refrain from giving lessons so that when we approach a government about human rights we can get a hearing.

In Africa right now many countries are going through a difficult political transition. In two years, for example, the country I was in – Cameroon – went from a single-party regime to its first multi-party elections in twenty-five years. It is very difficult for old habits and attitudes associated with a one-party state in terms of law-and-order apparatus to be turned around. It can be done, gradually, and helping the process along includes constant representation and raising issues in a way that shows sensitivity to the local cultural context.

Leahy had not been to sub-Saharan Africa until she was posted to Cameroon. The country – indeed, Africa itself – left a lasting impression upon her.

In Canada, you don't really get to know Africa. The few Africans we see here make an effort to adapt to us. I think it's really a world apart to which we should pay a lot more attention and make a greater effort to understand. It is far more complex and sophisticated than depressing development statistics convey.

On her return to Canada, in March 1992, Leahy became director-general of External's policy planning staff. Among her colleagues, she is regarded as one of the department's rising stars. She possesses the intellect, insight, and management skills needed to become the first female undersecretary. Her stated ambitions, however, are much more modest. "The physical environment is, to a certain extent, not so important. I wouldn't want to go to a country where war is raging. There is a trade-off between the relevance of the job and the minimum requirements for a decent life in terms of personal safety. I would want to go back to Russia."

Leahy attributes the fact that women have not been given the high-profile ambassadorial posts or been promoted to deputy minister more to lack of numbers than to discrimination.

These three posts [London, Washington, Paris] tend to be subject to political appointments or to be reserved for the most senior level of officials, for example, deputy minister, where women have not been legion.

Women who married had to leave right up until 1971; women didn't start applying in large numbers to join the foreign service until really the mid-'70s. Even today, efforts must be made to attract more women to write the foreign service exam, particularly francophone women who were barely 18 percent of those who wrote the foreign service exam in 1988.

In a few years, you'll see women in senior positions in headquarters because of the relatively larger intakes of recent years. I did a study a few years ago comparing the quitting rates of foreign service women and men; I found that the proportion was about the same but because there are fewer women, people tended to focus on them. In fact, the quitting rate in External is very low.

No, I don't see a glass ceiling in External. On the contrary, I think there have been very visible measures in favour of women in terms of assignments and promotion. Promotions are a sensitive subject with foreign service officers because there are so few openings every year. If you look at Louise Fréchette, former assistant deputy minister and now ambassador in New York, she went up like a meteorite and deservedly.

We adhere to the government's affirmative action policy, produce reports on equal opportunity and affirmative action every year. We were among the worst statistical offenders, apparently, for women in middle and upper management. This has a lot to do with the career concept of the foreign service and its "staffing to level" system and less to do with the fact that women are discriminated against. It could be very easy to put a lot of women in upper echelons here when all you have to do is take them from the outside. This would not be a popular move with either women or men foreign service officers who joined at the bottom of the ladder and want to protect their career prospects.

This department has for a long time, contrary to what people might say, assigned its promising officers in positions where they can prove themselves. Joe Clark should get a lot of credit for this; as minister, he took it upon himself, he insisted on it, and he probably moved women along more quickly than they might have otherwise.

Discrimination is an attitude ... which must be fought through the commitment of senior management. There are still some individuals who do not like the idea of women competing on an equal basis and I know that some women believe they have been set back by such men. However, I don't think there is institutional or systemic discrimination in External Affairs.

Explaining the "staffing to level" system in the department, Leahy asserted that the merit system works.

Many people will tell you it works very dismally because there are so few promotions every year. At least those who get them definitely deserve them; the problem is that there are many more who could have got the promotion as well had there been openings. It's because of the way the foreign service officer category is structured. Your level in any other government department depends on the position and you compete for that job.

In External, it doesn't work like that. In External you get your promotion in competition with everyone else at your level but not by direct competition. There are very few openings and in the context of government restraint and position cuts, there are fewer still.

Openings may be few; it is safe to say, though, that Anne Leahy's name will be on the short list.

CHAPTER SIXTEEN

ADVENTURE IN AFRICA
SANDELLE SCRIMSHAW

Long before the Canadian government sent official representatives abroad to promote trade and control immigration, Canadians themselves – missionaries, doctors, nurses, teachers – travelled to remote corners of the world and set up medical clinics, hospitals, and schools. They also built churches and spread the Christian gospel. A report on Canada's international relations, prepared in June 1986 by a special joint committee of the Senate and the House of Commons, recognized the connection between foreign policy and foreign aid.

> The impulse of Canadians to co-operate with people in the Third World is long-established and powerful. Since Confederation Canadian churches and voluntary groups have worked to improve the quality of education and medical care in the Caribbean, Africa, India and other parts of the world. Beginning with the first conference on the Colombo Plan in 1950, all Canadian governments have been concerned to promote the economic and social development of the poorest countries in the world. Over the years various reasons have been offered for this activity, but essentially it comes down to this: it is right and it is in Canada's self-interest that all peoples should enjoy well-being and a decent standard of living.

Despite the tradition of a strong Canadian presence in developing countries, the federal government for a long time was reluctant to involve

Courtesy of Sandelle Scrimshaw

High Commissioner Sandelle Scrimshaw with two other Canadian women who were heads of diplomatic missions in Africa in 1990. Scrimshaw is on the left; Raynell Andreychuk, high commissioner to Kenya, is in the centre; and Anne Leahy, ambassador to Cameroon, is on the right.

itself. For instance, the support External Affairs Minister Lester B. Pearson gave the Colombo Plan, founded at a conference of Commonwealth foreign ministers in Ceylon (now Sri Lanka) in 1950, was hardly altruistic. He saw development aid as the best way to keep communism and Soviet imperialism out of Third World countries. Communism may no longer be a worldwide menace, but the general argument about aid and democracy remains valid. People will not listen to exhortations about the benefits of democracy when their bellies are growling with hunger pains and their children are dying of starvation. If the rich democracies want to foster peace and stability in the world, they must feed the hungry and help them become self-sufficient and ultimately prosperous.

The Liberal government agreed that Canada would become a member of the consultative committee setting up the Colombo Plan. However, the Canadian delegation to the committee's first meeting in Australia was warned not to make any financial commitments, and was advised to avoid grandiose development projects. "Ordinary handpumps may be more suited to some regions than vast irrigation works; and ploughs may be more needed than tractors," the delegation was told.

Prime Minister Louis St. Laurent waited until February 1951 to approve Pearson's recommendation of a Canadian contribution of $25 million for the 1951-1952 fiscal year and to authorize him to negotiate with the Indian government the terms for sending $10-$15 million worth of wheat as part that contribution. To this day, food – especially grain from the Canadian prairies – remains an important part of our government's foreign aid program, which in terms of a yearly contribution has grown from $25 million in 1951-1952 to $2.8 billion in 1992-1993. This is impressive, but Canada's contribution has never reached 0.7 percent of gross national product. That was the benchmark set for prosperous countries in 1969 by the United Nations Commission on International Development, of which Pearson was chairman. External Affairs Minister Joe Clark promised in 1984 to reach the target by 1990, but he was undercut by Finance Minister Michael Wilson. His 1986 budget limited foreign aid to 0.5 percent for the rest of the decade. Since then, spending on development assistance has shrunk to 0.4 percent of GNP. In early 1993, the Mulroney government began to shift the main focus of Canadian aid away from developing countries towards those of Eastern Europe.

At the outset, External Affairs managed Canada's foreign aid program. A division of the department assumed administrative responsibility. From 1960 to 1968, the External Aid Office took over the program. In Ottawa and at posts abroad, foreign service officers supervised the money allotted to the projects.

External's direct involvement ended in 1968 with the establishment of a crown corporation, the Canadian International Development Agency (CIDA). It had its own president and its own staff, in Ottawa and in the field. At first, CIDA reported to Parliament through the External Affairs minister; from 1984 to 1993, the agency had its own minister of external relations and international development. Two individuals held the portfolio and both of them were francophone women – Monique Vézina and Monique Landry. When Prime Minister Kim Campbell took over the government in June 1993, she handed responsibility for CIDA back to her External Affairs minister, Perrin Beatty.

The shift to a crown corporation, changes in ministerial responsibility, and budget cuts notwithstanding, foreign aid continues to be an essential ingredient of Canadian foreign policy. Canada's aid projects in developing countries are of vital concern to Canadian diplomats. Indeed, at many posts in Asia, Africa, Latin America, and the Caribbean, officers dealing with development issues outnumber those handling either commerce or immigration. The relationship between CIDA and External is close. When CIDA employees go abroad, they are technically seconded to External and report to the ambassador or high commissioner. On their return to Canada, they usually go back to work at CIDA headquarters in

Hull. Occasionally, an individual whose foreign service career began in CIDA ends up an officer in External.

Sandelle D. Scrimshaw is one woman who made that transition. The road from development worker to diplomat was a roundabout one for her. After a year at the Université de Besançon in France, she earned an honours BA (and a gold medal) in French language and literature from the University of Western Ontario in 1973. Scrimshaw joined the public service as an administrative trainee, thinking that it would be a short-term job while she explored academic opportunities. She worked briefly for the Food Prices Review Board headed by Beryl Plumptre, spent another short period in the official languages division of the Secretary of State's department, and then moved to National Museums of Canada. She stayed there from 1974 to 1979. In the meantime, she also took courses in economics and political science at Carleton university.

During her tenure at National Museums, Scrimshaw worked on travelling exhibits with regional themes. At one time or another, she was museum interpreter, tour co-ordinator, media relations officer, and tour manager until her promotion to deputy director of the program. To improve her management skills and prepare her for senior management positions, she was then sent on a career assignment program that involved a three-month residential course followed by a series of management-training assignments.

Once the course was successfully completed, Scrimshaw spent nine months taking the Discovery Train – a travelling exhibition of Canadian history and culture – on its inaugural tour across Canada. It was a stimulating assignment that gave her a rare opportunity to see the country and meet Canadians from all walks of life. But when the train pulled into its last station, Scrimshaw's career seemed to have come to an end too. She began looking around, had a number of interviews, and chose CIDA. "Why was I interested in CIDA? I think, without knowing very much about the organization and having really a layman's perspective on development assistance, I felt that it was a field which had value and to which I could feel a commitment."

Sandelle Scrimshaw joined CIDA in 1979. Her bailiwick was Francophone Africa. She was senior project officer, country program manager, and finally deputy director of programming and evaluation. Although she made several field trips to Africa from her base in Ottawa, the prospect of living abroad did not materialize until 1983.

At that point there was a unique opportunity for lateral entry of CIDA officers into External Affairs. This was a time of foreign service consolidation; it was felt that it was important to have a cadre of foreign service officers who were specialized in development assistance. I entered that competition and was successful and so in 1983 I transferred to External Affairs as an FS2.

The next year, Sandelle Scrimshaw was posted to Abidjan, Ivory Coast as development counsellor, with additional responsibility for three satellite offices in Mali, Burkina Faso, and Niger. She talked about her eight-year adventure in sub-Saharan Africa.

I had the advantage of having worked on the Mali desk and on Francophone Africa programs in general before I went out and I was, therefore, comfortable with the issues and the programs. I had also travelled to the region a number of times. Occasional field trips cannot compare, however, to living and working in an environment which is so culturally different. My assignment to Abidjan wasn't perhaps a normal posting in that I travelled extensively, as much as 40 percent of my time, because of my regional responsibilities. I didn't have responsibility for Côte d'Ivoire. My focus was very much on the Sahel.

In geographic terms the Sahel – an Arabic word meaning "shore" – extends 3,000 miles along the southern rim of the Sahara desert, from Senegal to Chad, and includes parts of Ethiopia, Kenya, and Sudan. Scrimshaw put most of her energies into four countries within that vast region – Burkina Faso, Mali, Niger, and Chad.

My responsibility was to ensure the integrity of the aid programs, their relevance to the development needs of each country, and to ensure that the resources – financial, material and human – were well-managed. I provided guidance and direction to the staff and regularly engaged in policy dialogue on development issues with the host governments.

One of my frustrations was not being able to acquire the same depth of knowledge of each of the countries as those officers who were resident there. I was always left "sur mon appetit."

The most professional satisfaction, I think, came from the quality of the aid programs we have in those countries. We were probably the fourth or fifth largest donor and yet we had a credibility and an influence that went beyond the sheer volume of our assistance. Our programs were, first of all, very responsive to the critical needs of the Sahel in the early '80s. There was also a positive policy dialogue between the Canadian government and the governments of the Sahel. We were seen as not having a colonial past so that gave us a relationship with both the governments and the people that was very special. I think the other rewarding part was trying to build a strong and cohesive team of Canadian personnel for the Sahel, notwithstanding the communication challenges posed by distance.

Scrimshaw made some friends during the time she was based in Abidjan, but getting and keeping them was not easy when she spent so much time travelling. Although she described herself as someone who likes her life to be reasonably well-planned, organized, and predictable, she does not close her door to spontaneous adventures.

I did some interesting project visits overland in some very remote places: Timbuktu, Agadez, Zinder and the dunes of Mauritania. One night when we were in a small town in northern Mali – Gao – there was no accommodation so we slept on a rooftop. There were about eight of us travelling and we had been able to muster up some mattresses and we slept on the roof of a house of one of our cooperants – I think it was a CUSO volunteer in Mali.

So sometimes the conditions were not easy. We usually flew commercial flights although I remember taking a military flight up to northern Mali and sitting on those benches along the side, holding on, wondering – Russian-trained pilots in a Russian plane that's poorly maintained? I also have very vivid and colorful memories of sitting under a tent drinking camel milk in a remote corner of Mauritania; of overcrowded, unsanitary refugee camps and feeding stations during the drought of the early '80s; of women and children left to fend for themselves as their husbands left to find employment in the city.

Sandelle Scrimshaw found the work so challenging and absorbing that she requested and was granted a year's extension on her assignment to Abidjan. Then, instead of coming back to Ottawa in 1987, she was cross-posted to Accra as Canada's high commissioner to Ghana and also accredited as ambassador to Togo, Benin, and Liberia.

Scrimshaw spoke of her time in Accra.

> It was a professionally satisfying and personally reward-ing posting for me from all points of view. I thoroughly enjoyed being head of mission; it was my first opportu-nity, really, to have responsibility for programs other than aid. I also welcomed the challenge of trying to manage resources and a broad range of programs in a way which would maximize benefits to Canada.
>
> Our interests in Ghana are largely development-related and my experience at CIDA was therefore of tremendous assistance. Canada's development co-opera-tion relationship with Ghana is excellent. We also have a shared Commonwealth heritage which is, perhaps, more important for us than for Ghana, a country which is now a republic. And then there are relationships between Canadians and Ghanaians which go back for so many years. These bonds have resulted in an openness, a favourable predisposition to Canadians, that made my job much easier.
>
> I also found it easier to do business in Ghana than in some other West African countries. It was not neces-sary, for example, to go through the foreign ministry for an appointment with ministers. After the initial courtesy call, I was often afforded direct access.
>
> I travelled extensively in Ghana. I visited almost every Canadian project, maybe not some of the small, community-based initiatives, but the major ones I went out to a number of times. I also visited projects undertaken by Canadian companies and by the NGO [non-governmental organization] community. I some-times did regional tours to try and get a feel for what was the basis of the economy and how Canadian interests could be further engaged.

Besides gaining a better knowledge of Ghana, I felt it was important to see what was going on in the field with our projects – there is an accountability of the head of mission for that – and to provide support and encouragement to the Canadians and Ghanaians who were working on the projects. It is often a morale-booster for them and they seemed to look forward to the visits. Also, to be quite honest, I think it projected a very positive image of Canada. It raised our profile.

Scrimshaw was the first woman to be Canada's high commissioner to Ghana. She joined two other women among the forty-five heads of mission in Accra when she arrived. One was the ambassador for Burkina Faso, who left shortly after Scrimshaw came; the other was an American representative to the United Nations Development Program, who had been ambassador to Mali in the early 1980s.

Because of her mandate and her personal interests, she too was very much development-oriented. Both of us tended to receive extensive coverage in the papers and on television because of our interest in grass-roots development, a priority for the Rawlings government. I am sure that our gender also influenced our visibility.

The chief of protocol used to tell me that unless there was a requirement to respect precedence in the allocation of seating for official functions, protocol preferred to place the female heads of mission in the front row. I was also called upon to represent the diplomatic corps at functions where Canada was seen to be an influential multilateral player, i.e., World Food Day.

Diplomats are seldom off duty. Luncheon, cocktail, and dinner parties are as important as are high-level meetings with government ministers or field trips to development projects. For single women, social functions sometimes can be trying. Scrimshaw, with her perky manner, easy friendliness, and casual good looks, rose to every occasion.

There were some complications, challenges and funny moments. I remember distinctly my first courtesy call on the Japanese ambassador. We had never met and when he walked in you could tell he was taken aback. I think at the time I was thirty-six which was relatively young for a head of mission and it was very young in the Japanese context. My Japanese colleague, in an unusually direct manner, practically exclaimed, "How did you get to be a head of mission, an ambassador, so young? This would never, never happen in my country." He went on at some length about this "anomaly." I can also vividly remember my call on a North African ambassador who was the acting dean of the corps. This was my first call on a diplomatic colleague. I went in and he sat at one end of the sofa and invited me to sit at the far end. Not once did he look at me during our brief meeting. There was absolutely no eye contact. He would simply smile and ask questions as he looked across the room. I asked myself, "Is this what it's going to be like?" We ended up becoming quite good friends and I soon realized that his initial manner reflected nothing more than shyness and perhaps not knowing how to relate to a female head of mission.

Another interesting challenge which I regularly faced were dinner parties, particularly those hosted by Arab or South Asian colleagues, where women and men tended to congregate in separate corners of the room with virtually no interaction except once seated at the dinner table. "Aperitifs" and "digestifs" separated the men from the women. My dilemma was to diplomatically find a *terrain de compromis* as clearly I had more in common professionally with my male colleagues than with their spouses. I resolved the problem by first greeting the host and hostess and then, after paying my respects to the women, I would join their husbands for pre-dinner drinks. I would then make a point after dinner, when they separated into their two groups, to spend some time with the women, thereby covering both angles.

I did find it somewhat of a challenge being a single head of mission. Perhaps my single male colleagues have experienced the same difficulties of trying to manage office affairs and run an official residence at the same time. I entertained regularly, from smallish lunches to larger dinners for about twenty-four to twenty-six people to receptions for up to three or four hundred guests. The domestic staff were called upon to assume more responsibility than during my predecessor's tenure when there was a spouse willing to manage household affairs.

I thought it was an advantage being a woman diplomat in Ghana and I think that is the case in many countries. I think it can open doors. Because there are so few women at senior levels of most foreign services, there is an initial curiosity and interest surrounding the assignment of a woman as head of mission. For those doors to remain open, however, one has to perform, to demonstrate competence.

I also think that women are able to establish a different type of rapport with government and private sector interlocutors. At least, that has been my experience in West Africa. Perhaps we are less threatening, perhaps it is our "softer" side. But I did find that members of government opened up, consulted and even confided in me more than I believe they did with my male diplomatic colleagues. During my farewell call on Chairman [Jerry] Rawlings, he commented, "You have brought a human dimension to our relationship." He appreciated the fact that I was concerned about the social dimension of economic development, that I tackled difficult political issues with sensitivity and that I had travelled to even the most remote areas of Ghana to support community-based initiatives. I know that the women in rural areas and market towns were always excited when I would visit their projects and especially delighted when I would join them in dancing to celebrate the commissioning of their projects. One felt a sense of solidarity, of understanding. That sense of immediate rapport may have been more difficult for a man.

Ghanaian women no longer have as much political clout as they had in the early years of the former British colony's independence, when Kwame Nkrumah ruled first as premier and then as president until he was ousted by a military coup. However, they still have substantial economic power and are the "king-makers" in the matriarchal Akan society. Women have the authority to make decisions about the succession of tribal power at the village and community level. Scrimshaw found "extremely competent, well-educated Ghanaian women in all fields of endeavour," but she observed that they were under-represented in government.

> During my stay in Ghana, I tried to bring together peri-odically a group of Ghanaian women from different milieu, an informal women's group. Most of them knew each other; there were businesswomen, there were women from the universities, politicians. These were dynamic, fascinating women who enjoyed the opportu-nity to spend an evening with their "sisters" and to engage in lively, informed and sometimes satirical debate on the political, economic and social issues of the day.

The ease and grace with which Sandelle Scrimshaw performed her diplomatic duties in Accra makes it hard to believe that Canada's first high commissioner to Ghana, Evan Gill, had reservations about posting a female officer to the Ghanaian capital. In a memo to Bruce Williams, head of personnel at External, on 25 November 1957, Gill wrote: "I think that a woman officer might encounter some difficulty in travelling through the country and there is also the consideration that a woman finds it less easy to deal with native servants than a man does."

Scrimshaw returned to Ottawa in 1990 to take charge of the depart-ment's Asia Pacific South bureau. It was a long way from Africa to south-ern Asia, and she had much to learn.

> My background since my early CIDA days has been in Africa. The learning curve has been quite steep. First of all, this is the first time I have actually worked physically in the Pearson building because I went abroad shortly after I joined the Department of External Affairs. Each organization has its own corporate culture and each its own networks which one must establish to be able to work effectively, particularly at the more senior levels of the public service.
>
> And then there are the issues. Asia Pacific South is a large, diverse region where Canada's foreign policy prior-ities are clearly engaged. It is a region which has enjoyed a remarkable level of economic performance over the last twenty years and one which is central to the realization of Canada's prosperity agenda. The priority which we

attach to international peace and security and sustainable development is also reflected in Canada's relations with this dynamic and challenging region.

In mid-1992, when the government dissolved the social affairs stream in the foreign service, Scrimshaw had to decide whether to go back to CIDA and continue working on aid and development issues or stay in External where she could transfer to the political-economic or the trade stream. She chose the political-economic. "I opted to stay with the department because of the greater scope it seemed to offer at this point in my career," Scrimshaw said. "Notwithstanding my decision, I am still involved in development issues and maintain a close dialogue with CIDA on their programs in the Asia-Pacific region. This is perhaps the region where the linkage between development co-operation strategies and foreign policy priorities is the most pronounced."

If logic prevails, Scrimshaw's next posting would be to a country in the Asia-Pacific region. In External, though, logic cannot be counted on, and Scrimshaw will take what comes. "My preference would be for another assignment in the developing world because I think that I could use my strengths better there than I could in a developed country." She has no grand ambition to be External's first female deputy minister.

> I don't think in terms of long-term professional goals; I don't set my sights, for example, on a position or level which I would like to reach. It's important for me to achieve, to feel that I'm doing well, that I'm contributing, that I'm getting something in return and that I'm enjoying what I'm doing. To me, those are the benchmarks … not the next level, the next promotion, the achievement of the ultimate goal.

Her "laid-back" approach gives her a high rate of acceptance among her colleagues.

> I would say about 90 percent of my experiences in External Affairs have been positive. One invariably encounters a colleague or two who have gender biases but they are the exception rather than the rule. I have been fortunate; I came into government at a time of expanding opportunities; the government was also promoting bilingualism and affirmative action. Gender was

not an issue, at least not an impediment to my career advancement. On the contrary, I have consistently found management to be very supportive.

I believe firmly that one's attitude is critical. I didn't see my gender as a problem and it never became a barrier. Perhaps others did. I am happy with who I am – with the woman I am. That is important. Success in an organization which is still male-dominated depends not on playing the "male game," but rather on being yourself – true to yourself.

CIDA has been one of the more progressive government agencies in supporting and promoting women over the last fifteen to twenty years. There has also been an informal but strong women's network which has fostered a high degree of information-sharing, mutual support and collegiality.

Scrimshaw observed that it is difficult to sustain a women's network in External, even though the number of women coming into the department has increased steadily.

I understand that a few years ago there was an active group of women officers but interest seems to have waned, perhaps a reflection of a larger department and a rotational lifestyle. More recently, women trade commissioners in Ottawa have started to meet periodically.

A network can be a tremendous asset for officers at all levels, especially more junior officers who are new to the service. Women at more senior levels have a responsibility to provide support and guidance to those who represent the future senior management of the department.

I think the ratio [of women to men] is much better now than it used to be. In fact, there is probably an equitable representation at the FS1 and FS2 levels. It is at the executive levels where there is a serious under-representation. How do you solve this problem? While "stretch" assignments and "fast-track" career progression may help, it will take time to develop a sufficiently large cadre of women to fill senior management positions. The alternative is recruitment from outside the department.

Sandelle Scrimshaw remains single. In 1991, she became a single parent. "I wanted to have a child very much and as I saw the years creeping on I thought it was now or never." Her decision makes her one of the few unmarried women in the department who has a child. It is also proof of Scrimshaw's security in herself as a person and a woman.

PART THREE

The Contenders

Verona Edelstein

CHAPTER SEVENTEEN

MEETING IN MAPUTO
VERONA EDELSTEIN

In the summer of 1977 independence for Namibia was once again near the top of the agenda at the United Nations Security Council. The former German colony known as South West Africa had been administered by South Africa beginning in 1915, first under the terms of a League of Nations mandate and then, after the Second World War, by authority of the United Nations Trusteeship Council. In the 1950s, as more and more African states gained independence from their colonial masters, the people of South West Africa sought their own independence.

The drive for independence was spearheaded by the South West African People's Organization (SWAPO) and was vigorously – often violently – resisted by South Africa. In 1966, following passage of a resolution in the General Assembly, the U.N. ordered South Africa out of Namibia. South Africa was defiant. Instead of withdrawing, it used Namibia as a staging-ground from which to wage war against the Marxist government in Angola. When Cuba sent troops to Angola, South Africa used Namibian independence as a bargaining chip in an effort to dislodge the Cubans. Despite the fact that the U.N. had set up an eleven-member Council for Namibia to prepare the way for independence, there was little progress.

Guerrilla warfare broke out between SWAPO rebels and South African troops. The South African government imposed the death penalty for what it called terrorist acts in Namibia. When the U.N. General Assembly in 1976 demanded the withdrawal of all South African officials and the installation of a temporary U.N. administration, South Africa countered with its own independence plan which would have given authority to ethnic homelands. When its own plan failed to gain any support, South Africa appointed an administrator-general for Namibia.

As a member of the Security Council in 1977 and 1978, Canada joined four other western countries – the United States, Britain, France and West Germany – in an effort to resuscitate independence plans. The Contact Group, as the five countries were known, had to devise a proposal acceptable to both Pretoria and SWAPO.

Verona Edelstein, counsellor at the Canadian Permanent Mission to the United Nations in New York and Canada's alternate representative on the Security Council, was one of two Canadians (the other was Ambassador William Barton) most directly involved with the Contact Group. It was a highlight of her foreign service career.

Canada's role in the discussions was pivotal. Canadian representatives had good contacts with most countries in southern Africa and with SWAPO. The Africans trusted Canada because it had no history as a colonial power, and that same trust was enhanced by the scope of Canadian development programs on the continent.

At the same time, the United States had begun to take a more constructive attitude toward African issues. President Jimmy Carter and his Democratic administration had taken power in Washington, and Andrew Young, a black American, was U.S. ambassador to the United Nations. Instead of looking at African issues in the context of the Cold War and the imperative to contain communism, Carter and Young began to deal with Africa on its own merits. They sought advice, said Edelstein, from the other members of the Contact Group and particularly from Canada.

> It was an exciting experience because the five countries actually meshed their foreign policy machines in support of one objective. And for myself, I came to understand to a much greater extent the foreign policy-making processes of each of the countries, including, in particular, the United States.
>
> Turning to personal memories, I actually managed to break a certain logjam in terms of the initiation of the process. The five countries had met and had developed a basic approach to the issue and needed to engage the South African government and SWAPO in the discussions. The South African government was reluctant but, nevertheless, because of the importance of several of the countries to their economy, they at least did not refuse to discuss the issue of what they call South West Africa.

SWAPO, on the other hand, was extremely elusive. We were attempting to discuss the matter with the president of SWAPO, Sam Nujoma, and we were looking for him all over the world. It was reported that he was in Angola, it was reported that he was in Moscow, or he was elsewhere in Eastern Europe, but nobody could find Sam.

The search was still going on in the summer of 1977 when Edelstein went to Mozambique to attend a major U.N. conference on both Namibia and Rhodesia. Stepping off the plane in Maputo, she was greeted by the associate undersecretary of the Mozambique foreign ministry whom she had met in New York when he was still a leader of the country's pre-independence liberation movement.

He took me into the VIP lounge and there I found two people, Sam Nujoma and the ambassador of the OAU [Organization of African Unity] in New York, who is also an old friend of mine from our days on the decolonization committee.

I heard Sam Nujoma give an extremely negative interview to an African news service basically critical of any thought that the western "imperialist capitalist" countries could conceivably be serious and honourable in their intentions vis-à-vis a Namibia solution and indicating that SWAPO would have no part of it.

This was an important test for the Carter administration because at that point there were real doubts in the minds of the Africans as to whether Carter could be trusted. They didn't trust previous Republican administrations and they certainly didn't yet have confidence in the apparently new American policy.

Edelstein told the OAU ambassador that she and her Contact Group colleagues were concerned about Nujoma's negative stance. They wanted a meeting with him to explain the new U.N. proposals for Namibia. The ambassador took her message to Nujoma. He said, "Listen, Sam, there are some people who have been trying to talk to you and you should talk to them." Nujoma, who had met Edelstein in New York, where he often appeared as a liberation movement leader, replied that he would not meet Edelstein's colleagues but he would talk to her. He also asked for a copy of the position paper that she was carrying. She tactfully refused. The air-port conversation did produce a more conciliatory approach on Nujoma's part, but not before he did some face saving.

When the Mozambique conference opened, Nujoma circulated a paper, obviously prepared by SWAPO much earlier, that bitterly denounced the Western efforts, despite the fact that those efforts drew the approbation of delegates from China and Byelorussia. Nujoma's speech at the conference was much more moderate. He agreed to talk to the western five. Edelstein said, "The plan formulated eventually did serve as the independence plan for Namibia, once political will to imple-ment it was in place."

By the time an independent Namibia came into being with Sam Nujoma as its first president – on 21 March 1990 – Verona Edelstein had had six different assignments and was well into her seventh as director of Eastern and Southern Africa at External Affairs headquarters in Ottawa.

Edelstein was just thirteen years old when she decided that she want-ed to be a diplomat. Born in Regina, Saskatchewan, in 1942, as a teenag-er she lived in Hong Kong where her father was a businessman. The Canadian community there was a small one, everyone knew everyone else, and it was the junior trade commissioner from the Canadian com-mission in Hong Kong who suggested that Verona join External. She took the suggestion seriously.

At the University of British Columbia, Edelstein studied political science, French, Russian, and German. When she asked the U.B.C. campus-based chairman of the External Affairs interview board about of a foreign service career, she was told that External needed good secre-taries. The remark was eerily reminiscent of a response *Globe and Mail* reporter Kay Rex received in September 1960, when she asked about women in External. As there were only sixteen female officers in the department at the time, C.E. McGaughey of the personnel division took pains to point out in his reply to Rex, "I might add that we are fortunate enough to have many college graduates numbered among our stenographers."

Edelstein left her forty minute interview with the distinct impression that External was not interested in hiring women as officers.

> What would happen would be that there would be one
> token appointment every year of a woman who had a
> Ph.D. and spoke several languages. I then realized that I
> was not going to be selected for External Affairs through
> any normal interview process and so I decided that I

would finish my studies and do some travelling and then I'd come back and I'd find some way or another to join External Affairs. I was convinced that there had to be a place for people who did not have a Ph.D. and speak several languages.

Edelstein earned her bachelor's degree from UBC in 1963, attended Commercial College in Calgary the same year and in 1965 spent six months travelling in Europe. On her return, she wrote two public service examinations, one for the foreign service and the other for secretaries. Within two weeks, she was hired as a secretary. She learned the results of the foreign service tests in a roundabout way during an interview with the director of External's European division. Apprised of her background in political science, languages, and foreign travel, the director asked why she had not considered the foreign service. Edelstein replied that she had written the examinations and already had been interviewed. The director immediately made some inquiries and found that Edelstein had been successful and was on the list of prospective appointees.

Cheerfully abandoning secretarial duties, she started work as a foreign service officer the very next day. It was March 1966.

During her first two years as a budding diplomat, Edelstein worked in Ottawa, learning the ropes in a number of divisions – United States, personnel operations, Africa, and the Middle East. After obtaining a promotion, she was posted to London as second secretary and consul at Canada's high commission, a post she remembers primarily because Charles Ritchie – "a marvelous man" – was high commissioner.

Back in Ottawa in 1970, Edelstein became desk officer, with responsibility for social and humanitarian affairs, in External's United Nations division. She also made an important decision affecting her personal life. The decision established her reputation in the department as an outspoken, self-styled "ginger" person who knew her rights and brooked no infringement of them. She had met Robert Sandor, a trade commissioner, and they were married in December 1971, the same year that External lifted its ban on married women officers.

When we decided to get married, it was on the understanding that we would both pursue our careers. When we put forward the proposal to the department, in fact asked for permission to marry which is required in terms of the security clearance arrangements in External Affairs, there was dead silence for nine months.

There was quite a debate that proceeded in the department at that time with every element of the foreign service community involved – everyone from the older officers to the younger officers to the secretaries and clerks to the wives of diplomats – and it was quite a passionate debate examining the role of women in the department but also the role of wives in the Canadian foreign service.

In the end we proceeded with the marriage and got only a rather guarded comment from management to the effect that they had noted our intention to marry and that the single undertaking they would make in respect of our careers was to consult. The two departments would consult on the issue of assignments, nothing more.

In the discussions that led up to that understanding, I was asked whether I was not, in effect, demanding to be posted uniquely to cities where we had two or three missions, such as Brussels or Washington or Paris or London, and my comment was, "No."

We were first secretaries at that time, were at the same level and in different streams; he was, in fact, an employee of a different government department at that time – Trade and Commerce – though part of the foreign service. And they were, in fact, suggesting that we wouldn't be fully rotational, we would be restricting our rotationality to just two or three cities, and this was not acceptable.

Characteristically thorough, Edelstein had combed the pages of *Canadian Representatives Abroad,* an annual that lists the names of all officers at Canada's embassies, high commissions, consulates, and other posts in the world.

I had discovered that there were trade first secretaries and political first secretaries serving together at thirty missions ranging from developed countries to developing countries, countries where the conditions were very arduous. Their response was, "Well, that's fine at the first secretary level but when you go to counsellor level you'll be restricting yourself to just two or three missions." I said, "No." In fact, I had investigated that and there were thirty-five missions that had a political officer at a counsellor level and a trade officer at the counsellor level.

All we asked was that our family circumstances be given the same consideration as the family circumstances of other officers. I knew from my time in personnel that not everyone could move anywhere at any point in time, that you had to take into account health factors, the situation of the children, the health of the wives, the interests of the spouses in employment. And the director-general of personnel acknowledged that perhaps not more than half of the officers were really, truly, fully rotational.

Three months after her marriage, Edelstein went to Geneva as Canadian alternate to a meeting of the United Nations Commission on Social Development. Sandor called her to say that he had been posted to Jakarta. He wanted to know whether she, too, was going to Indonesia. She reminded him that External's posting assignments were not due for a couple of months; both of them realized that the consultation process had broken down before it even began.

When Sandor made inquiries in Ottawa, External's personnel officials said they had not been consulted about the possibility of a joint posting. Personnel officials in the trade department intimated that External should accommodate itself to the Trade Commissioner Service and, anyway, wasn't it a wife's duty to follow her husband? Edelstein related what happened next.

At this point External Affairs, in my mind, looked at the map to see which countries were near to Indonesia and sent a telegram to the ambassador in Indonesia saying, "By the way, Bob Sandor is married to Verona Edelstein and we're thinking of posting her to Kuala Lumpur, what do you think about that?" His response was that it wouldn't work at all because confrontation between Malaysia and Indonesia had just ended, it was very difficult to travel between the two countries, and both of us would probably be miserable at the separation. And, in any event, he knew me well and he would be pleased to have me assigned to any of the three first secretary jobs that were being created at the embassy in Jakarta that year.

And that's how the first assignment of an employee couple took place.

One year later, the department asked him if it wasn't problematic to have a married couple working together and he came back and said, "To the contrary, they're both doing an excellent job and that adds to the mission's effectiveness."

That summer, a number of other professional couples got married and were posted abroad together.

Foreign service officer couples are no longer oddities in External. The early days of fitful consultation have given way to more precise and sensitive routines. Posting a couple can even give the department two officers for the price of one.

There is a positive element for the department when they send a married couple abroad. It means they only have to rent one accommodation and there are some other savings. They only have to move one household and, if there are children involved, they only have to educate one set of children. So there are some real cost savings.

On the other hand, it's more complicated to arrange the posting. But with the emergence of a society in which both partners normally work, the whole business of posting people abroad has become immensely more complex. You simply have to take into account the employment aspirations of spouses.

Verona Edelstein and Robert Sandor have no children; however, that does not mean that it is easier to post them as a couple than it is to post couples with children.

The fact is that the competitive situation inside External Affairs, as inside any other major organization, is such that you typically work seventy-hour weeks and fitting a family into that kind of circumstance is really very challenging. On the other hand, younger women – only five years younger – did have children and they have indeed managed to balance their work and family responsibilities. Some of them married outside the foreign service –

> business people of different kinds, authors, educators –
> and they have managed to do this. Possibly had we mar-
> ried ten years later we might have looked at having a
> family and just dealt with the challenges as they came
> along.

Following her postings to Jakarta and New York, Edelstein returned
to Ottawa and became director of External's U.N. social and humanitarian affairs division. She also spent six months as the foreign service associate at the Paterson School of International Affairs at Carleton university
and a year as director of the Africa trade development division in the
department. In September 1983, Edelstein was posted as political minister at the embassy in Bonn, Germany. She was the first woman to hold
that position.

> I think it was the first time that a woman minister had
> been appointed at a major western embassy. Initially
> there was an atmosphere of incredulity but in a few
> months the mission – which included RCMP, military,
> trade, immigration personnel – came around to the idea.
> Two of them told me that they had not imagined that a
> woman could do a job which had always been done by a
> male senior officer.

Edelstein was welcomed more warmly by her German hosts than by her
Canadian colleagues.

> The Germans were wonderful. As far as they were con-
> cerned, I was the Canadian minister and they dealt with
> me accordingly. So I had excellent entrée with the military
> at the highest levels and also very good entrée with the
> foreign ministry and other elements of the German gov-
> ernment and society. There was no problem there at all.
>   I learned to speak German fluently while I was
> there. That was essential; you cannot function without
> it. I thought Canada's honour depended on me being
> able to speak German well. So I had had some German
> before I went to Bonn but then I really made it a point
> to become fluent there in that language.
>   I found out just by accident after I had been there a
> year or so that the presence of myself and my husband

in Bonn resulted in the German foreign service agreeing to sanction the employment of officer couples in their missions.

Edelstein was the political minister, and Sandor was the minister-counsellor responsible for commercial, economic, scientific, and environmental matters. They reported to the ambassador but not to each other. It was an essential component of External's policy on sending officer couples to the same post. Edelstein said,

> You can't have a conflict of interest or an appearance of a conflict of interest because our entire promotion process depends on the development of a rating report and your supervisor provides the rating report. On the basis of these rating reports you compete against all your other colleagues all around the world for a promotion to the next level. So it's essential that spouses not report to one another.

On her return from Bonn in the autumn of 1985, Edelstein spent an academic year at the National Defence College in Kingston. She then worked with External Affairs Minister Joe Clark and External Relations Minister Monique Landry on legislation establishing the International Centre for Human Rights and Democratic Development. When the centre opened for business in Montreal, Prime Minister Brian Mulroney appointed former New Democratic Party leader Edward Broadbent its first president. Her task of midwife to the new human rights centre finished, Edelstein took over as director of External's Eastern and Southern Africa division.

In her airy office in the Pearson building, a relaxed, elegant, and self-confident Verona Edelstein talked about her work as a director and about being a woman in External Affairs.

> Discrimination on the basis of sex permeates the Canadian society. This is a fact of life and anyone who was brought up in the '40s, '50s and perhaps the early '60s expected a certain pattern of society, a certain place for women in that society. As little girls we expected to grow up, get married and live happily ever after, and the notion of a long-term career was simply not present in our conditioning. Therefore the whole society has got to

adjust to the changes in the roles that women are playing and that men hope women play in respect of their
wives and their daughters.

So there is no doubt that there is entrenched discrimination and everyone is working throughout the
economy to try to deal with it. Naturally, the same situation existed and in a certain sense continues to exist in
External Affairs as in other government departments and
it will exist as long as women are a minority. Because
whatever the management intends or whatever provisions are put in place to ensure that all people are treated
equally, the reality is that women play on a different
playing field. It's not an even playing field, I think,
throughout the economy or External Affairs.

I think in External Affairs it is more challenging in
that the historical situation that I've described to you,
about recruitment of women and the mandatory retirement of women on marriage, has resulted in a smaller
percentage of women being officers of External Affairs
and that means that the minority factor is exacerbated
... There exists in External as elsewhere the kind of glass
ceiling where one obtains assignments in part as a function of previous performance but also as a function of
the confidence of a more senior person in your work.
The fact is that the management tends to be male and
tends to know better the qualifications of males who are
associated with them or with their friends and this is not
an approach that is limited to the male side of the
department.

I'm now a female manager and I, too, in my choice
of personnel or comments on assignments, take into
account what I know of a person or what my colleagues,
people I've worked with, say of that person.

But nonetheless I think the second factor is that,
with the rotational nature of the department, the
minorities – in this case women, previously it was fran-
cophones – find themselves obliged in a sense, when
they arrive in a new job, to prove themselves. They are
the minority, they stick out. They have to prove themselves and that takes extra time, energy and effort, and
it's still required in 1992 as it was when I joined in

1966. They [women] become known in the environment in which they work but then, three years later or four, when they're assigned elsewhere – to another geographic location – they have to start again. So I think that makes the challenge more difficult for women.

I don't think that I or other women have been the subject of specific discrimination; on the other hand, the playing field is not yet equal. It will take another couple of decades of determined leadership by our management to bring about greater equality.

The absence of a level playing field also accounts, at least in part, for the fact that career women have not yet been appointed heads of External's most sought-after posts – London, Washington, Paris, Tokyo, and Rome. Edelstein echoed Anne Leahy's thoughts.

It is simply a matter of numbers and levels. I have said that the playing field is not yet equal. Women are competing for promotions from the first level to the next level to the management level against hundreds of colleagues in all parts of the world. A minimal difference in a rating report – which may have been affected by male-female attitudes or by the particular challenges a minority person, woman, whoever, faces in the field or in Ottawa – can make the difference in terms of timing of promotions.

Now when you combine the relatively modest number of women who have been recruited into the foreign service, the modest number of women who have been retained in the foreign service – some very talented women have left, they have found better opportunities elsewhere – you then are left with a relatively small pool of women at the senior level.

Edelstein observed that the department sometimes failed to recognize the accomplishments of certain women. As an example, she cited what happened to Margaret Catley-Carlson on her return to External after having been senior vice-president, then acting president, of the Canadian International Development Agency. The vice-presidency of CIDA is equivalent to deputy-minister rank in the public service. After her return to External, Catley-Carlson was given a director-general's position, which is two levels below deputy minister and thus a demotion. It should have surprised no one that Catley-Carlson left External for the United Nations, or that she later rejoined CIDA as president and then became a deputy minister at Health and Welfare.

The government's decision in 1992 to transfer the social affairs stream of officers from External to Employment and Immigration made women even more of a minority than they had been previously. Edelstein regretted their departure.

> There was a higher percentage of women in the social affairs stream than exists elsewhere in the department and, as a result, you had a greater possibility of developing what I consider a critical mass in terms of the atmosphere in which people work in the department. When you have a meeting and the people around the table include 25 percent women, the atmosphere is quite different from that which prevails if there is one woman in the room. And that is a very constant situation. It's less typical now but it has been rather typical because of the small number of women involved. So I regret their departure.
>
> In terms of getting women to the top levels, I don't know what the impact would be. At the present time, the social affairs stream has fewer management positions, the top-level jobs. There aren't as many senior jobs classified or existing in the social affairs stream as in the political/economic or perhaps trade streams. So it's uncertain how quickly those women would have risen in the External Affairs competitive system. But on the other hand, their presence in the department would have provided more occasion for cross-stream fertilization, cross-stream secondment, and would have given the opportunity to develop the management skills of those women. Now, that can still be done, but the numbers of people who are likely to be seconded to management jobs in External Affairs or, say, deputy minister jobs, or places where they can become broadened and made capable of taking on heads-of-mission responsibilities, I think would be less than the present situation. So I think it's regrettable.

Edelstein's next posting may give the department a mild migraine. Both she and Sandor have reached the ambassadorial level; there are relatively few cities where Canada could send two such envoys. New York, with the consulate general and the U.N. mission, is a possibility. Paris and Brussels are also possibilities; both cities have Canadian embassies and are the headquarters of multilateral organizations to which Canada sends ambassadors. Commuting between Jakarta and Kuala Lumpur was ruled out earlier in their careers, but commuting between Copenhagen and The Hague, for example, might still be considered, especially now that the European Community has abolished frontiers. If Verona Edelstein has a preference, she is not expressing it publicly.

CHAPTER EIGHTEEN

MAKING A DIFFERENCE
LUCIE EDWARDS

External Affairs Minister Barbara McDougall paid an official visit to South Africa in early April 1992 and had top-level discussions with President F.W. de Klerk and African National Congress Leader Nelson Mandela. For one of the Canadians accompanying McDougall it was a sentimental journey.

Lucie Edwards, a keen, young foreign service officer who had been in South Africa on a posting from 1986 to 1989, took advantage of the trip to examine the fruits of her earlier labours. What she saw confirmed a long-held belief.

> What you have done makes a difference. I went to see a co-operative I helped found with some women, a clothing co-operative in a colored community, and they do everything from design the textiles to make the clothes. And from a tiny little hole-in-the-wall shop – the original shop was in Cape Town – they set up branches in seven cities. This is incredible; these women are very dynamic business women and they have done it all themselves.

Making a difference has been Lucie Edwards's major motivation since she began her foreign service career in 1976. Her choice of a career in the foreign service was due more to serendipity than actual planning, even though she had been exposed to international affairs from childhood. Her father was a career military officer who had taken part in Canadian

Courtesy of Lucie Edwards

Lucie Edwards, right, with some of the friends she made in South Africa during her diplomatic posting there from 1986 to 1989.

peacekeeping activities. He was also a man who thought teaching and nursing were proper vocations for women.

Born in Ottawa in 1954, Edwards fed her interest in world affairs during her high school years by taking part in model U.N. assemblies and mock Commonwealth conferences. She chaired the first mock Commonwealth conference when she was in grade thirteen. She attended her first real Commonwealth conference, a heads-of-government summit in Ottawa in 1973, working as a "geisha." Young male university students were employed to look after the conference delegates, and females (she was not yet at university then but got the job anyway) looked after the press. "We wore these very fetching orange uniforms so it really was very much of a geisha function." By the time Edwards attended her second Commonwealth summit, in Vancouver in 1988, she was no longer a decorative "gofer" but a full-fledged foreign service officer.

Lucie Edwards attended Trent University in Peterborough and graduated with an honours degree in history and economics. A summer assignment the year before graduation gave her a taste of what the future might hold for her and sparked a lifelong interest in the Middle East. She went to Egypt on a seminar sponsored by the World University Service of Canada. "I did a lot of work in upper Egypt, looking at conditions of women on the upper Nile, and I found it absolutely entrancing and wanted to go overseas again." As soon as the seminar was over, Edwards went backpacking around the Middle East and nearly became one of those consular disasters that gives Canadian diplomats prematurely gray hair. Her bus was hijacked in Lebanon. Fortunately, the incident ended without mishap and Edwards's lust for adventure remained undiminished.

Returning to Trent for her final year and hoping to attend law school, Edwards pursued some development studies related more to the Canadian north than to the Third World. Somebody suggested that she try the foreign service examinations; they were free and would be good preparation for the law school entrance tests.

> So I wrote the exam and really enjoyed it and proceeded through the rest of the year and was invited for the interviews. I don't think I took any of it very seriously because it just seemed so completely unlikely and uncertain and I was eventually offered a position at External. I thought I was too young, I thought there were other things I wanted to do, but I was keen to go overseas and it sounded like a good way of doing that and I thought that I could always go back to school. Famous last words!

Bright-eyed, eager, and twenty-one years old, Lucie Edwards arrived at External in 1976 and started her training program in the Middle Eastern division. It was like learning to swim by being pushed off the dock.

> I was assigned as the most junior possible person on the Israel-Arab desk and the day I arrived I was informed that the director and the senior officer on the desk were both proceeding on holidays and if anything happened I should just get in touch. I was just absolutely terrified for the next two weeks, convinced that an Arab-Israeli war was going to break out and I was going to have to handle it all by myself.

The two weeks passed peacefully. Her work in the division, plus the memories of her travels in Egypt and Lebanon, set her heart on a posting to Israel. Having finished a number of other assignments required during her training year in the department, Edwards decided "to short circuit the system, all of this in the spirit of the most breath-taking naiveté," to gain a posting to Tel Aviv.

I started doing Hebrew lessons on my own with the Jewish Community Centre here in Ottawa. I figured that by the time they were making their decision about posting people, I would be the only person who had any Hebrew so I might be a better qualified candidate. Of course, in this department, that's almost a guarantee you would end up in Buenos Aires, but something went wrong with the system and I ended up getting posted to Israel.

There were some anxious days before Edwards left for Tel Aviv. The department, which in 1958 had chosen Israel as the country to which to send Canada's first female ambassador, was reluctant to send a woman there in 1977. Edwards was slated to be the junior officer at the embassy. As such, she would be responsible for keeping tabs on Israel's relationship with the Palestinians in the occupied territories. She said that there was "this undertow of concern over whether or not a woman could do a job that was basically dealing with Arabs, and they thought three times before sending me to Tel Aviv." The department also squelched Edwards's offer to learn Arabic.

Besides reporting on the occupied territories and on Israeli domestic politics, Edwards helped develop a Canadian studies program in Israel. It was an immediate success and gained such momentum that fifteen years later the president of the Canadian Studies Association of Israel was head of the worldwide International Canadian Studies Program and presided at an important Canadian studies conference in Israel in 1992. The program convinced Edwards that her work as a foreign service officer could have a lasting and positive impact.

Returning to Ottawa in 1980, Edwards spent an unhappy six months trying to work on trade policy while being treated for parasites which she had picked up in Gaza. Margaret Catley-Carlson, then director general of economic policy in External and one of Edwards's heroes, came to her rescue by assigning her to aid policy work. Edwards was to work within the division as well as with the Canadian International Development Agency. About eighteen months later, when the International Trade and External Affairs ministries were integrated, Edwards was given responsibility for food and agricultural policy in both its trade and aid aspects. In 1982, she was reassigned to the Middle East division, just after Israel invaded Lebanon.

I was the Lebanon desk officer. We opened our embassy in Jordan, we had Lebanon to cope with, I was doing

quite a lot on Israel and Palestinian affairs as well, and
had an absolutely marvellous nine months with that. It
was really a lot of fun doing it at that time but it was
one of the times when things moved very rapidly, a bit
like the environment now, and I really enjoyed it. It was
a bit of a shock to the system. They had to find someone very quickly, they'd lost the previous officer and I
don't know if it would have been something that they
would have normally given to me to do but it was great
fun while it lasted.

In September 1983, Edwards enrolled in the Master of Public
Administration program at Harvard for the academic year.

I think in retrospect it was an enormously important
year. There was some scepticism about sending me
because the department has never been really good
about long-term training for people and the MPA program was really geared for people with about ten years'
more experience than I had. I was still twenty-nine at
the time. I'd just been promoted FS2, it's usually a program for people beginning the EX1 stage. But I wanted
to look at alternative theories in conflict resolution,
whether there were ways outside of the formal state-to-
state settlement for dealing with intractable problems in
the Middle East; got interested in South Africa there.

Had a very good year working with all the different
people working in negotiations theory at Harvard. A lot
of work going on in arms control; tremendous amount
going on in the Middle East. I think it was an important
year for me because, in a sense by coincidence, I have
been able to do some things in the department in promoting alternative, grass-roots negotiations work with
community groups. We are very, very good in this
department at negotiations but we are very good at it in
a very structural kind of sense, working in multilateral
and bilateral government structures. We are just beginning to support grass-roots work and reconciliation
work, so on, something that is still a bit alien to our
experience.

During her year at Harvard, Edwards also took a number of management courses – organizational development and management theory – which she immediately put to use on her return to the department, as deputy director of a new resource management division. The division's mandate was to conduct the department's negotiations with Treasury Board.

> The idea was that managers in the department would get one-stop shopping on anything they needed about either their personnel, their person-years – not staffing but person-years – and their dollars, and we would do all the negotiations on their behalf with the board ...
>
> It was a wonderful two years because I found I loved working on the money issues. My father's training in accountancy had been put to good use. I loved the work with the board and we were doing a lot of the crucial decisions, at that point, about cutting posts, re-allocating resources, and so on, and had a very good two years. After that, was ready for change, was desperate for posting. It had been six years, a long time.

Working in resource management gave Edwards an insider's knowledge of where the department was headed and of its more interesting assignments. She had been helping External Affairs Minister Joe Clark formulate the government's commitments to Southern Africa and Canada's opposition to apartheid in South Africa. She knew that a position would be created at the embassy in Pretoria, which would deal with black politics, labour, and human rights. External initially intended to fill the post with an official from a Canadian trade union; when that fell through, Edwards sought it for herself.

> I volunteered and got the job and arrived in June 1986 with the imposition of the state of emergency in South Africa. I was responsible for sanctions management there. So we were very busy that first year, all of the human rights work, all the black politics work, so had an absolutely amazing period there. Got promoted, I think, eighteen months later, to the EX group, and stayed on for a further eighteen months. They were amazing years in South Africa.
>
> You know you talk about the different kinds of

things you can do in this department and every so often you get a job where you wake up in the morning and you know that what you are doing is probably the most important thing you will do in your life. It was very much like the experiences that my parents and my husband's parents talked about during the Second World War when they were all involved in rather important war work. And it had that sense to it – it was a kind of Spanish civil war atmosphere. The Canadians were somewhat embattled because the South African government was so angry with us, probably at what we were doing and the role we were playing. At the same time, support we got in the townships was unbelievable.

We were given the tools by the minister and the department to do a colossal amount of good. Including the creation of something called the Dialogue Fund which was very important to me because, in fact, it was putting a lot of the ideas from Harvard to work: if you couldn't work on a political level with this government in bringing an end to apartheid you could still work at a grassroots level and mobilize people to work at a community level in terms of breaking down barriers and reconciliation. It was very important and, I think in retrospect, one of the better programs we've ever implemented anywhere.

As her 1992 return visit to the clothing co-operative indicated, Edwards also found her work in South Africa so satisfying in a personal sense that it was hard to leave.

We never knew if we would be able to go back. We left just after President de Klerk's election in 1989 ... It was a rather painful farewell. We had it in Soweto, the first time diplomats had ever had anything like that in Soweto, and hundreds of people came. It was a great party, incredible singing.

In Ottawa, Edwards was assigned to run a newly reorganized domestic communications division. Her job was to explain the Department of External Affairs to Canadians. It was a daunting challenge, given the abysmal level of public knowledge and interest in the diplomatic service.

Edwards was less than three months into that job when South Africa once again claimed her attention. She was appointed chairperson of the department's task force on Southern Africa, succeeding John Schioler on his retirement.

> There was a tremendous emphasis on communications to the public and the chair had unusual authority to do things like talk to the media, do speeches, organize meetings for community outreach, travel in Canada, and get the word out there on a policy that the government was absolutely convinced was a winner and they could only benefit from having the broadest possible community involvement.
>
> But it also had its very traditional aspects. We were chairing the Commonwealth committee on Southern Africa so there was a whole series of meetings to mount, sanctions management which is very complicated in trade policy areas. I rather enjoyed being back to doing trade policy. Altogether quite a difficult job.

At the outset, there were thirteen people on the task force. As the political climate in South Africa improved, Canadian sanctions were eased, and the number of people on the task force slowly decreased. When it was disbanded in February 1992, only seven people were left. By then, Edwards was appointed director of the Middle East relations division. It fulfilled her dream of returning to the Middle East, Edwards said in an interview in her Pearson building office.

> With the Middle East Refugee Conference and the multilateral peace process and so on we were in a position that was remarkably similar to where we had been when I started in South Africa. We had to get a task force under way in support of the Middle East peace process. There was a sort of obvious pattern of experience in terms of what we needed to do, but particularly in terms of our role in the peace process, and that's keeping us very busy indeed right now.
>
> We are going to be holding the big refugee conference in mid-May and there's a big job just in mounting something like that.
>
> For the task force we have twelve people downtown

working on it full-time ... and we are involved in a lot of ways in terms of bilateral process and consultations with different parties and so on. It's a wonderful time to be working in the Middle East.

We've also been doing some things that people said couldn't be done, like holding, for the first time, briefings for the ambassadors for the Middle East that had both the Arab and the Israeli ambassadors at the same meeting. We've had the Arab and Jewish community groups at the same meeting; we've had academics with diametrically opposed views come to advise us about the conference.

We have, for the first time this year, women's groups who are invited to meetings on the Middle East. We have certainly been much more forthright. One of the things in the minister's mandate to me was, "I want people to start thinking about women's issues in the Middle East, we cannot walk away from this issue." So it's something we have been doing with Kuwait, in particular – it has been an obvious target area – but looking at it very much for other countries in the area.

A lively, spontaneous person with a sparkling manner and no affectations, Edwards was both enthusiastic and thoughtful about her foreign service career. She has more heights to conquer.

I think I've been enormously lucky that the headquarters jobs I've had have always given me at least the illusion of having an impact, of making a difference in terms of policy, and that's important. Even the jobs that I had when I was quite junior, like working on aid policy, in the nature of things were ones where they were not ministerially dominant – they were things like African Development Bank policies and so on that the ministers did not have time to think about – and therefore you, as a desk officer, could have a disproportional impact.

Certainly working on Lebanon during the war, you had a tremendous impact. Here and in the Southern Africa task force, the same sort of thing. You felt that you could make a difference, to use Mr. Clark's classic expression about what External Affairs is all about.

In terms of being abroad, I'm still astounded that people pay me to do that. They are giving me a three-year open sesame to learn everything I can about a fascinating foreign country, absolutely everything from the culture, the politics, the people and the economic system, to start little projects, to make friends. Everything matters for twenty-four hours a day, whatever you are doing, it's all part of the learning process.

Edwards does not have specific career goals, but she does have a sense of direction.

I've got a pretty clear sense of what jobs I like to do abroad, which are not the great chancelleries of Europe and not multilateral work full time, but working on politically difficult, politically intractable issues in highly volatile societies, but I don't mean in a dangerous society, I mean volatile in a sense of an articulate, passionate, engaged society when changes are happening.

We are in constant change. At the moment, there are far more options. All of Eastern Europe is now much more interesting, compared to the days when it was congealed in political mud. So this is a wonderful time to be doing this kind of work.

A diplomat in post-Cold War western Europe is apt to spend a great deal of time talking to the host government about other parts of the world – South Africa, the Middle East, Russia, the former Yugoslavia. Edwards would prefer to be in a country where things are happening. "You can do a lot more good if you're in Belgrade," she said.

And for most of the European missions, if you are dealing with Canadian interests, you are talking about fish. I've done fish, I did agricultural trade policy, thank you. I've paid my dues.

In the United States, I am fascinated with the congressional system. I really enjoyed my time in Boston. In some ways, I think I'd probably have more fun with a big consulate, simply because the opportunities to schmooze and get things done in the States in the consulate are just fabulous. If you were in a key position in

> the New York consulate general right now, you are doing
> Wall Street … you are doing the national unity crisis,
> you are doing aboriginal issues. I mean, this is where the
> decisions are being made in the international communi-
> ty over whether Canada's going to make it or not. Now
> that strikes me as a really worthwhile job.

Married to author and environmentalist Tom Roach, Edwards said
that they manage postings "infinitely better than I think most people
do." Roach, a former forester, writes on forestry policy and environmental issues. According to Edwards, he has "one prerequisite per posting and
that is that the country has to have trees or alternatively, if it has no trees,
the prospect of planting the trees." When they were in Israel, Roach
wrote his first book and a number of articles; in South Africa, besides
writing, he completed a master's degree at the University of
Witwatersrand. They have no children.

Lucie Edwards's career in External Affairs has gone steadily upward.
She recognizes that without a shred of false modesty; she also knows that
for a woman in the department, the road upward can be very steep and
filled with potholes.

> One of the positions I was interested in before I went to
> South Africa was Damascus. Again, there was some
> scepticism about this. It wasn't that it was ever anything
> overt or officially written down, it was just a kind of
> squeamishness over risk-taking. So in that sense I sup-
> pose if I had been completely motivated as a Middle
> East specialist and nothing else, I would have been very
> frustrated …
>
> The only thing that one would say would be overtly
> discriminatory – and I almost hesitate to say it because I
> can hardly complain – is the first time I was being con-
> sidered for promotion to the FS2 level. I was one off the
> list and when they called me to say, "Consolation prize,
> you didn't get it but you did very well," the person who
> had been the chair of the board came to me and said,
> "Well, you know, you were a very strong candidate and
> so was the other candidate but he had a wife and chil-
> dren and we thought he needed it more." That would
> never happen today.

You know, it's terribly marginal if you are choosing between candidate number nine and candidate number ten anyway. And I was promoted the next year. And ever since then the promotions have been very fast. Nobody in this department would say that Lucie has the right to complain about no promotions.

During Edwards's early years in External, it was conventional wisdom that women should be grateful just to be in the department. There were also some issues that continued to be the preserve of men.

One of them was trade policy, GATT, and the other one was defence relations. I was never hugely interested in defence relations because my father had already whipped that out of me a long time before but trade policy did interest me. I had a good background in economics and I found the experience during those six months a very unwelcoming one. They weren't interested in experiments and they weren't interested in wasting positions on women. They didn't see me as part of the boys' club. It's not an area even now that is hugely welcoming to women.

There is no glass ceiling in External, Edwards said, because there are not enough women to warrant one. Instead, there is the "Golda Meir syndrome." Edwards's opinion on this echoes that of Ingrid Hall.

The department likes to pick on one woman almost per decade and say, "Look she's doing so outstandingly well, we don't have any problems, this department's doing great." In the '70s it was clearly Maggie Catley-Carlson – she zoomed up at an incredible rate – Louise Fréchette in the '80s. I would like to think, and I know Louise and Maggie would both concur heartily in this, that we're through that period.

What we don't need is a new woman for the '90s. What we need is a critical mass of excellent women moving through the system, so that it becomes very natural and normal and organic for women to be in senior positions in this department. It's relevant, this is very symbolic, but when Jean McClosky was named head of

Investment Canada and then within weeks Louise Fréchette was named head of our mission at the United Nations, we had no women in the department on the executive committee and there was no senior woman upstairs going to the meetings, apart from the minister's chief of staff who comes from a very different perspective as an observer rather than as a manager of a department. And that's very troubling to me.

If you move one of the senior women to an important job overseas or in another department, as they did with Jean or with Louise, it's at a cost of something else. It isn't because there's another one ready to fill their place. You're just rotating the same number of marbles around the table. There are four senior women in the department at the moment who go on occasion to executive committee for their branches and that's it. There's Kathryn McCallion, Sandelle Scrimshaw, Anne Leahy and me. Not enough. And again, in terms of the minister's very real commitment to equality of opportunity and the minister's commitment about women abroad, well, if you lose a Louise Fréchette or if I go abroad this summer, the number goes down.

There are two reasons for the absence of senior women at the executive committee level, Edwards said. Not enough talented younger women in the department are being promoted. In 1991, Edwards was one of only four women promoted to the EX2 level; in 1992, just one woman was promoted to that rank. There are also too few women entering the department, and it takes a long time for them to work their way up to executive levels. New officers all come in at the bottom level and it can take eleven years – assuming an officer gets every promotion the first time around – to reach the executive group.

No women were recruited into External in the two years immediately before and after Edwards joined. In 1976, forty-five new officers came into the department, among whom were five women. Only three are left. Of those three, Edwards is the most senior; another was promoted to FS2, and the third returned to the department after taking an extended leave of absence because she married a very senior man in the department, who took a senior position outside of government. The other two women recruited with Edwards have left External, one to teach law in New Zealand and the other to be a consultant and lobbyist in Washington.

To try to improve the situation for women, Edwards has conducted her own small recruitment crusade. Whenever she visits a university to make a speech about foreign policy issues, she tells the campus career office that she would be happy to give a seminar on foreign service careers and advise any students who might be interested. She has done this on annual visits to her alma mater, Trent, as well as at universities in Ottawa and British Columbia. She remarked on the frequency with which female students responded to the seminars by saying, "I didn't know you'd even consider recruiting women for the foreign service."

At the end of January 1993, Lucie Edwards was posted to Nairobi, Kenya as Canada's high commissioner. One of her last assignments, a few days before her departure, was to talk to a group of female students in Ottawa about women who have had distinguished foreign service careers. A less dedicated person, getting ready to move to Africa for three years, would have delegated someone else to make the speech; that is not Lucie Edwards's way.

Nairobi is her first assignment as a head of post and comes naturally in the steady progression of her diplomatic career. Interviewed in the spring of 1992, Edwards anticipated becoming an ambassador or its equivalent on her next posting.

> I have a sense being an ambassador sometimes is a bit like being Prince Charles. You end up with people painting everything before you come and having to be on their best behaviour and buying a new frock. This is not the kind of experiences that I'm interested in. I'm interested in travelling up some dirt road for ten kilometres and seeing what's at the end of it, and meeting the people there, and finding out what life is like.

With Lucie Edwards as high commissioner, the Canadian mission in Nairobi might find a four-wheel drive more useful than the official limousine. But the Kenyans on whom she comes calling do not have to erect a Potemkin village in her honour; Canada's down-to-earth high commissioner with the ready smile and the brisk handshake wants to get to know them just as they are.

CHAPTER NINETEEN

ELECTRONIC-AGE DIPLOMACY
KATHRYN HEWLETT-JOBES

Prime Minister Pierre Elliott Trudeau's incisive intellect and swash-buckling style made him an instant celebrity wherever he appeared on the world stage. Widely travelled before he entered politics, Trudeau easily charmed such world leaders as Fidel Castro, Anwar Sadat, Julius Nyerere, Jimmy Carter, and Helmut Schmidt. At home, however, Trudeau managed to miff the mandarins of External Affairs when, on a national television program, he remarked that "the whole concept of diplomacy today is pretty outmoded," and that modern methods of communication enabled the government to get as much useful information about international events and conditions from a good newspaper as from diplomats' dispatches.

The sun had begun to set on the glory days of Canadian diplomacy, which reached their zenith when Lester B. Pearson was foreign minister. Scarcely a dozen years after Pearson won the 1957 Nobel Peace Prize, the Trudeau government was pre-occupied with national unity, bilingualism, and a faltering economy. A drive to curb government expenditures forced External to reduce staff both in Ottawa and at posts abroad; the people who were left had to put most of their efforts into promoting foreign trade, not political reporting. External's prominence was briefly restored in 1979 when Ambassador Kenneth Taylor and his staff at the Canadian embassy spirited five American diplomats out of Iran, following an attack on the U.S. embassy by Shi'ite fundamentalists.

By 1980, the year the Trudeau Liberals defeated Joe Clark's short-lived Conservative government, life in the foreign service had changed so much, and morale in External Affairs was at such low ebb, that a royal

Kathryn Hewlett-Jobes

commission was warranted. In his letter appointing Pamela McDougall royal commissioner, Trudeau returned to his earlier theme:

> Traditional concepts of foreign service have diminished relevance in an era of instantaneous, world-wide communications, in which there is increasing reliance on personal contacts between senior members of governments, and in which international relations are concerned with progressively more complex and technical questions.

Trudeau's ruminations about the role of a diplomat in a world of computers, facsimile machines, satellite television transmission, and summit meetings may have upset the Pearsonian mandarins. Today's new breed of foreign service officer not only echoes Trudeau's theme but also takes the technology for granted and uses it effectively.

Kathryn Hewlett-Jobes, one of that new breed and director of External's personnel policy and planning secretariat, talked about the new diplomacy during an interview in her Ottawa office.

> The department has changed. The Pearson-era emphasis on academic excellence and on analysis I think has given way to a department which has shorter time-frames to deal with. We live in a CNN world; we don't have time to produce scholarly, thoughtful papers on what's happening in Yugoslavia.
>
> In the olden days, about twenty or thirty years ago, they used to write these marvelous telexes, beautiful language and real, thoughtful analysis, but articulated in such a thorough and elegant fashion. But the world didn't move quickly then. Wars still happened, wars happened quickly, but what the Canadian government needed, or Canadian business people needed, in terms of analysis, was much slower because their needs were dictated by the ship era rather than the instant cellular-telephone era. Now, our prime minister will get, has a requirement to have, a full analysis the next day, if not sooner, about anything that's happening.

Media demands have changed, too, Hewlett-Jobes observed. Twenty years ago, government officials and even the prime minister could respond to media questions about world events with vague expressions of grave concern and even vaguer assurances that someone was working on the problem.

> This was the normal response for the first week or two to events. Now, if the prime minister said that, he would be regarded as a waffling wimp. So because a lot of the product of our department is to provide analysis for the government, we just don't deal with those time-frames any more. The definition of excellence is changing in the department. I think the ability to provide decent analysis quickly is much more important than scholarly analysis in the long run.

In Hewlett-Jobes's view, journalists have become the diplomats' competitors and are constantly challenging the foreign service.

> We have to have a better product than journalists or else we'll become irrelevant because journalists are quicker, they are there; you just need to turn on your TV set and they are there. But to a very busy politician who is being sandbagged by journalists, it [diplomatic analysis] has to be delivered in a way that will feed the media. Public policy has that aspect to it now, which is very real and, in my personal view, it's extremely regrettable.
>
> There is a fairly common perception that the media are not interested in knowing the complexities or in understanding that things don't always add up, and there's also, I think, the assumption that a lot of media are just hostile, plain hostile to government, that all they're looking for is the thing you've done wrong, not the ninety-nine things you've done right.
>
> Good news doesn't mean that you are presenting an erroneous picture, but it's not the truth to report only the weaknesses of an organization, to report only the problems encountered, that's not the truth either. But in this age of scepticism, the only kind of truth that people seem to believe is the negative aspect, so I don't think we're as open to the media. People used to give quite free background briefings. In the olden days – ten years

ago – even fairly junior officers would be authorized to give background. Now, no way.

What's the upside? You make one slip-up, or you say something that comes out in an awkward fashion, and you've done yourself harm and perhaps, which is far worse, done the department or the government harm. And the upside is very intangible. The problem is that the upside is important; the upside is having a media that understand better because they're fed more information. But that's tricky.

The role of the department has changed, and recently recruited foreign service officers have had to adapt to that change. Instead of young people in their early twenties joining External straight out of university, and being given tasks of increasing complexity until they are moulded into proper diplomats, more mature and experienced men and women are coming to External. "They arrive and they produce from day one," Hewlett-Jobes said.

I think we have to have people with brains and fire and drive and a lot of chutzpah too. And by and large we get it because we are very under-resourced. I know that the outside world will probably find that hard to believe but our people work extremely hard. Here, to leave at 6 o'clock at night, you feel very apologetic. You go to other government departments, after four thirty it's just like wandering through the middle of the night. But here, I just wish we could take some of our critical media types and let them wander around at seven and eight o'clock at night, night in and night out, and see the number of people who are still working, really producing. It's not that they had a three-hour lunch and then are making up for it, it's also not that they're doing stupid things, they're producing.

Kathryn Hewlett-Jobes, who was born in Red Deer, Alberta, in 1951, was in her twenties when she joined External in 1975. A graduate in economics from the University of Calgary, Hewlett-Jobes worked for two years as assistant policy advisor on international aviation, in the office of the then minister of transport, Jean Marchand. She represented the minister during negotiations for bilateral air agreements. She got a first-hand look at embassy operations when she went abroad with negotiating teams, and she was on the receiving end of help from Canadian diplomats in various capitals. She was sufficiently intrigued by what she saw to write the foreign service examination. Having passed that hurdle, she chose the trade commissioner service because that was her primary interest at the time.

Hewlett-Jobes spent her training period on various assignments in Ottawa and at Canada's mission to the United Nations in New York. Next she was posted as second secretary commercial to the embassy in Switzerland. After three years in Berne, she went to Argentina to perform a similar commercial function at the embassy in Buenos Aires.

Like other female diplomats who have been posted to Argentina, Hewlett-Jobes has warm memories of working there. As a female diplomat, she had better access to the Argentines than her male colleagues had. It was partly because the Argentines were curious about her, but it was mainly because the macho tradition has a positive aspect.

> They tend to be terribly polite to women, feel a sort of gentlemanly obligation and, as a diplomat, when your main trade is obtaining information to understand a situation or explaining a Canadian position in one way or another, it made it just very, very easy. In Argentina they treated you as if you were something terribly special – you must be extraordinarily intelligent to have the position – which was flattering. And the social life was great.

In 1981, Hewlett-Jobes took a leave of absence from External and worked for two years as assistant manager of trade services for the Royal Bank of Canada. When she returned to the foreign service in 1983, she was promoted to FS2 and posted to the Philippines as first secretary commercial at the embassy in Manila. By this time, she had married Claus Jobes, a former officer in the German foreign service, who gave up his diplomatic career to pursue sculpting and photography. The couple's two daughters were born in Manila. Hewlett-Jobes talked about becoming a mother while on a diplomatic posting.

> Maternity leave was a luxury back when I had my children. Now eight years doesn't seem like that long ago but, just to let you know some of the context, back then, according to the regulations at the time, we could not use sick leave for any pregnancy-related illness and there

was no maternity-leave provision in the foreign service contract. What it meant was that, if you took any time other than your holidays, not only did you lose your salary, your allowances and so forth, but you were liable for the full cost of the residence that the government had put you in, the staff quarters. And at that time in Manila rents were very high and the cost of where we were living was some $2,500 a month, which was a lot, and faced with the total loss of income and having all those additional expenses, basically I was back at work three weeks after having my first. Again, not recommended practice because it wasn't good for my health but you do what you have to do.

Although maternity-leave provisions have improved since Hewlett-Jobes had her children, and the financial penalties are less severe, a female diplomat who gives birth while abroad has other factors to consider. She has to feel comfortable with the medical care system available at the post, and she has to deal with the health of the "corporation." According to Hewlett-Jobes,

It's very hard on our posts when people do have children abroad and avail themselves of the full benefits of the maternity leave provisions because we are very small. You take one person out of a three-person operation and you've taken a significant percentage away. So I've seen that for many of our officers – when it's a choice – there's a tendency to choose to have your children when you're in Canada or, indeed, not to avail yourself of the full maternity leave benefits.

Finding good child care can be as difficult for foreign service officers as for other professional women. Much depends on where the diplomat is working. In what diplomats call "the nanny belt" – the African and Asian countries – their incomes allow them to pay the going local rate for full-time help in the home. In Denmark, where she was commercial counsellor at the embassy in Copenhagen for three years after leaving Manila, Hewlett-Jobes found child care more expensive than in Canada. As every mother knows, sometimes the arrangements break down, as they did for Hewlett-Jobes one memorable day in Ottawa. She had a meeting she could not miss, and the sitter did not show. So Hewlett-Jobes took her six-month-old daughter to the office with her and parked her, asleep in a basket, next to her chair in the meeting room. When the baby started to whimper, Hewlett-Jobes picked her up, nursed her discreetly, and carried on with the meeting. After an initial jolt of surprise, the men in the room regained their equilibrium and calmly continued the discussion.

Child care is not the only concern parents have on being posted abroad. When Trudeau appointed the royal commission to examine conditions in the foreign service, he took special note of its disruption to family life. Hewlett-Jobes observed that the world has become even more hostile to foreigners than it was in 1981 when the royal commission reported. Parents, both men and women, are very concerned about their children's security and freedom. The first question they ask about a post is how it will affect their children's education and quality of life.

The ages of their children are a factor when diplomats evaluate postings. As an assignment officer in Ottawa, Hewlett-Jobes has found that it is usually fairly easy to post people with young children, but it becomes harder as the children grow older.

> Smaller children don't need as much freedom as teenage children do. So if you're in a relatively unsecure post where you must be very careful it's not a problem when you have small children because they'd expect to be ferried about here in Canada, too. But if you have a fourteen-year-old who's used to being able to take the bus and go across town to visit friends, it's very, very hard to say, "No, you have to wait until I can drive you to your friends," all the time.

Hewlett-Jobes has had postings abroad both before and after her marriage. Her husband has not yet attained an international artistic reputation. Consequently, wherever they are posted, he has to acquaint himself with the local artistic community and market his works. Despite the frustrations, however, Hewlett-Jobes still finds it easier to go abroad as a family.

> When you're single you have to cope with a much more intense level of loneliness when you first arrive at a post. When you go with your family, you have someone to play with. From the very beginning, you have someone to share your discoveries of the country with.

When you go as a single person you have to re-establish your network, and of course you will, and most of our single people are very, very good at this. And other single officers and staff in other embassies also are good at supporting because they recognize that it's very difficult. So if you're a person that finds it hard to reach out, hard to establish those networks, if you're married it doesn't matter so much, but if you're single it's deadly.

I'm talking about living outside of work. At work, we're all single; but it's what you do on the weekends, it's the Sunday afternoons. You know, weekends can be a very long stretch if you're new at a post and you're single.

The logistical part of life most of us learn to handle quite well, just getting your place set up and finding out where to buy the groceries, and all that. Some posts are easier than others. At some posts there's a more supportive network of Canadians than at others. I think single people are disadvantaged in accessing the informal support network because it's very often spouses and spouses sometimes aren't equipped to recognize the need when it's a single person as when it's another family moving in. But by and large we do that part well.

Because single women face more social restrictions than single men, the diplomatic life is often lonelier for women, especially in societies where a woman's behaviour is still circumscribed.

You go to South America and if you suggested to a male person you met that you have lunch or dinner or go to a movie, you'd nearly fall into the "painted woman" category. So that curtails one's freedom in making a network of friends. But it's lonely for the men too, although very few of them will really admit it. And I think the big difference is you'll find a lot of the men [who] sense [their] loneliness cure it by getting married. But it's a whole lot harder for the women to find someone that they can share this particular life with.

In some countries, the difficulties faced by women diplomats have more to do with being foreign than with being female.

> I'm thinking of the Japans of this world. The incremen-
> tal difference between being a foreign female diplomat
> or being a foreign male diplomat I think is very, very lit-
> tle. For the Japanese, it's being the foreigner that is, by
> far, the most important. And that's the same in Malaysia
> or in Pakistan with the exception of the urban areas. So
> in your dealings with government, the foreignness
> would be the issue, not whether you're male or female.

Hewlett-Jobes has a cool, detached, philosophical attitude on the subject of discrimination against women. External – and the foreign service internationally – remain very much dominated by men. She echoed the sentiments of numerous colleagues who see the situation changing as women enter the department in greater numbers. She cautioned women against seeing discrimination where none exists. For example, a supervisor's restrictive, unkind or generally detrimental behaviour may be due to personality traits and not to any bias against women. In that case, Hewlett-Jobes said, his behaviour probably will have an equally negative effect on the careers of both men and women.

> In general, I find that the value system in our organiza-
> tion is a very male value system. I think that the whole
> way that our assignments are done, the way careers are
> built in this department, depends very much on a word-
> of-mouth assessment of an officer's ability. It's not sup-
> posed to but it does. Now that can really tend to disad-
> vantage anybody that isn't a member of the club. Well,
> men who aren't members of the club either, but very few
> women are members of the club, very few.

She does see improvements and is optimistic for the future of women in External.

> When you look at the percentage of women that used to
> be recruited and the percentage of women now – the
> percentage of women at every level – you can see that
> there is a fairly large body of very junior female officers
> who, I think, as they work their way through the system
> are big enough to have an impact on attitudes. I've
> always thought you'd have to have about one-third
> women before the attitudes really started to change.

The percentages had been moving upward; the progress slowed, however, in 1992 when the government took the social affairs stream of foreign service officers out of External and returned it to Employment and
Immigration.

> It definitely has taken a pool of talented women away;
> women that will not now be available in the same way
> for access to those director positions because those posi-
> tions don't belong to this department any more. So while
> those women will still be moving up, they'll be moving
> up within another department's embrace, not ours. The
> department has also shrunk because we've moved that
> whole program area to the other departments.

Enthusiastic about her work, Hewlett-Jobes claimed to have "fallen
in love" with every job she has had. Assisting Canadian business has been
especially satisfying to her. She recalled a memorable trip to Pakistan. It
took place during her time in Manila. In her capacity as special liaison
with the Asian Development Bank, she travelled everywhere in Asia
except China and India. While in Pakistan, she visited a development
bank project in a frontier province where traditional customs were strictly
observed. To avoid giving offence and attracting "crowds of a hundred
ogling villagers," Hewlett-Jobes wore the customary cloaklike dress and
veil. The headcovering is actually a layer of five veils made of transparent
black chiffon-like material. A woman pulls just one of them over her face
if she is talking with someone she knows well, two if in a meeting with
government officials or others who are strangers but to whom she has
been properly introduced, three if indoors, and four or all five if out on a
public street.

> By the time you got all five of these sort of transparent
> scarves pulled down on your face, you couldn't see terri-
> bly well. But I found it fascinating. At first I was quite
> offended at the thought that I ought to do this, I wasn't
> going to do it, but we were going into fairly traditional
> areas where they wouldn't see too many people from a
> different culture and I didn't want to embarrass the
> Asian Development Bank team I was with and we were
> looking at a development project. I was the only woman
> and you want to show respect to the culture you're visit-
> ing. As well, it was very dusty and the grit gets right

through you and wearing one of these things keeps the grit away.

What I thought was so neat was that you could turn into a total voyeur – it's like wearing dark sunglasses – no one could see what you were looking at so you could just stare at people and they wouldn't know. And it was in a strange kind of way appealing, it was like walking in your own personal space the whole time. It wasn't an entirely negative thing. I wouldn't want to spend my life in one, though.

Since returning to Ottawa in the summer of 1989, Kathryn Hewlett-Jobes has worked in the Western Europe trade, investment and technology division and in the executive pool of the heads of mission division. She is currently director of the personnel policy and planning secretariat. In all these assignments at headquarters, she is honing her management skills for the day when she becomes a senior manager. She has the engaging personality, analytical acumen, and penetrating intelligence to achieve any goal which she sets for herself.

CHAPTER TWENTY

CONFIRM AND CONTRADICT
MARIE-LUCIE MORIN

Senator Patricia Carney, the Vancouver economist who first entered Parliament as an MP in 1980, had three portfolios in Prime Minister Brian Mulroney's Cabinet from 1984 to 1988. They were Energy, Mines and Resources, International Trade, and President of the Treasury Board. In all three departments, she found very few women. She wrote about her dismay in a foreword to *Beneath the Veneer: The Report of the Task Force on Barriers to Women in the Public Service.*

> When officials gathered in my ministerial office, they were normally all men. The few women who did attend were often in an "acting" capacity.
>
> When I asked where the women were, I was told: "We had one, but she left." Or I was told: "We have one, but she's not ready yet." Or worse, "She's too young." The picture was not totally bleak; in Trade, I had the rare opportunity of heading up at times an all-woman team: Ambassador Sylvia Ostry, Assistant Deputy Minister Jean McClosky, my Chief of Staff Effie Triantafilopoulos and myself. And I found some wonderful women holding down important jobs.
>
> But when I looked at the staffing list, I found very few women in the kinds of jobs that lead to the top levels.

Determined to find out why so few women were on the rungs of the management ladder, Carney appointed a three person task force in 1988. They were Jean Edmonds, Jocelyne Côté-O'Hara, and Edna MacKenzie.

Marie-Lucie Morin

They submitted their report in April 1990. To a considerable extent, their findings were predictable but contradictory, and they tended to prove that there are almost as many theories about why women do not move up in government, business, and industry as there are experts to expound the theories.

Simple discrimination against ambitious women is certainly a factor. Women's careers are often stalled if they marry and have children because society still expects mothers to bear the lion's share of responsibility for child-rearing. Women with backgrounds in the arts and the humanities are not seen as having the academic credentials, the experience, or the tough personalities needed to run a business or a government department. And the women who are trained in the law, economics, or finance too often find themselves shunted by their employers into low-status personnel or public relations work.

Women themselves are sometimes less than keen to compete for the top jobs. Flora MacDonald, External Affairs minister from 1979 to 1980, had some terse observations about the advancement of women.

> There has to be both a willingness at the top to appoint them and a labour pool to move forward. And sometimes women are reluctant to move forward. They know the hazards that exist; they've seen that the one or two or three who have gone out had, I won't say to suffer hammer blows, but really to contend with fairly major obstacles, and they say, "Who needs it?"

Marie-Lucie Morin, director in 1992 of the financial and business services division of the Department of External Affairs, is one young female diplomat whose career and work ethic at once confirm and contradict the prevailing theories about the advancement of women.

A native of Sherbrooke, Quebec, and a graduate in international law from the University of Sherbrooke, Morin wrote the foreign service examinations while still at law school. She was admitted to the Quebec bar in 1979 and joined External the following year. Offered the customary choice among the immigration, political, or trade streams, Morin took the toughest department. "I thought that my more pragmatic nature would be best suited to dealing with commercial and economic matters," she said. So much for the theory that women choose soft jobs with glitter and instant gratification instead of those requiring long, hard slogging before results are achieved.

Morin is a wife and the mother of three young children. She now takes her family into account when plotting her career and attempts to avoid postings abroad which call for heavy social responsibilities. Her current job is a demanding one that requires her to put in long hours at the office and take work home. She has little time or inclination to prolong those hours by accepting social obligations but acknowledged that her attitude might change when her children are older. She also sees her reluctance to engage in social activities as a difference between men and women in the diplomatic service. She argued that men were more free to participate in social activities. If they had children, their wives handled household and child-care duties.

> I don't want to be chauvinistic about this myself, but the reality of the matter is that women, by and large, still feel very close to their children, which is not something to be ashamed of. As a result, I may not be prepared to make quite the same sacrifices as I see many male colleagues making. And this does not translate into a lesser commitment to the job, or less productivity, or anything of that sort. Ask around and I think you will find that, certainly in this department, women are not absent more often than men, they're by and large very hard working and all of that, but if we look at this other aspect of the career, I think perhaps that women are less keen about it.
>
> But you know, at the end of the day, I always think when you get close to retirement, do you wish you had spent more time working and more time socializing, or do you wish you had spent more time with your family? … You have to try to keep things in perspective. And this is a career where, if you're not careful, you can have an eighteen-hour day every day.

Morin's first year in External followed the usual pattern for a new officer: training in several divisions and some cross-country travel that helped her to understand Canada and Canadian foreign policy. During that first year, she used her legal training to draft orders-in-council, not a very exciting task for someone who had looked forward to a career in international affairs from a very young age.

After completing her training year, Morin had three successive postings abroad. The first took her to San Francisco as vice-consul and assistant trade commissioner at the Canadian Consulate General from 1981 to 1984. She then went to the embassy in Jakarta as second secretary commercial. While there she was promoted to first secretary. In 1986, she went to the high commission in London, again as first secretary commercial.

Each posting had something special about it. As a junior officer in San Francisco, she plunged into the traditional tasks of a trade commissioner. It was classical trade promotion: organizing visits of Canadians seeking markets; mounting trade fairs and trade shows; conducting market surveys for new products. In addition, she dealt with what she called the "daily bread of a trade commissioner" – issues of Canadian access to the U.S. market, customs work, the non-tariff barriers to trade, the standards and regulations surrounding the sale of a product or the provision of a service. She enjoyed living in the city, took advantage of its broad range of cultural and leisure activities, and travelled often. In the process, she "developed a nice, close relationship with my Australian and New Zealand colleagues because it's kind of a natural affiliation and the Canadian thing", and scarcely noticed that San Francisco did not offer the traditional rounds of diplomatic social life even though the city is host to some sixty foreign consulates.

In Jakarta, Morin promoted Canadian trade, examined trade policies, and reported to Ottawa on economic developments in Indonesia and the surrounding region. She saw much more of her fellow-diplomats than she had in California. In Jakarta the diplomatic community is close, she said, "because you are in a foreign and often hostile environment and as a result … a sort of magnetic phenomenon develops which can be an incredible source of intelligence and you should try to exploit that to the maximum." Even though she had little opportunity to venture outside Jakarta, her social life was the lively one of a traditional diplomat. "I was out five nights a week and you could not refuse because if you had refused you wouldn't have been doing the job."

London was her favourite of the three postings and remains her favourite city. She concentrated on trade policy with special emphasis on the Uruguay round of negotiations of the General Agreement on Tariffs and Trade (GATT). Because she had almost six years' experience, she took a more pro-active approach to her work, which made her very effective and gave her considerable professional satisfaction. Policy work put her in frequent contact with her fellow diplomats. Their exchanges of views on British policies and the politics of process within the European Community influenced Morin's own thinking. She found that the accuracy of her opinion on any given subject or situation increased according to the number of people with whom she shared her ideas and thoughts. As for living in London, it was wonderful.

> I think that London is an incredibly exciting place to live. It remains the centre of the world in terms of intellectual life, certain musical life, the theatre and all of that. I felt extremely privileged that I had been sent to London when I was. I just found it incredibly stimulating intellectually. The quality of the people that you

meet in London – they're not all British, they come from all over the world – it's as though great minds all converge towards a certain axis.

Morin returned to Ottawa in September 1990 as assistant director of External's financial and business services division, and she was promoted to director in December 1991. During a lengthy interview in her Ottawa office, she called her headquarters assignment the most exciting of her career thus far and explained why.

First of all, because I am a true manager for the first time. Secondly, because I deal with files that are very salient to the economic and political debate at the moment. I deal with export financing, which is very essential to competitiveness, for example, and I deal also with all of the service industries which traditionally have been perhaps forgotten in the whole process of promoting trade. So I think I have quite a challenge on my plate and I like that.

And I should say that, by and large, although a lot of us prefer being abroad because of the excitement of living in a foreign culture and all of these things which are reasons why we joined the service, assignments at headquarters are very exciting from a political point of view and from a career point of view because you can really make a difference if you are well plugged in.

Working in Ottawa gives officers access to the policy-makers which they do not have when they are abroad; with access, it's easier to get things done. Morin cited an example from her own experience.

In London I did a lot of work related to the Uruguay round, the multilateral trade negotiation process, and I was asked very frequently to meet with the press and explain to them what our position was on any one topic and report what their position was. And I found myself very much in a position of being a messenger back and forth and sometimes I felt that if I were back in Ottawa I could really make an impact on how Canada was handling this particular file.

Here, if I feel strongly about an issue, I can put pen

to paper and write a note to the minister and say, "Here is the issue and here's what I think we should do about it." And of course the minister is totally free to decide whether or not I'm a nut case. But at least you have that access. It's totally normal that if you're stuck in Indonesia having to deal with the daily pressures, having to deliver, you get a little bit more remote from what the government's agenda is.

If focussing on economic issues is the stairway to the top at External Affairs, Morin is taking it one step at a time, while holding firmly to the belief that her work makes a difference and that her career can make a contribution.

I don't have any goals in terms of where I want to be in the department in fifteen or twenty years' time. I think that as it is I'm doing very well, I'm doing a good job and I think the scope is there for me to really do well.

In terms of assignments, I certainly want to go back abroad at some point in time. My preference would be to continue doing work in both policy and trade promotion areas, a mix of both, which I find very stimulating. I would like to come back to headquarters after that and continue working on the economic side of things, trade/economic.

Personally, the lifestyle of the head of post does not appeal terribly much. This is very much a personal thing, I'm not very much of a social animal to begin with, although I enjoy managing very much and I think I'm a rather good manager. I think I would probably ultimately prefer managing here at headquarters than really having to embrace all the social hoopla that comes with being a head of mission.

Morin has clearly chosen the career path most likely to gain her promotion to upper management levels. At age thirty-five, she has displayed considerable managerial ability and expressed a desire to continue in that direction. At the same time, however, her career and her aspirations confirm the opinions of those experts who say that women are not as single-minded as men in pursuing their goals and that women's responsibilities to their families can be roadblocks to career advancement.

When I entered this department, I told myself I'm not going to be wedded to the career. Men are able to have fulfilling careers in the foreign service and have everything else, why can't we?

The challenge is greater for us because men by definition do not accept readily to follow a woman around so to find a suitable spouse is a greater challenge for us than it might be for a male colleague. But nevertheless, I look at my peers in terms of age and ranking in the system and most of them now are married and many of them have children.

My husband was working ten years in oil and gas and had to change careers in mid-stream because of my moving around and he's now working on East-West trade and he's been able to really make a name for himself in that field. But it is not easy, it takes a lot of perseverance and a lot of flexibility and you see a lot of stress in marriages as a result of our lifestyles.

Although women are a small minority among foreign service officers, Morin does not believe that she has been discriminated against because she is female.

I think that we have come to a point now where it's accepted that there are women in the service, and whereas you still have the odd case of men of another generation who basically – deep down – might prefer to deal with another man because they feel more comfortable, I think that that's much less prevalent than it might have been fifteen years ago, and certainly I don't have a problem at all in carrying out my duties because I am a woman. At times you might have to be slightly more certain and the qualities that are normally associated with being a woman might not be qualities that are appreciated in diplomatic life.

The bottom line is that I think it's a perfectly acceptable environment to be working in for a woman now, from my point of view. And I should add that as a trade commissioner, I think that we women have had even higher hurdles to overcome than our sisters from the political stream because it has been a bastion controlled by men to a much further extent than on the other side of the shop.

As for being a married officer with children, Morin said that her situation differed little from that of male officers with spouses and offspring, or from that of working mothers everywhere who must find child care. Like her female colleagues, Morin hires a nanny for the children.

> I don't see that as a major problem. I think you can cope with that quite easily. What is more difficult to cope with is the fact that most of us have husbands who want careers, who are not satisfied with being at home or just part-timing or freelancing, and they find themselves in frustrating situations.
>
> A number of people will come to me and say, "You women in the foreign service have a real big problem with your spouses," and I always turn around and say, "Well, you just wait, give it another five years, this will be a universal problem for anybody who is married, for two reasons." Number one because male and female, by and large, want to do something with their lives, they want something without necessarily wanting a big career, they want to do something that's fulfilling. They want to use their professional skills, they want to use their skills, period. The second aspect, of course, very crass, is called money. We're no different from anybody else, and most of us don't come to the service with a big inheritance. I mean, it used to be the case, back in the old days, that you would only become a diplomat if you were well off to begin with. But of course that's no longer the case, so that you start off as a junior officer and you're paid just enough to support a family. Ergo, the spouse has to work.

Morin added that the difficulties and aspirations which she described applied equally to husbands and wives. In the foreign service, as in Canadian society generally, the two-income couple has become the rule, not the exception.

The chances of a woman becoming deputy minister or head of post in Washington, London, Paris, or Tokyo are increasing as the pool of qualified women steadily increases, Morin said. But much as she likes being a manager and considers herself a good one, Morin has no such expectations for herself. Indeed, she sounded as though she would be more content as a middle-sized fish in a big pond than as a whale in a small one.

> If you were to ask me, "Do I think that most women in the foreign service really have as an ultimate goal to become a head of mission?" I would say, "Probably not." The career is very interesting and being head of mission doesn't necessarily suit everybody's interests and everybody's skills.
>
> Certainly from my own perspective, I don't regard becoming some day a head of mission as my ultimate goal. I think that, professionally, if I had the opportunity of becoming a number two, for example, in Paris or something like that, it would be just as good for me as being a number one in Cameroon. You see what I'm saying? Everything is relative. But is there some artificial barrier there, is there a Chinese wall that you cannot go beyond because you're a woman? I don't think that's the case. Look at Louise Fréchette. But you see, Louise Fréchette is an exceptional officer and the fact that she is a woman is really more or less irrelevant.
>
> You're dealing with a female population in the department of 15 percent; why should there be more exceptional individuals in that 15 percent than proportionately in the remaining 85 percent? You have to look at it all and, as a matter of fact, I know that the prime minister and ministers have been making tremendous pressure so that there are more female heads of posts on the list every year, more and more, they want more. And I would say, as a result, you probably have female heads of posts that are being made heads of posts ahead of their years, if anything, for better or worse.
>
> So I don't perceive that there is really a discrimination at the top and I can see the day that certainly there will be qualified women become deputy minister, undersecretary.

Marie-Lucie Morin, a vivacious brunette who exudes candour and charm as well as intelligence, would grace any embassy. She hopes and expects to go abroad again one day, but she is in no hurry. She is perfectly content to work in Ottawa, to have time to enjoy her family, and to wait her turn for the diplomatic prize that is sure to come. Frantic clawing is not the only way to get to the top. Nor is it Morin's style.

CHAPTER TWENTY-ONE

THE THIRD CANADIAN
ALEXANDRA BEZEREDI

For eleven days in June 1992, the eyes – and the hopes – of the world were on Rio de Janeiro. Leaders from 180 countries had converged on the Brazilian city for the Earth Summit, a conference sponsored by the United Nations. Its lofty objective was to make common cause among the rich nations of the north and the poor nations of the south in order to rescue the environment from the ravages of humans and their technology and to protect it from future assault.

Two Canadians captured headlines during the two years of negotiations leading up to the summit and in Rio once the meetings began. One was Maurice Strong, business tycoon-cum-international public servant, the summit's secretary general and advance man, who travelled the world promoting the event and emphasizing the importance of its goals. The other was Prime Minister Brian Mulroney, who attended the conference, hailed it for moving the environment "to the top of the international agenda," and attracted delegate approval for three specific acts. He signed the conference's biodiversity treaty for the protection of animal and plant species, even though U.S. President George Bush had refused to do so. Mulroney offered to cancel $145 million in debts owed Canada by Latin American countries, if they spent an equivalent amount protecting their rain forests and endangered species. And he announced Canadian contributions of $20 million for forestry projects in Brazil and $50 million in new aid for drought-stricken southern Africa.

There was a third Canadian at the Rio summit whose contribution to the success of its proceedings was just as important. She was Alexandra Bezeredi. Thirty-one years old, she was a first secretary at the Canadian

Alexandra Bezeredi

mission to the United Nations in New York, who had spent four years of her diplomatic career immersed in environmental issues. Working with her counterparts on the U.N.'s second committee – the one that handles environmental, economic, and financial affairs – Bezeredi had discussed, analysed, reported, and prepared statements on all the issues that were to appear on the Rio conference agenda. They included climate change, environmental security, driftnet fishing, toxic and hazardous products

and wastes, drought and desertification, and the role of women in implementing development and protecting the environment.

Bezeredi's work leading up to the Rio summit was typical of what
diplomats do – long, often tedious, slugging behind the scenes to hammer out positions, negotiate trade-offs, draft resolutions, and secure
agreements. Of course, all praise (or blame) went to the politicians. The
work was also "one of the best jobs I'll ever have in my life," Bezeredi said
during a wide-ranging interview in her New York office a few weeks
before the conference took place.

When she was posted to the U.N. mission in 1988, Bezeredi's friends
and colleagues in Ottawa commiserated with her because she was not
assigned to the Security Council. (Canada took one of its periodic turns
as a council member, from 1989 to 1990.) Their sympathy was wasted.

> I have no regrets. I like my work. You're left alone a lot
> of the time and you can also be put under pressure a lot
> of the time but it's a nice balance where you really get
> into your subject area and you have a devoted con-
> stituency and you believe what you are doing is helpful
> and that you are doing something positive.
>
> Here I am responsible for environmental issues at
> the U.N. and for the past four years I have been prepar-
> ing Canada for the Earth summit. In fact, I just came
> back from working on temporary duty in Ottawa where
> I'm working with the team to get the prime minister
> ready to go to Rio.
>
> It has been fascinating. I helped to draft the resolu-
> tion that was the precursor to a resolution that launched
> the conference – which I also helped draft – and so it
> has been a wonderfully stimulating, intellectually stimu-
> lating, and exciting area.

Bezeredi knew her subject so well that she was able to predict the
outcome of the summit with uncanny accuracy.

> I think they are going to adopt two conventions: one on
> climate change, which was recently adopted here in New
> York and I think they are going to sign it, and one on
> biodiversity which is being negotiated right now in
> Nairobi. They are probably going to adopt a Rio decla-
> ration, which is a statement of principles. They will

adopt Agenda 21. Agenda 21 is a sort of program of
action on sustainable development to the 21st century
and beyond and covers all kinds of factors: fresh water,
oceans, forests, land use, poverty, health, etc. It's not perhaps going to be as revolutionary as people would have
liked in terms of having all the countries of the world
say that they will really try to change their economic
planning to take into account resource use and protection of the environment, but I think it's an important
step, and it's not supposed to be the end of the process,
it's supposed to be the beginning of a continuing
process. I think a lot of people will say that it's a lot of
hype and the language of some texts is weaker than we
would have liked in terms of solid commitments dealing
with these issues but I think on the whole it will be
good.

Delegates to the conference in Rio in fact did adopt the conventions on
biological diversity and climate change, the Rio declaration, and Agenda
21. And, just as Bezeredi predicted, there were complaints that the meeting produced too many photo opportunities for world leaders, too much
overheated rhetoric, and too little action. She remains optimistic that the
conference enabled the U.N. to organize itself so that it could tackle environmental issues in a more effective and positive way.

Born in Vancouver in 1960 and a graduate in economics and modern
East Asian studies from Trinity College, University of Toronto, Alexandra
Bezeredi wanted to be a foreign correspondent. She was news editor of
the *Varsity* and worked one summer at the *Vancouver Province*. She wrote
the foreign service examination in 1981 while still at university, at the
suggestion of a friend who thought that the foreign service would be
good experience for an aspiring international affairs reporter. The paucity
of job opportunities in Canadian newspapers during the recession of
1982, and the prospect of an overseas posting, made External an attractive alternative.

Bezeredi spent her first year in Ottawa on a variety of assignments.
Chief among them was assistant desk officer in External's Western
European division. Her duties included analysing trade statistics and economic trends in the European Community and arranging visits for high-
level European and Canadian officials. Her first posting, to India in
1983, was the least satisfying in her career. Although she was an officer in
the political stream, she went to India to work on immigration. Nothing

in her young life had prepared this warm, sensitive, empathetic woman for the emotional impact of her job. She had to deal objectively and sometimes coldly with the many hopeful men, women, and children who arrived at the high commission in New Delhi seeking new lives in Canada.

> It is a difficult post and you have to have a thick and a thin skin at the same time and it is very difficult to maintain a kind of balance because everyone appears so desperate to come to Canada. At the same time, you are working with an act and regulations that you are questioning every day and you see a side both of India and Canada that is really not that glamorous.
>
> In a sense, the problem of the foreign service is that too often you are on this tertiary level of meeting the finest and the best and the brightest and you sometimes forget what you are really representing and who and what Canada and Canadians are all about. So in one sense immigration reminds you of the fact that there are all kinds of interests at stake in Canadian foreign policy and Canadian domestic policy but on the other hand it isn't glamorous work.
>
> And I discovered, much to my chagrin because I had seriously thought of becoming an immigration officer, that I didn't have what it takes. I care too much. So, unfortunately, that, in terms of my career, was not what we would call a good career move, but in terms of my soul, I like to think it was probably very wise. I was very young – I was twenty-two when I went to India – so I had a lot of growing up to do.

Bezeredi returned to the Western European division in 1985. As desk officer, she was responsible for bilateral relations with the Nordic countries, Ireland, and Switzerland. She also formulated policy on northern security and co-operation, kept tabs on the Anglo-Irish agreement on Northern Ireland, and organized forty visits of high-level officials to and from Canada.

For four months in 1986, Bezeredi was assigned to temporary duty as an assistant to Douglas Roche, the former Conservative MP who was then Canada's ambassador for disarmament. In Ottawa and in New York, she researched all aspects of arms control and disarmament and examined all the issues surrounding international peace and security. She wrote speeches, articles, reports, and memoranda on the ambassador's behalf and represented him at the U.N. General Assembly and other international conferences.

After the disarmament assignment, Alexandra Bezeredi moved to the NATO desk in External's defence relations division and stayed there for ten months. The Cold War had not yet ended, and the security of Western Europe remained NATO's major preoccupation. Bezeredi monitored and analysed NATO decisions and helped formulate Canada's defence policy within NATO. She attended several meetings at NATO headquarters in Brussels and was a member of the Canadian delegation to the 1987 foreign ministers' meeting in Reykjavik, Iceland. It was during this period that she took an introspective look at herself and the department.

> By the time I got to the NATO desk I had made up my mind that I had to take some time off because I was very unhappy with my life and with the way the foreign service was going at the time.
>
> There was a whole bunch of factors, some of it is personal and some of it is macro. Foreign policy is becoming increasingly complex, increasingly we are becoming ensemble players. I think there is a certain tension within the Canadian foreign service about being the kinds of bridge-builders we would like to be, in a sense, but a lot of this costs resources. What happens then is that the foreign service itself can become more fragmented, people don't have a sense, a cohesive picture, of what we're trying to accomplish. I suppose people understand that exports are very important to Canada and that's probably the most important pervasive message.
>
> Often people in the foreign service feel as if they are spending a lot of time generating information but they're not quite sure where it's going and what it does, and coupled with the fact that there are certain tensions within the service as to who is on the most important track at a given time. Morale since I've joined has been steadily declining.

The facile assumption that those who joined the foreign service and managed not to fall on their faces would become ambassadors no longer holds true, Bezeredi said.

It's extremely competitive and it's not always competitive in the positive way of excellence; that people strive, for example, to write great treaties or to write a seminal speech or to develop a coherent plan of action on a given issue. It's also positioning yourself to be as visible as possible to the most senior people in the bureaucracy and in the political machinery so that you'll be noticed and easily promoted. People play chess in the bureaucracy and use their intellect far more for that, I believe, than they do for dealing with the issues.

It's so rare that you can run into someone who says, "I was in a post and I found the country interesting on its own ground." It's always prefaced – almost always prefaced – with the term, "It was good for my career to be in post X or Y." This is a very personal reflection but I think there will be a few people who feel that.

Alexandra Bezeredi's disillusionment led her to think once again about journalism. She took educational leave from the department, secured a scholarship, and enrolled in journalism and international and public affairs at Columbia University in New York for the 1987-1988 academic year.

I had a very important year to me personally. I learned that it's very difficult to be a journalist, I learned that writing is something not only that you want to do but that you need to do. I was very humbled by the class-mates that I worked with and I guess I went through some serious soul-searching. I was set to probably take kind of a freelance job with a major newspaper when the department contacted me and asked me to help out on the Toronto economic summit and it was clear they were working on me to do a posting either to Washington or New York.

Having returned to External, Bezeredi spent May and June 1988 on economic summit issues. She prepared the G-7 briefing book for the prime minister and was a member of the Canadian delegation to the summit in Toronto. Afterwards, just as she had anticipated, she went to New York as second secretary at Canada's mission to the U.N. She later became first secretary.

Although preparation for the Earth summit took a large part of Bezeredi's time during her four years in New York, it was not her only responsibility. She was also the New York co-ordinator for the Canadian delegation to the preparatory committee of the United Nations Conference on Environment and Development. She was concerned specifically with oceans, and legal and institutional issues. She was a member of the Canadian delegation to the U.N. environment programme governing council and the Economic and Social Council. And she sat on the U.N. committees dealing with sustainable development, new and renewable sources of energy, natural resources, and science and technology.

Her work at the U.N. earned her the accolade of her peers. At a 1991 gala dinner at the National Arts Centre in Ottawa, the Professional Association of Foreign Service Officers gave her its second annual Canadian Foreign Service Officer Award. Maurice Strong presented her with a scroll and a $1,000 cheque. The scroll was framed and hung in a prominent place on the wall behind the desk in her cluttered but homey New York office.

Enthusiasm for the challenge and the importance of her U.N. work did not blind Bezeredi to the pitfalls which women encounter in an environment almost exclusively male.

> The vast majority of your colleagues are male. There is still a problem. It's not easy. It is almost unheard of for a woman to be asked to chair something. There's a perception that women are emotional and unbalanced. I mean, a man can yell and scream and that's perfectly acceptable. He can disrupt a meeting for hours but if a woman does the same, she's a shrew.
>
> I have an Iranian colleague who is actually quite a nice guy. He refuses to shake my hand. I grabbed his hand once anyway and made him do it.
>
> I was in a negotiating session once on a very minor matter concerning a little resolution on energy and the Iraqi delegate made a very off-colour comment in front of sixty people, with translation, about how essentially he's been trying to get into my pants. I just ignored him and carried on to make my point. I remember my Danish colleague – a lady – came to me afterwards and she said, "You know, it's a tough call in a situation like that whether to ignore it or to turn it into a diplomatic

incident and demand an apology on the spot." I said it was so nerve-racking when you have to take that microphone and there's translation and sixty people and they're all listening to you and it's probably going to go on a Telex that night if you make a firm point of one kind or another – when you sort of have got that train of thought – it takes some guts to do it in the first place and then someone disrupts you. Nine times out of ten your reaction is just to carry on because it's so nerve-racking as it is. So that's just what I chose to do.

Yes, you get a lot of that, unfortunately. You get chairmen thoughtlessly saying, "The pretty delegate from France and the pretty delegate from whatever," and if that happens I go back and I say, "Well, thank you, the most handsome chair in the world." In other words, the message I would be trying to send is, "Sexuality is equal. You want to call me beautiful, okay, I'll take that, but then I'm going to call you handsome." And you know, they find it very embarrassing; they all blush and it's a "touché" which they instantly understand and it's good-humoured.

I have seen some women say, "You can't do this." I have seen other women brush it off. And there's always this duality that you are a person but you are also a country and you get into this problem of, if they're going to disrespect me because I'm a woman, they have to remember that I'm Canada, too. They have to live with that whether they like it or not and if they think they can disrupt a meeting for four hours on a minor issue of principle, well, I can do the same and I have. I absolutely have. I don't care any more what they call me because the people who think like that are usually actually relatively unimportant in the grand scheme of things. They are very unprofessional anyway.

I have been slighted in various ways and you have to say to yourself, "Well, I believe in choosing my weapons carefully and my times carefully for making a point about this kind of treatment," and/or ignoring the person, or saying, "Look, we're one of the strongest economies in the world, we have some clout here at the U.N., this is what my country is saying whether you like

it or not, and I'm prepared to hold up consensus on this
and call this sucker to a vote if you don't listen to me.
You want to play the same tactics, so will I."

Bezeredi recalled being disheartened when she first arrived in New York
to find that so few women were appointed to senior positions in the
United Nations' secretariat. The situation worsened early in 1992. U.N.
Secretary-General Boutros Boutros-Ghali, bent on reforming the U.N.
bureaucracy to save money and make it more efficient, eliminated fourteen under-secretary positions and lost two senior women. One of them,
Canadian Thérèse Sevigny, was replaced by a man. The only other
woman of senior rank was demoted.

Later in the year, following complaints about sexual harassment by
female staff members, the U.N. reluctantly moved to draft and adopt
guidelines to deal with this persistent problem. On another front,
Boutros-Ghali recommended the appointment of Elizabeth Dowdeswell,
an assistant deputy minister with Environment Canada, as executive
director of the U.N. environment program. Bezeredi called the
Dowdeswell appointment "a coup for Canada and for the promotion of
women to senior managerial positions in international affairs."

Despite that appointment, the U.N. bureaucracy seems little more
hospitable to women now than it was when Flora MacDonald was
External Affairs minister in 1979-1980. Boutros-Ghali's predecessor,
Javier Perez de Cuellar, was "impossible to talk to on this subject,"
MacDonald said. She continued:

> He and his staff were adamantly against the appoint-
> ment of women on the secretariat or in the major U.N.
> agencies or to anything of that nature. ... It's dreadful to
> think that we've got major global organizations that
> don't set any kind of example whatsoever. The U.N. is
> the worst bureaucracy in the world when it comes to
> women. Yet it goes on and on prating about human
> rights and equality; you look at it and you're bound to
> say, what hypocrisy. So there isn't much encouragement
> to member countries to do much about the status of
> women.

Bezeredi was ambivalent about the prospects for the advancement of
women in the Canadian foreign service. She referred to the affirmative
action programmes at Columbia, where young black students from

wealthy families attended university on full scholarships while other students struggled and complained about unfairness.

> We are in a phase right now when the promotion of women is being encouraged. There have been numerous cases in which, between an equally qualified man and a woman, the woman has been given a push. The women who have been given the push are extremely good. So I don't think there are hard feelings in that sense, other than the fact that numerous of my male colleagues have complained and said, "Look, I have to wait two or three extra years for a promotion or a good job that will get me a promotion, whereas this person doesn't, it's not fair."

Bezeredi's pertinent reply to such complaints is that it was not fair for women twenty years ago and redress is overdue.

> I have worked in situations where I genuinely felt that the people I worked for just felt I couldn't do the job as well as a man. I have worked in a couple of instances like that and you're constantly being reminded of the fact that you're, in a sense, doomed because chances are you won't be able to find a spouse who's able to travel with you, therefore you're doomed to singlehood. How unfulfilling that must be. And so you get a lot of that. That means if you're unfulfilled you're unhappy and therefore that will affect your ability to work with others and to manage. So you carry all these stigmas around, talk a lot about it, I think that some women network.
>
> One little thing that I've always noticed is there is a group called the policy planning group and right now the director general is a woman, Anne Leahy, who was the ambassador to Cameroon. She is the first woman since I joined the department who has actually worked in that bureau at a senior level. They may have had women but I always felt that particular group, policy planning group, was the "old boys" network.' This idea that only men have the intellectual ability to sit and map out the great foreign policy strategy for Canada – because that is what that division does, it's a very important division and they do a lot of writing and a lot of thinking – I've com-

plained for years about that. Why don't you see women being assigned to that particular division?

I have run into veiled sexism of one kind or another, some more overt than others. I have felt it is very important to promote people on merit. At times I have been concerned about the morale problem when you are pushing a group because you feel you have to rather than purely on merit. But lately, over the last couple of years, I've really started to realize that the more you run into people who are difficult, the more you start to realize the policy of trying to promote women is not a bad one. Even if it makes some people mad. There is just so much hostility, veiled hostility I would say, it is all very skilfully concealed.

Bezeredi contrasted her own situation with that of a female foreign service officer twenty-five years ago. This young woman, engaged to a journalist, was offered a posting to Washington. They would marry and her husband would accompany her to Washington where he planned to work as a freelance correspondent in a city providing fertile ground for such endeavours. If the roles had been reversed – if the diplomat had been a man and the freelancer a woman – the posting would have been so routine as to go unremarked. But External adamantly refused to post her to Washington with her spouse. She left the service.

Alexandra Bezeredi experienced a similar situation but the outcome was different. Her spouse, who had been working at the Bank of Canada, took a job with the International Monetary Fund in Washington. Shortly after the Rio summit, Bezeredi was posted to the Canadian embassy in Washington as first secretary economic. She said the reason for her cross-posting from New York to Washington, without an intervening period in Ottawa, was "to accommodate my desire to be with him because the department knows I have been commuting for four years – three to Ottawa, one to Washington." If Bezeredi ever leaves the foreign service it will be for professional, not personal, reasons.

At the end of March 1991, more than half of Canada's 112 missions abroad had reciprocal employment agreements giving spouses and dependents access to jobs in other countries. It is indicative of the department's changed attitude toward married officers and its acceptance of the recommendations of Pamela McDougall's 1991 Royal Commission on Conditions in the Foreign Service. Bezeredi reflected on the changes.

Now what we are doing in the foreign service is bending over backwards to accommodate spouses and some of my colleagues have fought very hard for this and believe in it and I'm of two minds. I really have very mixed views about it because it is a problem being a spouse. It is no fun, especially if you've been working and you've got talents and professional abilities, having to take off big chunks of time. I don't think it's particularly easy but at the same time this is something you should have sorted out before walking into this arrangement.

In any event, the Canadian foreign service has decided that it's going to do its best for spousal employment, encouraging them to sign up for contracts or special things that become available in missions, or special projects, things like that.

In some countries, you can't even work as a volunteer. You have to get permission from the government and then you get professionals saying, "Why should I work for free as a doctor or nurse or whatever? I get paid a good salary for this and it's very difficult for me to do that free of charge." But more and more, women officers are getting married. They marry people from all walks of life – teachers, engineers, freelance writers or journalists – and they're working things out. Clearly the problems of the male officer married to a woman are the same as a female officer married to a guy.

A couple of my female colleagues have had children and they've had to take time off. Usually they take a year off per child. They've said that it's very difficult to manage a career like this, a marriage and a family, and you hear the old axiom that you could probably do two out of three well but to do all three something usually has to suffer.

But to me the problem is deeper than the foreign service, in that this is a social problem, a societal problem. We run ourselves ragged and we work incredibly long hours and it's the fact that we're prepared to drive ourselves silly right through to our forties and fifties. For what? For something that we don't have time to enjoy and we sacrifice so much of our personal time and our family time, it just seems to me as if our priorities as a

society are wrong. And so, in a sense, we are getting
caught up in this in the foreign service as much as doctors or lawyers on Bay street in Toronto are. Everybody
is getting caught up in the same problem.

Alexandra Bezeredi may solve the problem for herself by leaving the
foreign service. At the moment, however, she is enjoying her assignment
in Washington. It began at an exciting time of transition. There was a
change of guard at the White House, from George Bush to Bill Clinton,
and a change in Canada's ambassador to the United States, from a career
foreign service officer, Derek Burney, to a career military officer, John de
Chastelain. No woman has been Canada's ambassador to the U.S., the
crown jewel of Canadian diplomatic postings. Bezeredi doubts that a
woman will get that posting in her lifetime, but she does expect a woman
to become undersecretary in the department in Ottawa.

There is still a perception that women are operators and
they can get the job done and everything, but they are
not intellectual heavyweights, which is why I'm concerned about the policy planning bureau. Because those
are the kinds of jobs where you can really prove that you
are an intellectual heavyweight and show your depth
and, still, that just eludes women.

There's just not that many of them who could sit
and write a seminal speech or foreign policy outline.
There's just not that many who are interested in sitting
down long enough to do that and not playing the
bureaucratic games because you have to sit still for a
couple of years and really study an issue. But, you see,
it's that kind of thinking that gets you ambassador to
Tokyo or ambassador to Moscow or ambassador to
Washington, because you have to have that kind of
depth so that someone can lean on you and say, "Well,
it's thirty years, it's all here, now off you go to
Washington and make it happen."

That is a pessimistic view from someone as bright and gregarious as
Alexandra Bezeredi. But it contains a kernel of truth and realism for every
woman now in External or contemplating a foreign service career.

CHAPTER TWENTY-TWO

GLAMOUR AT A CATTLE SHOW
MARISA PIATTELLI

Traditional diplomacy as practised by political officers is not as important as it once was in international relations. Heads of governments and foreign ministers still depend on their envoys for information on the what and why of current affairs. At the same time, however, government leaders have access to instant information on world events from the mass media, especially television, and they are able to conduct their own personal diplomacy with their foreign counterparts. It is as easy as picking up the telephone.

While the role of diplomats as political reporters diminishes, their role as trade promoters grows. The international marketplace is becoming more and more competitive. Every diplomat is a hawker and a hustler as every country seeks to expand the market for its goods and services in an atmosphere of intense rivalry.

For Canadian diplomats, it is almost as though the wheel has come full circle. After all, the first Canadians sent abroad to represent their country were trade agents. When the political officers succeeded the trade agents, they quickly ascended the diplomatic pecking order, causing considerable tension and one-upmanship in Ottawa and at posts abroad. That tension did not disappear completely with the merger of the departments of External Affairs and Industry, Trade, and Commerce in 1982.

Members of the older generation of political officers see their diplomatic careers threatened by the growing emphasis on trade in Canada's international relations. Those of the younger generation, meanwhile, recognize and accept the change in direction. They have met the challenge

Marisa Piattelli at the United Nations Security Council in 1992.

of an intrusive mass media, and they have learned to play two roles – political reporter and trade promoter.

Marisa Piattelli, first secretary at the Canadian mission to the United Nations in New York, is one of the new generation of foreign service officers who move comfortably from trade to politics and vice-versa.

Piattelli arrived in New York in 1990 when Canada was finishing a two-year term on the Security Council. Even when Canada is not on the council, our representatives carefully monitor its activities. It was Piattelli's job to coordinate the coverage. Interviewed in New York, in May 1992, shortly after the first Canadian peacekeepers were sent to the former Yugoslavia, she spoke about how Canada's membership on the Security Council affected her work.

> I thought the change would be more dramatic. When you're off the council a certain amount of pressure is off, so the reporting requirements are a little different. But in practice, of course, nothing has changed. During our Security Council term, Ottawa became accustomed to a certain level of reporting with a certain timeliness; the department wants that and it's more difficult to get the information because you're not sitting in the council, you're not sitting in the informal consultations where the real discussion happens, you're waiting outside the door.
>
> Moreover, with the increased media focus on the U.N., diplomats find themselves in competition with journalists, especially now that you have live CNN coverage, that kind of thing. It's essential to try to get information to Ottawa before they hear it in the media.
>
> So I think the pressure to get the information to Ottawa accurately and in timely fashion is still there. For instance, the [Security Council] report yesterday on Yugoslavia, I made sure that it was in Ottawa at 8 o'clock this morning. Senior management meets at that time; National Defence will need to know, there are 1,200 Canadians there.
>
> So while we're not on the Security Council, those kinds of reporting requirements haven't changed at all. The Security Council is now focusing on issues of major interest. This is a busy, busy post.

In addition to keeping an eye on Security Council affairs, Piattelli has specific responsibility for East-West relations, including the former Soviet Union and Yugoslavia, and handles the mission's relations with the media.

Born in Toronto in 1959, Marisa Piattelli graduated from the University of Toronto in 1982 and joined the foreign service that same year. John Holmes, a former diplomat, who by then was teaching several courses in international relations, taught Piattelli and steered her towards External. On his advice, she wrote the foreign service examinations. She passed them and spent her training year in Ottawa, in the North Asia and Pacific division of the department. Then she went to Italy on her first posting, as vice-consul and assistant trade commissioner in Milan.

Piattelli found the Italian assignment enormously satisfying. Her account of it indicates how easily the new breed of diplomat moves between trade and political functions and finds value in each.

> The posting in Milan was very interesting because it was a cross-stream assignment from the political-economic stream to the trade stream. Assisting Canadian exporters to market their products, to set up the contacts, arrange the meetings, go in and do the translation if necessary [she's fluent in Italian], and get the order placed is a very practical, immediate result which you don't necessarily get on the political-economic side.
>
> I recall when I arrived in Milan I was given a wide range of trade portfolios as the junior officer, including the agricultural sector. One of my first assignments was to attend the Cremona Cattle Show. I had a list of Italian importers to see, particularly a long-standing importer who had been doing business with Canadian Holstein-Friesian breeders since just after World War II. When I met up with this particular gentleman, he insisted upon showing me one of his prize Holsteins – a cow with, apparently, quite a distinguished Canadian genealogy.
>
> We went to his trade stand where I found quite a magnificent cow. He yanked me down so he and I were squatting under this enormous cow. "You must feel her udder because only Canadian Holstein-Friesian stock have udders like silk." I thought, so this is the glamour of the foreign service; squatting under this enormous cow with this little old gentleman rubbing the udder of a cow and saying, "Yes, yes it does, in fact, feel like silk."

> The trade section of the consulate was able to facili-
> tate dozens of business deals – importing, licensing,
> joint ventures, agreements. It was enormously satisfying.

Her three years in Milan gave Piattelli some insight into the advantages and disadvantages of being a woman in the foreign service.

> Because I was female and, at the time, quite young, I
> think there was a bit of a curiosity element for local con-
> tacts and perhaps, as a result, a greater willingness to
> return a phone call and to set up a meeting and that
> kind of thing. But that's the extent to which my gender
> assisted me in any way.
>
> What really assisted was the fact that I could speak
> the language; when local business contacts called the
> office they usually asked for me because they didn't want
> to go through the difficulty of trying to speak English
> with one of the other trade commissioners. They would
> rather have spoken about their business in their own
> language. That was what helped more than gender.
>
> I worked in Milan with a trade commissioner, an
> old-school, old-style trade commissioner, who I think
> thought it was "sweet" that the junior trade officer was
> female and therefore used little terms like "dearie" and
> that kind of thing. I considered it neither harassment
> nor discrimination, it was simply another generation
> talking.

Piattelli said that she had not been subjected to harassment or discrimination – in Milan or elsewhere. In Ottawa, she continued, "There is
an awareness that one can't discriminate against women and an acknowl-
edgment that this was done in the past." However, Piattelli also has found
that women must prove themselves again and again in ways that men do
not.

> I think there's also a residue of perhaps tension between
> male and female officers by virtue of the fact that every-
> one is aware that the department is interested in pro-
> moting its women, interested perhaps in making up lost
> ground. Therefore if you have two equally competent
> people for promotion, I feel that as a female officer I

want to prove that the promotion is deserved and not a number-crunching exercise by the department. The latter defeats the purpose. I want it to be clear that a promotion is merited and not solely gender-related.

On her return to Ottawa, Piattelli spent two years in the international financial and investment affairs division. Next she went to Toronto on an executive interchange programme and worked for the Ontario government for two years before she was posted to New York. She still makes frequent trips to Toronto. Piattelli, a new breed of foreign service officer in her personal as well as her professional life, is married to a professor at the University of Toronto. They see each other every two weeks in Toronto or New York.

Piattelli talked about having a commuters' marriage, about the difficulties encountered by both men and women who try to combine marriage with a foreign service career, and about the effects of having children.

Compromises are necessary. In many ways, the foreign service is more than a career, it's a lifestyle, it's like joining the army. It dictates how you live your life, where you are, all that. And so I'm involved in making the compromises now. My husband is in Toronto and I am in New York. This posting has worked out personally to the extent that Toronto-New York is a reasonable distance, more or less like Ottawa-Toronto. Every two weeks, I fly up or he flies down. Enormously expensive and probably untenable over the long term. If I were in Kenya, for instance, unaccompanied, where we couldn't see each other every two weeks, I'm not sure really how that would work.

I do think it's going to take a superhuman effort on the part of female foreign service officers who wish not just to maintain personal relationships but who want to have a family and pursue a successful career. Frankly, I'm not sure whether it all pulls you out of, or at minimum lengthens, the promotion track. Women will have to take time off to have a family and if you aspire to senior rank I'm not sure how that affects one in the end. Certainly, like in every other institution in the private or public sector, I think women have to work doubly hard to maintain the pace.

By the same token, I have many male colleagues who are also commuting, whose wives are in Montreal or Toronto or in a very good job in Ottawa who don't wish to go abroad for four years and perhaps curtail a very successful career. Some of these officers have had either to forego certain postings or do the posting on an unaccompanied basis. So to a certain extent it's a shared problem of both male and female foreign service officers though, as I've said, women officers have to cope with particular realities.

The continued political upheavals in Eastern Europe and the increasing violence that has the republics of the former Yugoslavia teetering on the brink of civil war keep Piattelli busier than she may want to be. When she is not up to her eyebrows in work, or spending rare but precious time with her husband, she "networks" among her colleagues in other missions and at the U.N. secretariat. "There's a very efficient female network here in New York; absolutely, it's very useful. We exchange an enormous amount of information, see each other socially, and it's become a group of friends."

All in all, Marisa Piattelli is the very model of a modern diplomat, facing a bright future with a realist's eye and a pragmatist's mind.

CONCLUSION

NOT FOR THE FAINT OF HEART

Forty-six years after women officially became foreign service officers, the Department of External Affairs remains a man's world run by an old boys' network. Statistics show that men are in the majority. In 1992, there were 674 men and 169 women in External's political and trade streams in the foreign service. At 20 percent of the total, that is a slight improvement from 1984, when 14 percent of officers were women. In the executive ranks, however, women in External lag well behind their counterparts in other government departments; in 1992, women made up 7.8 percent of the executive group in External, but in the public service as a whole women accounted for 16.1 percent of the executives.

The optimists in the department, women and men, subscribe to the "critical mass" theory: as the number of women increases, their chances of becoming middle- and upper-level managers will increase. Some day a woman will be deputy minister of the department, or high commissioner to London, or ambassador to one of the high-profile posts: Washington, Paris, Tokyo, Moscow, and Bonn.

The realists recognize that the odds still favour the men. The size of the foreign service is being reduced as part of the government's cost-cutting measures. Since few officers are being recruited, it is unlikely that there will be an increase in either the number or the proportion of women. The return of the social affairs stream of officers from External to Employment and Immigration, in 1992, diminished the number of women whose experience had set them on an upward career path. While they are still eligible, in theory, for ambassadorial appointments, they will not be rising through the ranks in External where the majority of such appointments are made.

When Flora MacDonald was Canada's first female foreign minister in 1979-1980, she did not think that there were enough women in the department. Now chair of the International Development Research Centre, television commentator, and a frequent traveller to Third World countries, MacDonald's view has not changed. In a 1992 interview, she said:

> I still think that is so and I was very anxious to encourage young women, in particular, to move upwards. I think that there is still a reluctance on the part of senior officials in the department to move women forward. There's been a fairly major increase, particularly while Mr. [Joe] Clark was secretary of state for external affairs; there was an effort to have women moving into posts at the intermediate level and I'm pleased, when I go out now travelling, to meet these women in key positions. But I think it's still very difficult for them to go up the ladder to the top positions.

Canada's first women ambassadors – Margaret Meagher, Pamela McDougall, Marion Macpherson, and Dorothy Armstrong – were often the only female members of the diplomatic corps in the cities to which they were posted. Meagher went to Israel as Canada's first female ambassador in 1958, but nine years elapsed before McDougall went to Poland to become Canada's second female ambassador. As late as 1984, there were only two women in charge of Canadian missions abroad.

MacDonald is a member of the board of the Institute for Research on Public Policy. Until the institute's budget was cut in 1991, it sponsored an annual conference of academics, bureaucrats, and business people from the G-7 countries, prior to the G-7 economic summit. Material produced at the conference was forwarded to the participating governments before the summit convened. As the only woman at one of those conferences, in Brussels in 1990, MacDonald drew attention to her minority status.

> There were perhaps forty people at it, all of them involved in the international scene. I was the spokesperson for the Canadian delegation so I had spoken at the beginning and I was one of the people to wrap up the conference. And I said, "Some of you are not going to like what I have to say but I'm going to say it anyway

because it's a tenet with me that I express these views wherever I go." I then went on to say, "It's deplorable that we're sitting around here and you have no idea of the resources that you're not calling on." The idea that in that day and age only one of the forty delegates would be female is just shocking to me. So in these major conferences, I still see a tremendous dearth of women. It's due in part to the political scene, it's also because of the public service structural biases against women. Look at the Commonwealth conference in Harare last October; there was one woman leader on the scene, the prime minister of Bangladesh. But even in the entourages of other leaders, there were very few women. At that level there's still very, very little breakthrough.

In *Beneath the Veneer: The Report of the Task Force on Barriers to Women in the Public Service* (1990), there is this observation about External:

> The network of "old boys" who have served together in posts abroad over the years can be a formidable obstacle for women in the Department. The nature of the assignment system means that it is often necessary to "lobby" the directors of different divisions in the pursuit of good assignments. Most of these positions are held by men, and the number of female mentors and role models is small.
>
> One woman recently assumed a position normally filled by someone at a lower level than she had achieved. She was reluctant to do so, but was told there were no other opportunities. She had requested another vacant post, which was commensurate with her current level, but was told that there was already one woman in a similar position, and that they couldn't have two women in those posts. The position she wanted was then filled by a man who was at a lower level than the position required – a "stretch" assignment for him. (p. 98)

The notion that one woman per post is enough goes back at least to 1965 when Pauline Jewett, a brilliant woman who was then a Liberal Member of Parliament, discussed the possibility of a cabinet appointment with Prime Minister Lester B. Pearson. Pearson already had Judy LaMarsh in his cabinet; having another women was apparently out of the question. He never did have a cabinet with more than one woman in it. Such tokenism was commonplace in the 1960s; that it persists in the 1990s is appalling. A brief to the barriers task force was critical of External's management for paying more attention to the appointment of women as ambassadors than to their promotion within the ranks. Tokenism again: appointing a female ambassador attracts favourable public attention; appointing a female director general or assistant deputy minister goes unnoticed by the public but may ruffle male feathers within the bureaucracy. Yet the middle-level promotions are vital, as the task force was told: "To appoint one woman is significant, to appoint two will provide impact, but to appoint three is to begin the process of critical mass." The report added: "Women at all levels in the public service told us that they felt better able to relax and do their job once they were no longer an oddity – a single example of their kind – but part of a group of at least three. Once this point has been reached, progress accelerates."

There is a consensus in External and among outside observers that when Joe Clark was minister, he accelerated both the recruitment and advancement of women in the department. Jodi White, Clark's chief of staff from 1984 to 1988, talked about his efforts:

> He also really pursued some women in the department and outside the department to try to get them to take positions, and on several occasions he interviewed women, or called them himself, and said, "Would you take a post and be appointed ambassador?" That included some women who were in the public service in other departments and it included women within External Affairs who perhaps weren't getting on to the list because it wasn't considered they were quite ready yet. I mean, there is a whole process, when you're running a career service, of making decisions at what point people are ready to start to be appointed to the top jobs. And there were several that he pursued and had appointed perhaps prior to when they might have got those appointments. And the women, I must say, were quite aware of it and not terribly supportive of that; I mean, when you're working in a career service as External is, you're aware that your time will come and you should take it when your time does come and not before.

There's a lot of women who don't want to be treated differently just because they're women. I have some sympathy for that. People don't want to get promoted just because they're women. Now the counterbalance to that is, most people would say, there's all sorts of men who have been promoted because they happen to be buddies or something, it's not always on merit by any means, so that women should start to accept that.

Louise Fréchette, Canadian ambassador to the United Nations, is one of the officers who was awarded what is called a "stretch" post at Clark's prodding, White recalled.

When they sent her to Argentina, it was a little earlier than she might have got it otherwise. She decided to accept it and I'm glad she did; she did a fabulous job and she was really glad she'd accepted it and could see that it was an opportunity and it shouldn't have taken only Joe Clark to have insisted on that happening. She's very, very able. When we went down to Argentina when she was there it was clear she'd made an impact with the government and was doing very, very well.

Clark's one-person affirmative action program may have helped some women move up, but it had less impact on pervasive attitudes. White found External very male-dominated. No woman has been undersecretary at External, she said, and there have been very few female assistant undersecretaries. Had Clark remained in External instead of moving over to Constitutional Affairs, she added, he would have insisted that a woman be appointed deputy minister by mid-1992. (As an aside, White remarked that when she travelled with Clark, she often encountered ambassadors who were uncomfortable with a minister who had a female chief of staff.)

Pamela McDougall, who was an ambassador and a deputy minister (but not in External), expanded on the theory of critical mass:

There haven't been all that many women assistant undersecretaries really, I don't think, and if you look at who they've been there are a number who were not career, not what I would call career, foreign service officers. I think the point about needing more, a larger base of women, is certainly true. You've got to have the real-

ization that the women are there and they can go
through the progression, they don't have to be picked
out of somewhere else and given the job. I think it all
goes back to the question of the number of women in
the department.

Trying to combine family life with a foreign service career hinders
women, McDougall said.

You are always going to have fewer career women in
External Affairs if it continues to be a rotational service
which I suspect it will be, in one way or another. You are
never going to have as many there as you have in an
Ottawa-based department simply because it can't be
hacked.

Single women who become ambassadors, as McDougall found when
she was one, also have adjustments to make.

I found it extremely lonely. It's lonely at the top, there is
no question about it, particularly when you're in a place
like Warsaw. I always found at a post being a single
woman was a great advantage in that you knew everybody and you associated with everybody, from the head
of post down to the lowliest security guard. You'd find
yourself inviting them to your house for drinks, or going
to their house, and it didn't matter who it was.

In a way, the single woman, I think, performed a
certain pulling together of the staff. [Margaret Catley-
Carlson called it being "the glue in the system."] The
married couples have set their own agenda, they have
their children, they have their problems, they're tearing
their hair, the wife is unhappy, etc. So very often they
can't perform that function. I think a single woman does
do that. I certainly did and I found it easy to do and I
enjoyed doing it, liked knowing everybody.

But when you are the head of post that's difficult,
you're still entertaining them but you're in a different
kind of position, it's not as easy.

Kathryn McCallion called External "a male bastion" and expressed
concern about the future of women in the foreign service.

I think things got better for a while and I think things are on a down trend again. I think people became complacent. I think they thought they had reached the beachhead before they actually got there. Taking certain things for granted, for instance, once the door was open that it would stay open.

I don't think people should assume that because there's a group of people doing something, that one of them will be a woman, one of them will be a francophone. I think you still have to remind people. I don't think we have been successful in making the foreign service appear to be a wonderful career for women, I don't think we've broached that issue either.

I think the recruitment process is at fault; they go out and they talk to the university students, but I don't get a feeling from the incoming officers that it's seen as a job that women can instinctively do well and grow fast in. Unlike the medical profession, for instance, where the beachhead has been reached, and law as well. There may be prejudices in law firms or certain hospitals or certain sub-sectors of both professions, such as why would a woman do criminal law? But it is very much accepted and I don't think that we in External have reached that point yet. I don't think it's a sure thing any more.

The promotion of women to key jobs at various levels within the department is very much an in-house issue. There is still a hesitancy to put women in certain jobs. Now, to be fair, there is not that large a pool primarily because years ago they weren't being hired and we have to rise up through the system. There is strong resistance to lateral entries. There wasn't enough activism by the women because they believed it would be detrimental to their individual careers.

I'm concerned about the women in the department and as a senior woman myself I do what I can to help but I'm not an activist. I am not in favour of promoting all women, just the good ones, otherwise what is the point? We will lose in the end.

Although the External Affairs department is still male-dominated, the women's movement has had a profound influence on the lives of all diplomats. A staff paper prepared for McDougall's Royal Commission on Conditions of Foreign Service recorded the movement's effect on diplomats' spouses.

> Of all the social changes that have affected life in the foreign service, the women's movement has had the strongest impact. Many of the traditional approaches to foreign service described at the opening of this paper were established and maintained by foreign service spouses. Today, most overseas communities of Canadians reflect the new reality in Canadian society in general. They are made up of spouses with diverse expectations, needs, desires – some want to work, others want a career and still others prefer a more traditional role and want to be recognized for their part in representing Canada abroad. (p. 140)

Dorothy Armstrong described the effect of the movement on female officers.

> I would say that Betty Friedan's extraordinary book, *The Feminine Mystique,* was the one that started raising public consciousness – a giant step beyond Simone de Beauvoir's early work on the subject – and when I read it I found myself saying, "Yes, oh yes." It was full of recognition for me; she was right, it seemed to me. And she was the first one who had written it down, said it out. Those of us who were in positions that were regarded as traditional male bastions in those days were going through some of the very things that she talked about and she was able somehow to organize it all into a synthetic whole which suddenly made sense. More than that, a brilliant revelation. I think it spoke to women everywhere and helped to begin one of the giant "waves" of the century. Germaine Greer's more esoteric work, *The Female Eunuch,* also carried this on and I think they both had a very catalytic long-term effect.

The women of External, like women in other walks of life, also encounter sexual harassment, although no one talks about it openly or for attribution. The hand on the knee at meetings and the inappropriate remarks are commonplace; the promise of promotion in return for favours is rarer but not unheard-of. Of course, support staff are particularly vulnerable; officers tend to protect themselves by letting offenders know that their behaviour is noticed and not welcome. One young officer went further; when a colleague grabbed her breast while they were bantering in a corridor, she kneed him in the groin and told him, in no uncertain terms, not to do that again. He never did.

Margaret Catley-Carlson described the men and women of External Affairs as "a very elite corps ... of highly motivated, highly aware, highly engaged, involved personnel who live in a bunch of different cultures [and] care very deeply about what they do." Many of the women say that they want "to make a difference" in Ottawa and in the countries where they represent Canada. Not every woman wants to be an ambassador or an undersecretary or even a manager at a lower level. As Janice Sutton said, some of those jobs are no longer very challenging or satisfying.

> Head of division in Ottawa has almost no authority any more. There are so many levels above him that it's demeaning. Let alone the desk officer. You do a memo to your minister, put it to your head of division who okays it, then it has to go to the director-general and then to the assistant undersecretary and a half dozen more other places and the whole thing gets changed all the way along the line and the poor desk officer often doesn't even know what's happened to his memo.
>
> You didn't have enough authority, you were just another cog in a large wheel, and there's an enormous amount of stress, enormous pressures on heads of division and heads of posts.
>
> The complexity of the questions that the department is dealing with has grown, the feeling that the political side of things is under threat with trade becoming so important. At one point the trade officers were really cocks of the walk. "Trade is what runs the world, we earn money for the government and External Affairs; political just costs the taxpayer money." So I think a lot of political stream people really are running scared and

feeling very pressured.

And then you have so many more demands on you. In CIDA while I was there as project officer we had to deal with not only managing a project and all the problems that can be involved in managing a project but then we had to deal with equal opportunities. We had to make sure that every project had an equal opportunity element, a women in development element, all of which takes time and thought and expertise, and you've probably got to hire a consultant to do a study and all this costs money and time and contracts and so on. And then came the requirement for a human rights element and, just as I was leaving, the environment was coming in, there would have to be an environment component in every project. There was no extra time, no extra money, no extra human resources given to you to deal with these questions but you have to include them in your paperwork.

I think analogous things were happening in divisions in the department; there were demands, demands, demands and the poor directors were just keeping so many balls in the air all the time.

Despite the odds, or perhaps because of them, there are women who are having satisfying and challenging careers in the foreign service. The foreign service needs more women, not to increase their chances of promotion, but because they have a contribution to make. As Pamela McDougall said,

I think women in a particular situation do bring a different point of view. They look at problems a different way and they attach different priorities. Their views are necessary, their input is necessary. But this is not just true of External Affairs, it's true of every walk of life, every government department, and every level, and it should be to the highest level.

The degree of male domination in diplomacy, McDougall said, is no greater than it is in politics or the professions. "If you look at the professions and at politics, if you look at politics particularly, that's the worst. And women haven't yet made it. Individual women have, thank God for that, but not as a group. So I think that there should be women, certainly, in every aspect of government and things would be run better."

Although many Canadians travel abroad and some even have a chance to meet their country's representatives, an aura of mystery and intrigue continues to surround the practice of diplomacy. In a thoughtful memorandum, Dorothy Armstrong sought to disperse some of the shadows.

> We are forever being asked by people, "But what does a diplomat do?" I suppose we must sometimes appear a bit mysterious and removed. But it is really quite straightforward. An ambassador must:
>
> (a) Analyse and report on conditions in the country of the posting: political, economic, commercial, cultural, social (including labour relations) and just about anything else that could shed light on understanding. We all spend hours at our desks writing – or these days at the computer.
>
> (b) Present and promote Canada's views to the host authorities as persuasively as possible, according to our government's priorities of the day; nowadays, as global issues assume more prominence, much effort is spent on supporting bilateral undertakings *with* the host country – joint ventures in business. (1) Backing Canadian firms in their efforts to sell our products, participating in workshops, fairs and seminars to push investment and technology transfers – a big priority these days – and calling on heads of firms personally to make the point. (2) Putting Canada's best foot forward culturally – promoting the work of performing artists, visual artists, writers and publishers in the country of one's posting. If possible, get CanLit going in the local university.
>
> (c) Looking after Canadians abroad through normal consular services and assistance to Canadians in distress. This can be among the most demanding but at the same time most fascinating aspects of our work.
>
> (d) Be an efficient manager: a helpful guide to both the Canadian and local staff, a vigilant watchdog of Embassy budgets and accounts and masterful at achieving much with little in running both Chancery and Residence.

Diplomacy is not a career for the faint-hearted. However, it can be an immensely satisfying one for a woman with a sense of adventure, a thick skin, a yen to travel and live in foreign countries, a desire to make a difference, and a gambler's instinct to beat the odds.

BIBLIOGRAPHY

ARCHIVES

National Archives of Canada. Files 12141-40; 2795-AB-40; S-1-AA; 156-F; 156-C-1; 1895-12-3; 1883-7-18; 1895-6-20.

INTERVIEWS BY THE AUTHOR

Dorothy Armstrong, Ottawa, 23 June 1992

Alexandra Bezeredi, New York, 13 May 1992

Margaret Catley-Carlson, Ottawa, 22 June 1992

Colleen Cupples, Ottawa, 22 April 1992

Verona Edelstein, Ottawa, 23 June 1992

Lucie Edwards, Ottawa, 22 April 1992

Louise Fréchette, New York, 14 May 1992

Ingrid Hall, Ottawa, 23 September 1992

Kathryn Hewlett-Jobes, Ottawa, 23 June 1992

Julie Loranger, Ottawa, 25 June 1992

Anne Leahy, Ottawa, 21 April 1992

Flora MacDonald, Ottawa, 22 September 1992

Marion Macpherson, Ottawa, 21 September 1992

Kathryn McCallion, Ottawa, 23 June 1992

Pamela McDougall, Ottawa, 24 June 1992

Margaret Meagher, Halifax, 4 July 1992

Marie-Lucie Morin, Ottawa, 24 June 1992

Marisa Piattelli, New York, 14 May 1992

Sandelle Scrimshaw, Ottawa, 24 April 1992

Janice Sutton, Toronto, 13 November 1992

Jodi White, Ottawa, 22 September 1992

Note: Interviews were taped and transcribed, and the transcriptions were edited by the interviewees.

OTHER INTERVIEWS

Alison Taylor Hardy. Interview by Mary Burnett. Transcript of taped interview for the Oral History Project of Queen's Women. Queen's University, Kingston, 1968.

SECONDARY WORKS

Burke, Angela. "See Canada Approaching Time for Appointment of Woman Ambassador," *Toronto Star*, 7 November 1957.

Cadieux, Marcel. *The Canadian Diplomat, An Essay in Definition*. Toronto: University of Toronto Press for the Canadian Institute of International Affairs, 1963.

Campbell, Ruth V.G. "Woman is Head of New Canadian Legation at Beirut, Lebanon," *Windsor Daily Star*, 22 June 1955.

Canadian International Development Agency. *Annual Report 1990-91.* Ottawa: Supply and Services Canada, 1992.

———. *Sharing our Future: Canadian International Development Assistance.* Ottawa: Supply and Services Canada, 1987.

Cox, Corolyn. "Our First Woman Diplomat," *Saturday Night*, 8 May 1943.

———. "Safekeepers of the Secrets and Conscience of External Affairs," *Saturday Night*, 17 May 1945.

Documents on Canadian External Relations. Edited by John F. Hilliker. Vol. 11, *1944-1945*, Part II. Ottawa: Supply and Services Canada, 1990.

Edmonds, Jean, Edna MacKenzie, and Jocelyne Côté-O'Hara. *Beneath the Veneer: The Report of the Task Force on Barriers to Women in the Public Service.* Ottawa: Supply and Services Canada, 1990.

External Affairs and International Trade Canada. *Annual Report 1990-1991.* Ottawa: External Affairs and International Trade Canada, 1991.

Farrell, R. Barry. *The Making of Canadian Foreign Policy.* Scarborough: Prentice-Hall, 1969.

Ferguson, Alan. "U.N. 'men's club' freezes out women," *Toronto Star*, 29 September 1992.

Foreign Policy Association, Inc. Information Service. *Foreign Policy Reports.* Vols. 1, 5, and 6, and Supplement 1 to Vol. 2. New York: Kraus Reprint Co., 1969.

Fraser, Graham. "Sexual Politics: Why so few women run for office," *Globe and Mail*, 26 January 1993.

Fraser, John. "Canadian diplomat copes with crisis," *Globe and Mail*, 7 November 1984.

Freifeld, Sidney A. *Undiplomatic Notes: Tales from the Canadian Foreign Service.* Toronto: Hounslow Press, 1990.

Gessell, Paul. "Stonewalling Female Diplomats," *Ottawa Citizen*, 13 June 1992.

Goar, Carol. "Merit no longer counts at External Affairs," *Toronto Star*, 5 May 1992.

———. "Ex-spymaster shakes up External," *Toronto Star*, 21 May 1992.

Granatstein, J.L. *A Man of Influence, Norman A. Robertson and Canadian Statecraft, 1929-68.* Toronto: Deneau, 1981.

———. *The Ottawa Men, The Civil Service Mandarins, 1935-1957.* Toronto: Oxford University Press, 1982.

Granatstein, J.L., and Robert Bothwell. *Pirouette: Pierre Trudeau and Canadian Foreign Policy.* Toronto: University of Toronto Press, 1990.

Gwyn, Richard. *The Northern Magus: Pierre Trudeau and Canadians.* Toronto: McClelland and Stewart, 1980.

Hardy, Alison Taylor. "Women: always diplomatic and more recently diplomats," *International Perspectives,* July-August 1976, 26-32.

Harper, Tim. "Big names, unknowns contend for plum post," *Toronto Star,* 1 December 1992.

Harvey, Alan. "Middle East Expert Working in Ottawa," *Globe and Mail,* 26 January 1959.

Heeney, Arnold. *The Things That Are Caesar's: Memoirs of a Canadian Public Servant.* Toronto: University of Toronto Press, 1972.

Hilliker, John. *Canada's Department of External Affairs.* Vol. 1, *The Early Years, 1909-1946.* Montreal and Kingston: McGill-Queen's University Press, 1990.

Hillmen, Anne Trowell. "A Remembrance: Elizabeth Pauline McCallum," *bout de papier,* Summer 1985, 14-15.

Holmes, John W. *The Better Part of Valour: Essays on Canadian Diplomacy.* No. 49, The Carleton Library. Toronto/Montreal: McClelland and Stewart, 1970.

———. "The Canadian Foreign Service at Middle Age." Unpublished papers at the Canadian Institute of International Affairs, Toronto.

———. "Diplomacy – Canadian Style." Unpublished papers at the Canadian Institute of International Affairs, Toronto.

Ignatieff, George. *The Making of a Peacemonger.* Toronto: University of Toronto Press, 1985.

LaMarsh, Judy. *Memoirs of a Bird in a Gilded Cage.* Toronto: McClelland and Stewart, 1968.

Lucas, Steve. "The Gatekeeper," *Saturday Night,* June 1984.

Macbeth, Madge. "Efficiency Does It," *Mayfair,* June 1943.

Mackay, Donald R. "From the President's Desk," *bout de papier* 9, no. 2 (Spring 1992): 3-4.

Markham, Carol N. "The Domino Effect," *bout de papier* 9, no. 2 (Spring 1992): 2

Martin, Paul. *A Very Public Life.* Vol. 1, *Far from Home.* Ottawa: Deneau, 1983.

———. *A Very Public Life.* Vol. 2, *So Many Worlds.* Toronto: Deneau, 1985.

McDougall, Pamela A. *Report of the Royal Commission on Conditions of Foreign Service.* Ottawa: Supply and Services Canada, 1981.

Morgan, Nicole. *The Equality Game: Women in the Federal Public Service (1908-1987).* Canadian Advisory Council on the Status of Women, 1988.

Nicolson, Harold. "Marginal Comment," *Spectator* (London), 23 January 1942.

Pearson, Lester B. *Mike: The Memoirs of the Right Honourable Lester B. Pearson.* Vol. 1, *1897-1948.* Toronto: University of Toronto Press, 1972.

——. *Mike.* Vol. 2, *1948-1957.* Toronto: University of Toronto Press, 1973.

——. *Mike.* Vol. 3, *1957-1968.* Toronto: University of Toronto Press, 1975.

"Our First Woman Consul Kept it Secret Six Months," *Toronto Star,* 10 April 1943.

Reid, Escott. *Radical Mandarin: The Memoirs of Escott Reid.* Toronto: University of Toronto Press, 1989.

Report of the Royal Commission on the Status of Women in Canada. Ottawa; Information Canada, 1970.

Report of the Special Joint Committee on Canada's International Relations. Independence and Internationalism. Ottawa: Supply and Services Canada, 1986.

Reynolds, Louise. "Agnes McCloskey" (unpublished background paper prepared for John F. Hilliker, *Canada's Department of External Affairs,* Vol. 1, *The Early Years, 1909-1946*). Ottawa.

——. "Women F.S.O.s. (unpublished background paper prepared for John F. Hilliker, *Canada's Department of External Affairs,* Vol. 1, *The Early Years, 1909-1946*). Ottawa.

Ritchie, Charles. *Storm Signals: More Undiplomatic Diaries, 1962-1971.* Toronto: Macmillan, 1983.

Sallot, Jeff. "Diplomatic corps feels the crunch," *Globe and Mail,* 24 April 1992.

——. "General named ambassador to U.S.," *Globe and Mail,* 7 January 1993.

——. "Lowering the flag to save money," *Globe and Mail,* 15 January 1993.

Sanger, Clyde. "Namibia, The Black Man's Burden," *Canadian Institute of International Affairs* 48, no. 4 (Summer 1990): 1-20.

Smith, Cameron. "Female Ambassador to Poland once a Government office clerk," *Globe and Mail,* 22 January 1968.

Teltsch, Kathleen. "Canadian Official Is Selected to Lead Population Council," *New York Times,* 12 June 1992.

Thibault, J.E., and Cheryl Moreau. *Canadian Heads of Post Abroad, 1880-1989.* Ottawa: External Affairs and International Trade Canada, 1991.

Willock, David. "Lady in the Striped-Pants World," *Weekend Magazine* 8, no. 43 (25 October 1958).